I wish to express my love and gratitude to my dearly departed friend Jean, who first introduced me to vegetarianism many years ago; to my partner Mike, a professional chef, for his knowledge and encouragement; and to my best friends Angela, Heather and Gretchen, whose work for animal rights and welfare continues to inspire me daily.

Written by Skye Michael Conroy

Email: michaelgconroy@yahoo.com

Website: http://thegentlechef.com

For those who not only dream of a gentle and compassionate world

But make the commitment to realize that dream…

Table of Contents

Chapter 7 – Soups, Broths and Stews   121

Please visit TheGentleChef.com for full color images of many of the recipes in this cookbook, along with new recipes, additional information about veganism and a list of vegan resources.

An Introduction

In the late Summer of 2010, I took PETA's 30-day pledge to adhere to a vegan diet. I never turned back. An individual who adheres to this diet subsists wholly on vegetables, grains, fruits, nuts, and seeds and excludes any and all foods derived from animal origin. This transition did not occur overnight, in fact, it was the culmination of many years of on-and-off vegetarianism. I was introduced to vegetarian cuisine in early adulthood and enjoyed it very much, but I also enjoyed many animal foods. Somehow the idea of slaughtering animals seemed wrong, but since I never witnessed or participated in the slaughter, I accepted it as part of the dark and ugly side of reality.

One day, I stumbled across a documentary entitled "Meet Your Meat", which exposes the horrors of factory farms and slaughterhouses (abattoirs). I was deeply disturbed by the film and immediately eliminated meat from my diet. But time passed and indifference returned along with my omnivore diet, as I rationalized that somehow these were isolated incidences. I just couldn't fathom that human beings, or our government, would allow such atrocities to occur. Yes, I was very naive.

Several years later, I became friends with a fascinating woman who just happened to be a vegan and animal rights activist. I found her lifestyle interesting and admirable but at the same time extreme - I could imagine a life without consuming meat - but a life without dairy and eggs seemed unthinkable. Sure, the health benefits were obvious, but that reason alone was not enough for me to maintain such a strict diet and lifestyle. I still hadn't made the mental and spiritual connection, or perhaps more accurately, I wasn't ready to make the connection because I knew it would involve some radical shift in the way I lived my life.

I think my defining moment came after viewing the documentary entitled "Earthlings". At that point, I finally came to the realization that animals exist for their own reasons and were not put on this Earth merely to gratify human desires. I knew then that if there was to be any change at all in how animals are treated, I was going to have to be part of that change. It was time.

Guided by this new level of awareness, I decided I would no longer consume animals or their by-products and I would reject, as far as possible and practical, all use of animal products for any other purpose. This practice of non-violence and non-exploitation of sentient beings became an intrinsic part of my spiritual path, as well as my philosophical beliefs.

There are many types of activists who confront animal rights issues from different angles. Vegan activism can take a wide range of forms, including protests and demonstrations; raising social awareness through media attention and distribution of literature; petitioning organizations and lawmakers; boycotts; and active involvement with liberation, advocacy, rescue and sanctuary organizations. We all contribute according to our individual abilities and talents.

My activism targets the individual by teaching how to change lifelong dietary habits through the replacement of animal products with those derived from plants. This may seem like a small contribution, but unless we can change our mindset about food, animals will continue to suffer needlessly. My goal is to make this dietary transition easier and enjoyable for anyone willing to make the change.

Some individuals avoid change because change always involves some degree of self-sacrifice, but vegan cuisine offers such a vast array of taste and texture, it will delight even the most discerning food critic. Once you learn what to purchase and how to prepare it, there really is very little self-sacrifice involved.

If the food is delicious, nutritious, satisfying, comforting and reasonably convenient and affordable, then one is more likely to embrace a plant-based diet.

I am still rather new to the vegan lifestyle, but my passion for cooking has existed since childhood. I have been inspired by some amazing cooks, both vegan and non-vegan, and some of my recipes reflect that inspiration - with my own personal touch added. Other recipes and techniques were created from my own imagination.

It's evident that my recipes focus heavily upon meat, egg and dairy imitations, and of course there's a percentage of the vegan population who, for their own reasons, shun any foods that resemble meat, eggs or dairy. My goal is not to reinvent the wheel of vegan cuisine for that percentage, as there are many amazing cooks and authors who already target that demographic. Maintaining a vegan diet is easy for individuals who have an aversion to animal-based foods. It's not going to be easy, however, for individuals who crave those flavors and textures. The reality is we live in a meat-centric society and many of us grew up on a diet of meat, eggs and dairy. This addiction to animal-based foods is woven into every fiber of our culture. It takes time to rewire our brains into accepting change, especially for those who perhaps never cared for vegetables and "health food" in the first place. More than likely, if you offer a plate of bean curd and sprouts to a die-hard carnivore, you're not going to elicit a positive response.

My goal then, is to create foods which will sway the greatest number of people over to compassionate cooking. People thrive on familiarity and if that familiarity can be satisfied, then there is a greater chance of success with this transition.

I'm not a nutrition expert, although I have done a great deal of personal study in this area. As such, you will not see nutrition tables included with the recipes. The purpose of this cookbook is to help relieve the suffering of farm animals and avert the impending destruction of our planet - it's not a manual for weight loss or health rejuvenation. Nevertheless, I do know from my own experience that the vegan diet has vastly improved my own health (confirmed by my doctor and blood panel results) and brought my weight down to an ideal range.

Keep in mind too, that in order to win people over to vegan cuisine, I'm aiming for the best taste and textures and not always the most low calorie, low-fat, low-carb or low-sodium options. However, I do encourage breaking the reliance on commercially prepared and heavily processed foods as much as possible and I provide detailed instructions for preparing many of the components of my recipes with unprocessed, wholesome ingredients. My philosophy is: "everything in moderation". Even vegan foods can be fattening if not consumed sensibly.

Regarding food allergies and sensitivities: I have none, and since this cookbook is based upon my personal adventures in vegan cooking, I heavily rely on gluten, soy and nuts as the foundation for many of my recipes. There are a few occasions where I do provide options for allergy-sensitive individuals. For a full range of recipe options, I suggest doing some research for cookbooks and websites that specifically benefit allergic and food sensitive vegans.

I wish you all the best upon your own adventures in vegan cooking and I sincerely hope my recipes can be of value to you. This cookbook is a chronicle of my experience.

Peace and Compassion,
Skye Michael

Chapter 1

Seitan, the Wheat Meat

An Introduction to Seitan

Seitan (say-tan) or wheat meat, is an amazingly versatile, protein-rich meat alternative made from wheat gluten. Gluten (from the Latin gluten, meaning "glue") is a protein complex that appears in foods processed from wheat and related species, including barley and rye. Wheat gluten is not a complete protein in itself, which means that additional ingredients must be added to seitan to complete its amino acid profile (nutritional yeast or bean flour, for example).

Unfortunately, some individuals cannot benefit from the nutrition and versatility of seitan due to gluten sensitivity or total intolerance (Celiac disease*), and must obtain their protein from vegetables, legumes and gluten-free grain sources such as quinoa, amaranth or buckwheat (which is actually not a grain but a seed).

*About 1 out of every 100 people have Celiac disease; however, if you have digestive problems, do not rush to blame gluten, as these issues can be caused by any number of different disorders. Blood testing can rule out Celiac disease, so see your doctor before making any drastic dietary changes.

Vital wheat gluten (or vital wheat gluten flour) is not the same as high gluten wheat flour. High gluten wheat flour is typically used in baking to give breads a chewy texture. It also contains a large proportion of starch, unlike the isolated vital wheat gluten. Ironically, high gluten wheat flour is used in the traditional method of making seitan. In this labor-intensive method, the wheat dough is continually kneaded and rinsed in water to wash away the soluble starch, thus yielding a rubbery mass of gluten. My recipes avoid this lengthy (and often inconsistent) process by using vital wheat gluten instead.

Vital wheat gluten can be found in health food stores, where it can sometimes be purchased in bulk, and many supermarkets now carry it as well. Bob's Red Mill™ produces a high-quality vital wheat gluten and this is what I use for all of my seitan recipes.

Of course, you can always purchase commercially prepared seitan, but it's much more expensive than preparing your own. It's also limited in its application because it's only packaged in small chunks. Commercially prepared faux meat products can be equally expensive and are often very processed. There's something inherently magical and wholesome about preparing food from scratch with your own two hands. Some cooks may think that making seitan is too complex and may feel intimidated by the process, but this concern is unfounded as long as one can follow a recipe.

Wheat gluten is not digestible in its raw state, therefore it must be cooked. The traditional method is to simmer seitan in a seasoned broth. Baking seitan is another successful method of preparation and steaming seitan wrapped in foil packages is a popular method used for creating a variety of vegan sausages. Initially, I didn't care for the baking and steaming methods, until I discovered that the proportion of water suggested in most recipes was insufficient for creating a "meaty" texture. The seitan always resembled the texture of dense bread. Once I found the correct water to gluten ratio, the seitan turned out deliciously moist and "meaty".

Many commercial vegan meat analogues contain textured wheat protein made from gluten. This produces the "stringy" texture which replicates real meat. Proteins, in general, can be textured to mimic the properties of real meat (chicken, beef, pork or seafood) using different processes such as spinning, jet-cooking, steam treatment and extrusion cooking. Among these processes, extrusion has been the preferred technology. Textured wheat protein is produced using twin-screw extrusion technology using a mix of wheat gluten and other processing additives to yield products that differ in size, shape and color. Obviously, these production processes cannot be duplicated in the home kitchen (nor can they be considered "natural"). Regardless, I feel that seitan prepared properly at home can produce textures that will satisfy most palates.

Preparing Seitan

Preparing seitan is an art and science unto itself, much like the art and science of baking. There is a molecular chemistry involved in the process, therefore adherence to recipe measurements is essential or you may end up with an inedible mess on your hands. Whether the recipe calls for a teaspoon (tsp), a tablespoon (T) or a cup (and fractions thereof), always use level measurements. And please, no "eye-balling" measurements - that may work for some cooking techniques but it doesn't work when making seitan. The recipes (or more accurately - formulas) provided here have been tested many times in my own kitchen and adjusted to produce appetizing results, so exercise caution when you wish to experiment with different measurements involving dry ingredient to liquid ingredient ratios. Also be careful when adding unspecified extra ingredients that contain moisture (for example, adding raw apple to sausage dough), as this can change the moisture content significantly and alter the results.

Tamari, soy sauce or Bragg Liquid Aminos™ are liquid seasonings which are often added to the water for making seitan dough and are specified in many seitan recipes, sometimes along with other liquid seasonings. For health purposes, purchase reduced-sodium tamari or soy sauce whenever possible. Although soy sauce (also known as shoyu) and tamari [tuh-mawr-ee] are both made from fermented soybeans, Japanese tamari has a smoother, more complex and well-balanced flavor compared to soy sauce, which is sharper due to the difference in raw materials and a stronger alcoholic fermentation. Since tamari can be somewhat more costly than soy sauce, save it for use directly in the seitan dough and use the less expensive soy sauce for the simmering broth (for which larger amounts are required).

Bragg Liquid Aminos™ are made from non-GMO* soybeans and purified water. This product can be used as a replacement for tamari and soy sauce and contains 16 amino acids, including the nine essential amino acids. Bragg Liquid Aminos™ have not been fermented or heated and are alcohol-free. The packaging label states that the product has only a small amount of naturally occurring sodium, but I find it to be just as salty tasting as tamari and soy sauce, so I use it in the same measurements as I would tamari or soy sauce.

*GMO (genetically modified organism) refers to agricultural products that are genetically altered for higher yields and insect and disease resistance. There have been no studies proving the long-term safety or danger towards human health from these modifications. Regardless, there's something inherently wrong about science tampering with Nature's design. Corn and soybeans are the most commonly modified, so purchase organic whenever possible. Many health-oriented and organic food companies will state "non-GMO" directly on their labels.

Nutritional yeast is another ingredient commonly included when preparing seitan. Nutritional yeast is a non-active form of yeast and a source of complete protein and vitamins, especially the B-complex vitamins. Some brands of nutritional yeast, though not all, are fortified with vitamin B12. The vitamin B12 is produced separately and then added to the yeast. It is also naturally low in fat and sodium and is free of sugar and dairy. Bob's Red Mill™ produces an excellent fortified nutritional yeast, and this is what I use in my recipes.

Tribest™ 16 oz Blender

Occasionally it will be necessary to grind herbs, whole spices or incorporate and emulsify thick ingredients such as tomato paste into the liquid ingredients for making the seitan dough. Using a blender is the best option and mini-blenders work especially well for this purpose. I use a Tribest™ 16 oz personal blender, and I have found that it is an invaluable appliance in the kitchen.

Garbanzo bean flour, or chickpea flour, is a gluten-free flour produced by grinding dried garbanzo beans. It is used in many of my seitan recipes to lighten the texture of the gluten. It is very affordable and can be found in most health food stores or natural markets. You can substitute with other bean flours such as soybean or fava bean. Bob's Red Mill™ produces an excellent garbanzo bean flour.

In some of my recipes, Gravy Master™ (aka "browning liquid") and liquid smoke are listed as ingredients. Gravy Master™ is an animal-free and preservative-free product used to create a rich brown color in broths and gravies. In seitan recipes, it is used as a color enhancer to produce a more appetizing appearance. It can be found in most markets where jar gravy is located. Liquid smoke is an animal-free product used as a seasoning to add a smoky flavor to seitan and is available in most markets in the condiment aisle.

Depending on the desired texture of the finished product, kneading is often utilized to develop the wheat gluten and add elasticity to the dough. Gluten forms as *glutenin* molecules cross-link to create a sub-microscopic network. Kneading promotes the formation of the gluten strands and cross-links, creating a seitan that is chewier in proportion to the length of kneading. The water added to the dough, as well as the absorption of water during simmering, enhances gluten development.

The addition of vegetable oil (fats) and other ingredients such as bean flour, and herbs and/or spice, inhibit formation of the gluten cross-links, and a less chewy and tender seitan is the result. In other words, fewer ingredients and more kneading produces a chewier seitan, which is desirable for creating certain mock meats such as "steak" strips or ribz; and additional ingredients and less kneading produces a tender seitan, which is desirable for creating chik'n cutlets, tender roasts and "meat" balls.

Simmering Seitan

A slow simmer is essential when cooking seitan using the traditional simmer method. This means that you will have to check the cooking pot frequently to adjust the heat. Do not set the timer and leave it unattended. There should be a gentle bubbling action but not a vigorous rolling action. DO NOT RAPID BOIL when cooking your seitan! Initially, the broth is brought to a rapid boil before the dough is added, but is immediately reduced to a simmer during cooking. Continuous rapid boiling will produce a brainy, spongy texture and no amount of pan frying will save your finished product. Soaking in hot broth without simmering will produce a tough, rubbery texture, as not enough liquid will be absorbed.

The trick to seitan is to find that happy medium which will produce a nice meaty texture and this is accomplished by gentle simmering. Also, seitan will expand up to twice its size through absorption of the broth; therefore, you will want to season the simmering broth generously to enhance the flavor of the gluten. If the broth has little flavor, it will "leach" the flavor from the gluten.

Some cooks suggest the "cold start" method, which means placing the dough in cool broth and then bringing it to a simmer, but in my experience this resulted in a spongier texture. Also, it's more difficult to dissolve bouillon or release the aromatics of herbs and spices in cool water, and I like to have my broth seasoned perfectly before adding the gluten dough.

Better Than Bouillon™ vegetarian bouillon bases are excellent for creating homemade simmering broths. They're a staple in my vegan pantry. They aren't always easy to locate, but most health food stores and natural food markets carry them. If you can't find them there, they can be purchased through Soupsonline.com and Amazon.com.

There are three vegan flavors to choose from: Vegetable Base, No Chicken Base and No Beef Base, and each one is useful in various flavor applications. Do not purchase the Mushroom Base - it contains whey, an ingredient derived from dairy.

A general rule of thumb is 1 tsp of bouillon base per cup of water (6 tsp or 2 T for 6 cups of broth) - or more or less to taste. Keep in mind that a generously seasoned broth is going to produce a more flavorful seitan.

There are also quite a few vegetarian bouillon cubes on the market which work well for creating your own broths. Be sure to read labels to make sure ingredients are both vegan and wholesome. A general rule of thumb is 1 cube per 2 cups of water (3 cubes for 6 cups of broth) - or more or less to taste. Again, keep in mind that a generously seasoned broth is going to produce a more flavorful seitan. You can also use commercially made, "ready-to-use" vegetable and mushroom broths that come in aseptic cartons. Just be sure to season them to your satisfaction.

As an alternative to commercial broth products, I've provided recipes for homemade broths which can be found in the chapter 'Soups, Broths and Stews'. There you will also find a recipe for Chik'n Broth Powder (pg. 122), which makes an instant and delicious chik'n broth when pressed for time.

Additional seasonings may also be added to the simmering broth to enhance the flavor of seitan. Sliced fresh ginger root is a nice addition to enhance flavor for Asian recipes. Bay leaves add extra flavor for both chik'n and beaf broths.

An important point I'd like to mention is water quality used for broth, or in any other recipe for that matter. Do not use unfiltered tap water if at all possible – the seitan absorbs water readily and tap water is full of impurities. Faucet mounted filters (PUR™, for example) are a godsend for ensuring clean water. They're also economical and kinder to the environment than disposable plastic water containers.

After simmering, seitan is essentially cooked and edible. However, I have found that refrigeration after simmering helps firm and improve its texture. Before refrigerating, the seitan first needs to be cooled to room temperature, preferably in its cooking broth. For this reason, I recommend preparing seitan early in the day, or the day before, as it should refrigerate for a minimum of 8 hours before using in recipes.

When refrigerating simmered seitan, always include about 1/4 cup of the simmering broth in an airtight container or zip-lock bag. This will keep the seitan moist. It can be refrigerated in this manner for up to 10 days. After that, it can be stored in the freezer for up to 3 months and then thawed before using.

Simmered seitan is not very appealing served "as is" (although, small diced pieces work well in soups and stews). The real magic occurs in its final preparation. Pan-searing with a small amount of Better Butter (pg. 62), Savory Butter (pg. 29), vegan margarine or a misting of vegetable oil in the skillet will enhance the taste and texture of simmered seitan. This technique produces a golden brown and lightly crispy exterior while keeping the interior moist and tender.

The seitan can then be served immediately or further glazed, simmered or sautéed with various sauces or reductions. Pan-searing has health advantages too, because it does not add excess grease and calories commonly associated with deep-fat frying. Of course, seitan can also be breaded and fried when you wish to indulge a bit.

The high moisture content of simmered seitan makes it suitable for pan grilling or grilling on an outdoor BBQ, but be sure to "season" your grill with a little oil to keep the seitan from sticking. Also, the seitan needs to be brushed generously with vegetable oil before grilling. This applies even if you are using a sauce. There is little, if any, fat content in seitan, other than the trivial amount of oil that was added when preparing it, and fat (oil) is what will keep the seitan tender, juicy and flavorful when grilling.

I highly recommend using a hand-pump spray mister whenever a misting of cooking oil is needed for pan-searing seitan. This eliminates excessive landfill waste from aerosol cans, as well as pollution from propellants which may be present in commercial products. And it's much more economical too. Simply add your favorite oil; vigorously pump the top a few times and you're ready to spray.

Baking Seitan

Traditionally, wheat gluten is simmered in broth to create seitan, as discussed previously. But baking is another successful method for cooking gluten and is especially useful for creating seitan roasts and other specialties such as seitan ribz, pepperoni and bacun.

For the roast recipes, the gluten dough is rolled or wrapped in aluminum foil before being baked. This not only creates and holds the shape but seals in moisture. It is very important that you use heavy-duty aluminum foil when baking gluten. Regular foil can easily rupture from expansion of the gluten as it cooks, and from steam pressure which builds up inside the foil. Always err on using too much foil rather than not enough and when in doubt, rewrap with an additional sheet of foil.

Seitan roasts are always finished by browning in the skillet with a pan glaze (pan-glazing). This creates a crispy brown exterior, while the interior remains moist and tender. Detailed instructions are provided with the recipes.

Steaming Seitan

The foil wrap and steam method is a popular way of making a variety of vegan sausages. You will need a large pot with a lid and a steamer insert for this method. The gluten dough is then rolled and sealed in aluminum foil before being steamed. This not only creates and holds the shape of the sausage but seals in moisture.

It is very important that you use heavy-duty aluminum foil when steaming gluten. Regular foil is too thin and easily tears when twisting the ends of the foil wrappers. It can also easily rupture from expansion of the gluten as it cooks, and from steam pressure which builds up inside the foil. Always err on using too much foil rather than not enough and when in doubt, reroll with an additional sheet of foil. Refrigerating after steaming will help firm the sausages and optimize their texture before grilling or browning in the skillet.

Regarding the use of aluminum foil for wrapping seitan sausages and roasts: Some individuals may express concern for their food coming into contact with aluminum - this is the reason why cooking in aluminum pots is not recommended, as aluminum ions may (or may not) transfer to the food. I don't believe there is a health concern when using foil to bake or steam seitan, but if there is any doubt, there is a solution: simply cut a piece of parchment paper to line the foil before rolling or wrapping. This will keep the dough from coming into contact with the foil.

Basic Seitan and Beaf Seitan

Basic and beaf seitan are essentially the same, except beaf seitan contains an additional ingredient to enhance color and is simmered in a "beef" flavored broth, rather than a basic vegetable broth. "Beaf" is a word derived from the consonants of the word "beef" and the vowels of the word "wheat".

Seitan can be shaped in many ways prior to simmering, depending upon its intended application; the shaping techniques are explained in the recipe.

For the best texture, simmered beaf seitan should be refrigerated for a minimum of 8 hours before final preparation; so plan accordingly. This recipe makes about 1 and 1/4 lb (20 oz).

Sift together the following dry ingredients in a large mixing bowl:

- 1 cup vital wheat gluten
- 2 T garbanzo bean (chickpea) flour
- 1 tsp onion powder
- 1 tsp garlic powder
- 1/4 tsp ground white pepper

For the liquid ingredients, mix the following in a separate bowl or measuring cup:

- 3/4 cup water
- 2 T nutritional yeast
- 1 T tamari, soy sauce or Bragg Liquid Aminos™
- 1 T vegetable oil
- 1 tsp Gravy Master™ or other browning liquid (for beaf seitan)

For the simmering broth you will need:

- 6 cups vegetable broth for basic seitan (see pg. 121 for broth options)
- 6 cups beaf broth for beaf seitan (see pg. 123 for broth options)

Technique:

In a large saucepan, set your broth over high heat while you prepare your seitan dough. You will want to bring it to a rapid boil. Add the liquid ingredients (not the simmering broth) to the dry ingredients in a large bowl and mix well.

Turn out onto a work surface and knead vigorously with the heel of your hand for several minutes to develop the gluten. The dough will become very elastic.

Now, you will need to shape the dough prior to simmering, and there are different ways to do this depending on your application:

- ❖ If you need thin slices for a recipe, form the dough into a rounded loaf shape and cut in half with a sharp knife. Simmer and refrigerate as directed, then slice as needed.

- ❖ If you intend to later thread your seitan onto skewers for grilling, divide the dough into 6 to 8 pieces. Squeeze and shape the pieces into slender 3 or 4-inch long "tenders" and slightly flatten them with the palm of your hand. Simmer and refrigerate as directed, then skewer.

- ❖ For "steak" cutlets, which can later be cut into "steak" strips if desired, divide the dough into 4 to 6 pieces. Stretch and flatten each piece with the heel of your hand. Let the dough rest for a few minutes and then flatten again to form very thin cutlets. Simmer and refrigerate as directed, then use in your intended recipe.

Next, add the shaped dough to the boiling broth. The addition of the dough may temporarily halt the boiling action. Once the broth begins to bubble again, immediately adjust the heat to a gentle, lazy simmer and set the timer for 45 minutes. Be sure to leave the pot uncovered. If you've divided the dough into strips or cutlets, simmer for 30 minutes.

The first ten minutes of simmering is the most crucial, as this is when the texture is set. Watch the pot and continue to adjust the heat by increments, up or down as necessary to maintain a gentle simmer. If you catch the broth rapidly simmering, simply reduce the heat slightly. Turn occasionally once the seitan pieces float to the top of the pot.

When finished cooking, remove from the pot from the heat and let the seitan cool in the broth until it reaches room temperature. It will be very soft at this point. Refrigerate the seitan with about 1/4 cup of the simmering broth in a zip-lock bag or airtight container for a minimum of 8 hours, or for up to 10 days, before final preparation. This will firm the seitan and optimize its texture. You can also freeze it for up to 3 months.

Reserve the remaining broth for other uses, but be sure to add back a little water if necessary, as the broth may have become very salty from evaporation during simmering.

Final Preparation and Uses for Basic and Beef Seitan:

Larger seitan pieces are at their best when sliced very thin and pan-seared in a small amount of vegetable oil. They can also be finely diced. The slices and dice hold up well in hearty soups, stews and pot pies. Try thin-slicing simmered seitan and serve with Skye's Best BBQ Sauce (pg. 208) on a bun; or glaze with Teriyaki Sauce (pg. 206) and serve over rice. Pan-sear seitan cutlets, then slice into strips for "steak" sandwiches. Cutlets can also be breaded and fried.

Seitan "tenders" can be used for shish-kabob or satay (see Seitan Satay, pg. 15). Be sure to brush them first with a generous amount of vegetable oil and then frequently with the marinade or sauce to keep them from drying out on the grill.

Ground beef seitan is an excellent alternative for any dish calling for pre-cooked and crumbled ground beef. Simply cut into chunks and grind in a food processor. Add to pasta sauce, or enhance with additional seasonings for Mexican cuisine.

Chik'n Seitan

Chik'n Seitan can be shaped in many ways prior to simmering, depending upon its intended application. The shaping techniques are explained in the recipe. For the best texture, simmered chik'n seitan should be refrigerated for a minimum of 8 hours before final preparation; so plan accordingly. This recipe makes about 1 and 1/4 lb (20 oz).

Sift together the following dry ingredients in a large mixing bowl:

- 1 cup vital wheat gluten
- 2 T garbanzo bean (chickpea) flour
- 1 tsp onion powder
- 1/2 tsp garlic powder
- 1/4 tsp poultry seasoning
- 1/4 tsp ground white pepper

For the liquid ingredients, mix the following in a separate bowl or measuring cup until the salt dissolves:

- 7/8 cup water (3/4 cup plus 2 T)
- 2 T nutritional yeast
- 3/4 tsp sea salt or kosher salt
- 1 T vegetable oil

For the simmering broth you will need:

- 6 cups chik'n broth (see pg. 121-122 for broth options)

Technique:

In a large saucepan, set your broth over high heat while you prepare your seitan dough. You will want to bring it to a rapid boil. Add a bay leaf, or a few slices of ginger root, for extra flavor if desired.

Add the liquid ingredients (not the simmering broth) to the dry ingredients in a large bowl and mix well. Turn out onto a work surface and knead the dough for about 1 minute or until it begins to exhibit some elasticity. Avoid over-kneading as this can make the chik'n less tender.

Now, you will need to shape the dough prior to simmering, and there are different ways to do this depending on your application:

- ❖ For chik'n cutlets: Cut the dough into 6 to 8 pieces. Stretch and flatten each piece with the heel of your hand. Let the dough rest for a few minutes and then flatten again to form very thin cutlets. Simmer and refrigerate as directed, then use in your recipe.

- ❖ For chik'n nuggets: Twist and stretch the dough and tear off small pieces about 2-inches in size. Squeeze and shape the pieces into nuggets. Simmer and refrigerate as directed, then use in your recipe.

❖ For chik'n "tenders", which are ideal for threading onto skewers: Cut the dough into 8 pieces. Squeeze and shape the pieces into slender 3 or 4-inch long nuggets. Simmer and refrigerate as directed, then use in your recipe.

Next, add the dough to the boiling broth. The addition of the dough may temporarily halt the boiling action. Once the broth begins to bubble again, immediately adjust the heat to a gentle, lazy simmer and set the timer for 30 minutes. Be sure to leave the pot uncovered.

The first ten minutes of simmering is the most crucial, as this is when the texture is set. Watch the pot and continue to adjust the heat by increments, up or down as necessary, to maintain a gentle simmer. If you catch the broth rapidly simmering, simply reduce the heat slightly. Turn occasionally once the seitan pieces float to the top of the pot.

When finished cooking, remove the pot from the heat and let the seitan cool in the broth until it reaches room temperature. It will be very soft at this point. Refrigerate the seitan with about 1/4 cup of the simmering broth in a zip-lock bag or airtight container for a minimum of 8 hours, or for up to 10 days, before final preparation. This will firm and optimize its texture. You can also freeze it for up to 3 months.

Reserve the remaining broth for other uses, but be sure to add back a little water if necessary, as the broth may have become very salty from evaporation during simmering.

Final Preparation and Uses for Chik'n Seitan:

Simmered chik'n cutlets can be used whole or sliced into strips for sautéing, or diced for soups, in which case you can use the broth too. Pan-searing in a small amount of vegetable oil will give the chik'n a golden brown and lightly crispy exterior. Chik'n "tenders" and nuggets can be skewered and grilled with your favorite sauce (see Seitan Satay, pg. 15) or breaded and fried (see Fried Chik'n, pg. 158).

Seitan Specialties

Seitan Mignon

This tender and petite "cut" is perfect for serving two to four people ("mignon" is French for "dainty"). For this recipe, the seitan dough is wrapped in cheesecloth to provide a uniform shape, and then simmered in a "beef" flavored broth. The real magic occurs during the final pan-glazing - the exterior becomes brown and crispy, while the interior remains moist and tender.

Slice into thin medallions and serve, if desired, with Beaf Au Jus (pg. 38), Quick Pan Gravy (pg. 29), Béarnaise Sauce (pg. 214), Creamy Horseradish Sauce (pg. 205) or smother in sautéed mushrooms and onions. For the best texture, simmered seitan mignon should be refrigerated for a minimum of 8 hours before pan-glazing and serving; so plan accordingly.

Sift together the following dry ingredients in a large mixing bowl:

- 1 cup vital wheat gluten
- 2 T garbanzo bean (chickpea) flour
- 1 tsp onion powder
- 1 tsp garlic powder
- 1/4 tsp ground white pepper

For the liquid ingredients, mix the following in a separate bowl or measuring cup:

- 1 cup water
- 2 T nutritional yeast
- 1 T vegetable oil
- 1 T tamari, soy sauce or Bragg Liquid Aminos™
- 1 tsp homemade vegan Worcestershire Sauce (pg. 206) or commercial
- 1 tsp Gravy Master™ or other browning liquid - optional

For the simmering broth, you will need:

- 8 cups of beaf broth (see pg. 123 for broth options)

For the pan-glaze, you will need:

- 2 T Savory Butter (pg. 29), Better Butter (pg. 62), vegan margarine or vegetable oil
- 2 T dry red wine or dry sherry (optional)
- a few pinches of coarse ground black pepper

Additional items needed:

- a double layer of cheesecloth, about 12" x 12" and kitchen string

Technique:

In a large soup pot, place your broth over high heat while you prepare your seitan dough. You will want to bring it to a rapid boil.

Add the liquid ingredients (not the simmering broth or pan-glaze ingredients) to the dry ingredients in a large bowl and mix well. Turn out onto a work surface and knead vigorously with the heel of your hand for several minutes to develop the gluten.

Form the dough into a loaf shape and place onto the cheesecloth. Roll the dough tightly inside the cheesecloth and tie the ends with the kitchen string.

Next, add the wrapped dough to the boiling broth. The addition of the dough may temporarily halt the boiling action. Once the broth begins to bubble again, immediately adjust the heat to a gentle, lazy simmer, partially cover the pot to vent steam and set the timer for 60 minutes.

Watch the pot and continue to adjust the heat by increments, up or down as necessary to maintain a gentle simmer. If you catch the broth rapidly simmering, simply reduce the heat slightly. Turn occasionally once the seitan floats to the top of the pot.

When finished cooking, remove the pot from the heat and let the seitan cool in the broth until it reaches room temperature. Refrigerate the seitan with about 1/4 cup of the simmering broth in a zip-lock bag or airtight container for a minimum of 8 hours, or for up to 10 days, before final preparation. This will firm and optimize its texture. You can also freeze it for up to 3 months.

Reserve the remaining broth for other uses, but be sure to add back a little water if necessary, as the broth may have become very salty from evaporation during simmering.

Final Preparation:

In a large, deep non-stick skillet, melt the butter or margarine over medium heat.* Add the seitan and roll it around to coat with the butter or margarine. Sauté, turning frequently, until it begins to brown lightly. Now, add the remaining pan-glaze ingredients. The mixture will sizzle and begin to caramelize, turning the seitan a beautiful deep brown color. Continue to roll in the mixture until lightly crisp.

* Exercise caution if using vegetable oil for pan-glazing, as some splattering of hot oil may occur, especially when adding other pan-glaze ingredients. Vegan butter and margarine contain an emulsifier that reduces oil splatter when pan-glazing.

Transfer to a serving platter and slice into thin medallions. If pan-glazing has not sufficiently reheated the seitan, wrap in foil and gently re-heat in the oven. Or you can briefly heat the slices in the microwave or in a warm skillet before serving.

Seitan Satay

These flavorful seitan "kabobs" are perfect for the outdoor BBQ but they can also be grilled or broiled indoors too. Be sure to generously brush the satay with vegetable oil before brushing on the sauce to prevent the seitan from sticking or drying out on the grill or in the broiler.

Technique:

Prepare Basic or Beaf Seitan (pg. 9) or Chik'n Seitan (pg. 11) as directed in the recipe and shape the dough into tenders or nuggets. Simmer as directed and let cool to room temperature, then refrigerate for a minimum of 8 hours for the best texture.

Soak your bamboo skewers in water for at least one hour to prevent them from burning on the grill. You can also use steel skewers if you prefer.

Thread the seitan onto the skewers. Brush liberally with vegetable oil and then with your favorite sauce or glaze. The vegetable oil is essential, as it will keep the seitan from drying out and sticking to the grill.

Grill over hot embers (no flames!), on both sides, just until the sauce or glaze begins to caramelize. Do not overcook! The satay can also be grilled on the stove using a grill pan or broiled in the oven. I have achieved superior results with broiling.

Seitan Kefta

Kefta is an aromatically seasoned Middle Eastern delight that is perfectly suited for the grill or BBQ. In Greece they're called "keftedes" and in Persian cuisine they're called "koobideh". Grilling over charcoal gives the seitan kefta an authentic smoky flavor. For the best texture, simmered seitan kefta should be refrigerated for a minimum of 8 hours before grilling and serving; so plan accordingly. This recipe makes 8 kefta kabobs.

Thoroughly stir together the following dry ingredients in a large mixing bowl:

- 1 cup vital wheat gluten
- 2 T nutritional yeast
- 1 T dried minced onion
- 2 tsp ground cumin
- 2 tsp dried parsley
- 1 tsp onion powder
- 1 tsp garlic powder
- 1 tsp paprika
- 1 tsp dried oregano
- 1/2 tsp ground rosemary
- 1/2 tsp coarsely ground black pepper

Mix the following liquid ingredients in a separate bowl or measuring cup:

- 3/4 cup water
- 1 T tamari, soy sauce, or Bragg Liquid Aminos™
- 1 T extra-virgin olive oil
- 1 T liquid smoke
- 1 tsp Gravy Master™ or other browning liquid - optional

For the simmering broth you will need:

- 6 cups beaf broth (see pg. 123 for broth options)

Technique:

In a large saucepan, place your broth over high heat while you prepare your seitan dough. You will want to bring it to a rapid boil.

Add the liquid ingredients (not the simmering broth) to the dry ingredients. Mix thoroughly until all ingredients are combined but do not overwork the dough or the kefta will not be as tender. Cut the dough into 8 equal pieces with a sharp knife. Roll each piece into a thin sausage shape.

Add the dough to the boiling broth. The addition of the dough may temporarily halt the boiling action. Once the broth begins to bubble again, immediately adjust the heat to a gentle, lazy simmer and set the timer for 30 minutes.

The first ten minutes of simmering is the most crucial, as this is when the texture is set. So, watch the pot and continue to adjust the heat by increments, up or down as necessary to maintain a gentle simmer. If you catch the broth rapidly simmering, simply reduce the heat slightly. Turn occasionally once the seitan pieces float to the top of the pot.

When finished cooking, remove the pot from the heat and let the kefta cool in the broth until it reaches room temperature. It will be very soft at this point, so carefully transfer the pieces (to avoid breaking) to a zip-lock bag or airtight container and add 1/4 cup of the simmering broth. Refrigerate for a minimum of 8 hours, or for up to 10 days, before final preparation. This will firm and optimize its texture. You can also freeze it for up to 3 months.

Reserve the remaining broth for other uses (I use it for the rice pilaf), but be sure to add back a little water if necessary, as the broth may have become very salty from evaporation during simmering.

Final Preparation:

Soak 8 to 10 bamboo skewers in water for at least one hour before threading and grilling your kefta.

Thread the kefta lengthwise onto a bamboo skewer, making sure you keep the skewer centered. This is actually much easier than it sounds. Season your grill rack or grill pan with oil and start your charcoal or heat your grill pan over medium-high heat.

Brush the kefta generously with extra-virgin olive oil and place on the hot grill (over glowing embers - no flames) or hot grill pan. Turn occasionally, brushing with extra-virgin olive oil every few minutes to avoid drying out. Sprinkle with a little ground red pepper if desired. Grill until nicely browned.

Kefta is wonderful when served over rice pilaf with Tzatziki Sauce (pg. 209). You can also grill fresh vegetables on bamboo skewers and serve along side. Tabbouleh salad, Hummus (pg. 88), Baba Ghannouj (pg. 90) and pita bread are favorite accompaniments with this dish as well.

Kali orexi! - That's Greek for "enjoy your meal!"

Seitan Meatballs

These tender and delicious meatballs are perfect for using in your favorite pasta sauce, soup, stew or for meatball sandwiches. Once browned, they hold up very well when added to cooking liquids and do not break down like commercial vegan meatballs.

For the best texture, simmered seitan meatballs should be refrigerated for a minimum of 8 hours before browning and serving; so plan accordingly. This recipe makes approximately 20 to 25 medium-sized meatballs.

Thoroughly stir together the following dry ingredients in a large mixing bowl:

- 1 cup vital wheat gluten
- 1/4 cup garbanzo bean (chickpea) flour
- 2 T nutritional yeast
- 1 T dried minced onion
- 2 tsp dried parsley flakes
- 1 tsp onion powder
- 1 tsp garlic powder
- 1/4 tsp ground black pepper

Variations:

- ❖ For Italian meatballs omit parsley and add 1 tsp dried oregano, 1 tsp dried basil and 1/4 tsp ground red pepper

- ❖ For Swedish meatballs add 1/4 tsp fresh grated nutmeg and 1/4 tsp allspice

- ❖ For Mexican meatballs omit parsley and add 1 tsp dried oregano, 1/2 tsp ground cumin, 1/2 tsp ground coriander and 1/4 tsp ground red pepper

- ❖ For Mediterranean meatballs reduce parsley to 1 tsp and add 1 tsp dried oregano and 1/2 tsp ground cumin

- ❖ For Moroccan meatballs add 1/2 tsp ground cumin, 1/2 tsp allspice and 1/4 tsp ground red pepper

Mix the following liquid ingredients in a separate bowl or measuring cup:

- 3/4 cup COLD water
- 1 T tamari, soy sauce or Bragg Liquid Aminos™
- 1 T vegetable oil
- 1 tsp Gravy Master™ or other browning liquid - optional

For the simmering broth you will need:

- 6 cups beaf broth (see pg. 123 for broth options) or vegetable broth (see pg. 121 for broth options)

Technique:

In a large saucepan, place your broth over high heat while you prepare your meatballs. You will want to bring it to a rapid boil.

Add the liquid ingredients (not the simmering broth) to the dry ingredients. Mix thoroughly but just until all ingredients are combined. DO NOT overwork the dough or the meatballs will be difficult to roll and will not be as tender after cooking. Cut off small pieces of dough and roll into small, round meatball shapes with the palms of your hands, about 3/4-inch in diameter.

Try to work quickly when rolling; the gluten in the dough becomes more elastic the longer the dough sits, and this will make rolling more difficult. The cold water used in mixing the dough is important, because it helps slow down the activation of the gluten. Some of the meatballs may look a little irregular in shape but don't stress about it - they'll be fine once browned in the skillet. Also, do not make the meatballs too large because they will increase in size when simmered.

Now add the meatballs to the boiling broth and immediately reduce the heat to a slow simmer. Cook uncovered for 25 minutes. Check frequently to maintain the broth at a very gentle simmer. DO NOT RAPID SIMMER OR BOIL! Turn occasionally once the meatballs float to the top of the pot.

When done cooking, remove the pot from the heat and let the meatballs cool in the broth until they reach room temperature. Refrigerate the meatballs with about 1/4 cup of the simmering broth in a zip-lock bag or airtight container for a minimum of 8 hours, or for up to 10 days, before browning in the skillet. This will firm and optimize their texture. You can also freeze them for up to 3 months.

Reserve the remaining broth for other uses if desired, but be sure to add back a little water if necessary, as the broth may have become very salty from evaporation during simmering.

Finishing the Meatballs:

Sauté the meatballs in a skillet with 2 tablespoons of vegetable oil over medium-high heat until nicely browned. Add them to your favorite sauce, soup or stew the last 15 minutes of cooking time before serving.

Corned Beaf

Corned beaf is delicious anytime of the year but is especially appropriate for celebrating St. Patrick's Day or the Spring Equinox. For the best texture, prepare a day ahead because the corned beaf needs to refrigerate for a minimum of 8 hours before final preparation. Leftovers are perfect for making Grilled Reuben sandwiches (pg. 22). This recipe makes about 1 and 1/4 lb (20 oz) of corned beaf.

Sift together the following dry ingredients in a large mixing bowl:

- 1 cup vital wheat gluten
- 1 T garbanzo bean (chickpea) flour
- 2 tsp onion powder
- 1 tsp garlic powder
- 1 tsp ground coriander
- 1/2 tsp allspice
- 1/2 tsp ground ginger
- 1/4 tsp ground white pepper

Process in a blender until caraway seeds are finely ground (mini-blenders work great for this):

- 3/4 cup water
- 2 T nutritional yeast
- 1 T tamari, soy sauce or Bragg Liquid Aminos™
- 1 T vegetable oil
- 1 tsp paprika
- 1 tsp caraway seeds

In a large stockpot add these ingredients to make the brine:

- 8 cups water
- 1 T plus 1 tsp salt
- 2 T red wine vinegar or apple cider vinegar
- 1 T whole juniper berries (or a tablespoon of pickling spice and omit the 10 whole cloves)
- 10 whole cloves
- 2 bay leaves

Additional items needed:

- a double layer of cheesecloth, about 12" x 12" and kitchen string
- 1/4 cup raw shredded red beet (for color)

Technique:

In a large pot, bring the brine ingredients to a boil while you prepare your seitan.

Process the blender ingredients (mini blenders work great for this, such as the Tribest 16 oz blender) until the caraway seeds are finely ground.

Pour the blender ingredients through a strainer into the dry ingredients (you want the flavor of the caraway seeds but not the particles). Stir well to combine; use your hands if necessary to incorporate the ingredients completely. The dough may seem a bit dry - this is normal.

Turn the dough onto a work surface and knead for 1 to 2 minutes to develop the gluten. Let the dough rest for a few minutes and then knead again. Form into an oval, flattened loaf and place on the double layer of cheesecloth. Now, fold the loaf inside the cheesecloth creating a flattened package. Tie the ends securely with kitchen string.

Add the dough to the boiling broth. The addition of the dough may temporarily halt the boiling action. When the broth begins to boil again, immediately reduce the heat to a slow-simmer and set the timer for 60 minutes. Check the cooking pot frequently and adjust the heat up and down as necessary to maintain a gentle simmer. DO NOT RAPID BOIL! When the loaf eventually surfaces in the pot, turn it a few times during the remaining cooking time.

When the corned beaf is done simmering, remove the pot from the heat and let it sit in the broth until the broth is lukewarm. Transfer to a work surface and remove the cheesecloth. Reserve 1/2 cup of the brine and discard the rest.

Thinly slice the corned beef and place in a zip-lock bag. In a bowl, stir together the 1/2 cup of reserved brine with the 1/4 cup shredded red beet. Let stand for a minute or two and then strain out the beet pulp. Add the colored brine to the corned beaf in the bag. Seal the bag and refrigerate for a minimum of 8 hours before final preparation (turn the bag occasionally to ensure even distribution of color). The corned beaf can also be stored in the broth for up to 10 days in the refrigerator, or in the freezer for up to 3 months.

Finishing the Corned Beaf:

Drain the brine from the corned beaf and lightly pat dry with paper towels. You can gently warm the slices in the microwave or wrap in foil and warm in the oven. The slices can also be warmed in the skillet. To do this, mist a skillet with a little cooking oil spray and lightly pan-sear the slices over medium-low heat.

Serve warm with grainy mustard or Creamy Horseradish Sauce (pg. 205) and a side of mashed potatoes and Caraway Cabbage (pg. 162); or use to make Grilled Reuben sandwiches (see the following recipe).

Grilled Reuben

The Reuben is a hot sandwich of layered seitan Corned Beaf, sauerkraut, vegan white cheese and a dressing which is then grilled between slices of rye or pumpernickel bread. The dressing is traditionally either Russian or Thousand Island.

Ingredients:

- Better Butter (pg. 62) or vegan margarine
- sliced rye bread or swirled pumpernickel/rye bread
- thinly sliced seitan Corned Beaf (see preceding recipe)
- sliced or shredded vegan white cheese that melts (Daiya™, for example)
- sauerkraut, drained and pressed well to remove as much moisture as possible
- vegan Thousand Island or Russian Dressing (pg. 108)

Technique:

Drain the brine from the corned beaf and lightly pat dry with paper towels. You can gently warm the slices in the microwave or wrap in foil and warm in the oven. The slices can also be warmed in the skillet. To do this, mist a skillet with a little cooking oil spray and lightly pan-sear the slices over medium-low heat. Set aside.

If desired, heat the sauerkraut in a saucepan over low heat or in the microwave for 30 seconds to 1 minute.

Lightly "butter" one side of all bread slices. Spread the non-buttered sides with a dressing of your choice.

On 1/2 of the bread slices, layer 1 slice vegan cheese (or sprinkle with shredded vegan cheese), as much corned beaf as you like and 1/4 cup sauerkraut. Top with the remaining bread slices, "buttered" sides out.

Grill the sandwiches until both sides are golden brown (a Panini press works great for this too). Slice in half and serve hot.

Bacun

Bacon has a flavor and texture that many people miss when they transition to a vegan diet. There are several steps to this recipe, but because this vegan version simulates the appearance and taste of real bacon fairly well, it's worth the extra effort. I think it's actually better than the commercial brands.

This recipe really isn't as complicated as it appears, so give it a try. It's wonderful served with tofu scramble at breakfast and especially for BLT sandwiches. For the best texture, you will need to refrigerate the Bacun for a minimum of 8 hours after baking before slicing and browning slices in the skillet; so plan accordingly.

In this recipe you will be making two batches of seitan to create your bacun. Dough 1 is for the darker marble layer of the bacun. Dough 2 is for the lighter marble layer of the bacun.

Thoroughly stir together the dry ingredients for Dough 1 in a large bowl:

- 1 cup vital wheat gluten
- 2 T nutritional yeast
- 3 tsp smoked paprika
- 2 tsp onion powder
- 1/4 tsp ground white pepper

Mix the liquid ingredients for Dough 1 in a bowl or measuring cup:

- 1/2 cup water
- 2 T tamari, soy sauce or Bragg Liquid Aminos™
- 2 T real maple syrup
- 2 T tomato paste
- 1 T liquid smoke
- 1 T vegetable oil

Thoroughly stir together the dry ingredients for Dough 2 in a medium size bowl:

- 1/3 cup vital wheat gluten
- 1 T nutritional yeast
- 1/2 tsp garlic powder

Mix the liquid ingredients for Dough 2 in a bowl or measuring cup:

- 1/4 cup water
- 1/2 tsp smoked sea salt (substitute with sea salt or kosher salt)
- 1 T liquid smoke
- 1 T vegetable oil

Preheat the oven to 325°F.

Dough 1 Technique:

Add the liquid ingredients to the dry ingredients and mix well to incorporate. Divide the dough into 3 pieces.

Dough 2 Technique:

Add the liquid ingredients to the dry ingredients and mix well to incorporate. Divide the dough into 2 pieces.

Now you will begin the layering process which will create the marbling effect for your bacun. Take a piece of Dough 1 and flatten and spread the dough on your work surface with the heel of your hand until it is about 1/4-inch thick. You don't need to worry about the shape. Place the flattened piece on a large sheet of heavy-duty aluminum foil.

Next, take a piece of Dough 2 and repeat the process. Lay this on top of Dough 1 on your foil. Repeat the process again with another piece of Dough 1, then with a piece of Dough 2 and finally with the remaining piece of Dough 1. If they don't stack perfectly, that's good - if you are too precise, the bacun will look like it was made by a machine.

With the palms of your hands, shape the dough into a rectangular "slab" about 1 inch thick. Once again, don't worry about being too precise; the dough will expand during baking to conform to the shape of the foil package. Sprinkle with a little black pepper and wrap (don't roll) the slab of bacun in the foil. You want to create a rectangular shaped package. Wrap again in another piece of foil. Place seam side down in a shallow casserole dish and bake for 90 minutes.

Cool the bacun in the foil at room temperature and then refrigerate for a minimum of 8 hours, or for up to 10 days, before browning in the skillet. You can also store the bacun in the freezer for up to 3 months.

Now unwrap it, slice it thin (but not too thin, or it will tear when trying to turn it in the skillet) and fry in a tablespoon or two of vegetable oil until lightly browned and crisp.

Transfer to a plate lined with paper towels to blot any excess oil. Serve or use on your favorite sandwiches.

Rack of Ribz

Perfect for an outdoor BBQ or anytime when using a grill pan or broiler. This is my original recipe for ribz that are chewy on the outside and tender on the inside with a wonderful "pull-apart" texture. The secret to the texture is the shredded onion.

Thoroughly stir together the following dry ingredients in a large mixing bowl:

- 1 cup vital wheat gluten
- 2 T nutritional yeast
- 1 T garbanzo bean (chickpea) flour - omit if you like you ribz really chewy
- 1 tsp onion powder
- 1 tsp garlic powder
- 1/2 tsp ground ginger
- 1/4 tsp ground white pepper

For the liquid ingredients, mix together the following in a separate bowl:

- 2/3 cup water
- 1/4 cup **shredded** onion
- 2 T tamari, soy sauce or Bragg Liquid Aminos™
- 1 T vegetable oil plus an additional 1 T for brushing on the dough
- 1 T liquid smoke

For the topping:

- Skye's Best BBQ Sauce (pg. 208) or Teriyaki Sauce (pg. 206) or your favorite sauce or glaze

Technique:

Preheat the oven to 350°F. Grease an 8×8-inch baking pan with vegetable oil. If you have parchment paper, cut a piece to line the bottom of the pan. This will ease removal of the ribz from the pan after baking. Thoroughly mix together the dry ingredients in a large mixing bowl. Combine the liquid ingredients in a separate bowl or large measuring cup.

Shred the onion with a cheese/vegetable grater (use the larger holes) or use a food processor with a shredding blade. The shredded onion will be very wet. Shred enough of the onion to pack 1/4 cup. Add the onion to the bowl with the liquid ingredients and stir.

Now add the liquid ingredients to the dry ingredients in the mixing bowl. Stir to completely combine but do not overwork the dough or it will become extremely elastic and difficult to spread in the baking pan.

Place the dough into the baking pan and flatten and spread so that it fills the pan evenly. The layer of dough will seem somewhat thin - this is normal. Take a sharp knife and score the dough into 6 strips; then turn the pan and score those strips in half lengthwise to form 12 pieces. Don't worry about cutting them perfectly or all the way through. Brush the top of the dough with vegetable oil. Place uncovered in the oven and bake for about 30 minutes. If the ribz feel springy in the center, they're done baking. If not, bake for 5 minutes longer. Do not exceed 35 minutes.

Remove the pan from the oven and let sit until cool enough to handle. Lightly re-score the ribz to ensure that they will pull apart easily later; avoid cutting all the way to the bottom of the pan. If you don't plan on grilling or broiling the ribz right away, invert them onto foil, wrap securely and store in the refrigerator for up to 10 days or in the freezer for up to 3 months.

Finishing the Ribz:

Prepare your grill pan or grill rack by "seasoning" with vegetable oil. Vegetable oil is essential for preventing the ribs from sticking to the cooking surface. If using a grill pan, place over medium heat.

Generously brush the ribz with sauce or glaze. Now carefully but quickly invert the ribz onto the hot grill or grill pan. Generously brush the exposed side of the ribz with sauce.

Watch closely to make sure that they don't burn (lift a corner with an extra-wide spatula to check). When the sauce or glaze begins to caramelize on one side, turn over carefully with the spatula and cook the other side, adding more sauce as necessary.

The ribz can also be broiled if more convenient. This is my preferred method because the ribz are being cooked from the top, so it's much easier to keep an eye on the browning process. For this method, line a baking sheet with foil. Brush the ribz with sauce or glaze and invert the pan onto the baking sheet. Brush the exposed side of the ribz with sauce or glaze and broil. When the top is nicely browned after about 5 minutes, flip the ribz over and repeat.

When done, remove to a platter and cut or pull apart the individual ribz to serve.

Seitan Roasts

To prepare a seitan roast, the gluten dough is rolled and sealed in aluminum foil before being baked. It is very important that you use heavy-duty aluminum foil when baking gluten. Regular foil can easily rupture from expansion of the gluten as it cooks, and from steam pressure which builds up inside the foil. Always err on using too much foil rather than not enough. When in doubt, rewrap with an additional sheet of foil.

Foil Wrap Technique for Seitan Roasts

The foil wrap technique applies to all seitan roasts and is described here to avoid repetition in each recipe.

On a work surface, lay out a large sheet of heavy-duty aluminum foil (18-inch wide). Place the dough directly on top.

With your hands, form the dough into a round mass. The dough will be very soft and somewhat difficult to shape but try to keep it as compact as you can. Now, lift the edge of the foil over the dough and begin to roll the dough inside the foil, pinching the ends closed simultaneously while rolling. The goal is to create a thick, compact package - not a thin sausage shape. This may take a little bit of practice, so be patient.

Now twist the ends tightly to seal, being careful not to tear the foil. Wrap with an additional large sheet of foil and twist the ends very tight to completely seal the roast.

Important! The seitan dough will expand under steam pressure while baking; therefore, it is crucial that the dough be wrapped in a minimum of two layers of heavy-duty foil and the ends twisted very tightly. If you fail to do so, the package may explosively burst open during baking.

Place the foil package into a shallow baking dish and bake for 2 hours, turning after 1 hour. Remove from the oven and transfer the foil package to a plate or work surface.

After baking, the roast should be pan-glazed to firm its texture, lock in moisture and create a lightly crispy exterior. The pan-glazing technique is described on page 28. The roast can be pan-glazed immediately after baking or refrigerated and pan-glazed later. This will depend on how you plan to slice and serve the roast:

- ❖ To immediately slice and serve the roast hot, pan-glaze after baking as directed (pg. 28) and then place on a cutting board or serving platter. Slice the roast as thin as possible with a sharp knife. For the sake of presentation, discard the end pieces if you find them unappealing, as they sometimes become misshapen by the twisted foil. Leftovers can be refrigerated and then reheated later or served cold for sandwiches. To reheat the slices you can either wrap them securely in foil and heat in the oven; briefly heat the slices in the microwave; dip the slices in hot au jus or gravy; or warm them gently in a lightly oiled skillet before serving.

- ❖ If you wish to create deli-quality "shaved" slices of roast, use a very sharp mandoline or an electric-deli slicer. Let the roast cool to near room temperature and then place in a zip-lock bag or covered container. Refrigerate for a minimum of 8 hours, as thorough chilling will make thin slicing much easier (the roast can also be stored in the refrigerator for up to 10 days before slicing or in the freezer for up to 3 months). The slices can be served either hot or cold. To reheat the slices you can either wrap them securely in foil and heat in the oven; briefly heat the slices in the microwave; dip the slices in hot au jus or gravy; or warm them gently in a lightly oiled skillet before serving.

❖ If you plan on browning and serving a roast at a future date, remove it from the oven after baking, let it cool to near room temperature and then refrigerate for a minimum of 8 hours in its foil wrapper. It can also be stored in the refrigerator for up to 10 days or frozen for up to 3 months. When ready to serve, remove the foil and pan-glaze the roast as directed (pg. 28). If the roast is frozen, thaw completely before pan-glazing. Slice thin and serve. If pan-glazing has not sufficiently reheated the roast, you can either wrap the slices securely in foil and heat in the oven; briefly heat the slices in the microwave; dip the slices in hot au jus or gravy; or warm them gently in the same skillet before serving.

Pan-Glazing Technique for Seitan Roasts

Let the roast rest at room temperature until it is cool enough to handle and then untwist the ends of the foil. For ease of removal, cut the ends off of the foil package with sharp kitchen shears. Peel away the foil and recycle. The roast will be soft at this stage, so handle it carefully.

In a large, deep, non-stick skillet over medium heat, add 2 tablespoons Savory Butter (pg. 29), Better Butter (pg. 62), vegan margarine or vegetable oil. Add the roast and roll it around to coat with the butter, margarine or oil.

Sauté, turning frequently, until the roast begins to lightly brown. Add any remaining pan-glaze ingredients as specified in the recipe.

Continue to roll the roast in the mixture until nicely browned and lightly crisp.

If wine is specified as a pan-glaze ingredient, use a dry-flavored wine such as Chardonnay for chik'n and turk'y roasts, and Merlot or Cabernet Sauvignon for beaf roasts.

* Exercise caution if using vegetable oil for pan-glazing, as some splattering of hot oil may occur, especially when adding other pan-glaze ingredients. Vegan butter and margarine contain an emulsifier that reduces oil splatter when heat contact is made with moisture from the roast and other pan-glaze ingredients, such as lemon juice, liquid smoke or wine.

Savory Butter

Savory Butter is a special blend of homemade vegan butter (or commercial margarine) and seasonings. It works beautifully for adding a flavorful crust to seitan roasts or for browning seitan cutlets, tofu or tempeh in the skillet. It's also excellent for topping potatoes, corn on the cob, cooked grains or cooked vegetables.

Ingredients:

- 1/2 cup Better Butter (pg. 62) or vegan margarine
- 1 T fresh lemon juice
- 1/2 tsp onion powder
- 1/2 tsp garlic powder
- 1/4 tsp ground black pepper
- 1/4 tsp sweet or smoked paprika
- 1/4 tsp fine sea salt or kosher salt
- dash of homemade vegan Worcestershire Sauce (pg. 206) or commercial
- 2 tsp minced fresh herbs of your choice (optional)

Mash all ingredients together in a bowl. Refrigerate in a covered container until ready to use.

Quick Pan Gravy for Seitan Roasts

To make quick pan gravy for any seitan roast, add 1/4 cup (4 T) Better Butter (pg. 62) or vegan margarine to the same skillet used for pan-glazing the roast and heat on medium setting until the butter or margarine melts. If you prefer, you can substitute with vegetable oil.

Whisk in 1/4 cup (4 T) flour (unbleached all-purpose wheat; rice or soy) until smooth and cook for a minute or two to eliminate any raw flour taste. Turn the heat to low and slowly pour while vigorously whisking in 2 cups of vegetable, chik'n or beef broth (see pg. 121-122 for broth options), loosening any caramelized bits of glaze as you stir.

Add a splash of dry-flavored white wine (Chardonnay works well) for chik'n or turk'y roasts and dry-flavored red wine (Merlot and Cabernet Sauvignon work well) for beef roasts, and salt and pepper to taste.

Increase the heat to medium-high and stir frequently until the mixture is bubbling and begins to thicken. Serve over sliced roast.

Herb Roasted Chik'n

This roast is a favorite with friends and family. The real magic occurs during the final pan-glazing - the exterior of the roast becomes golden brown and lightly crisp, while the interior remains moist and tender. Try serving warm with Quick Pan Gravy (pg. 29). The roast can also be refrigerated and sliced ultra-thin for superb deli-style sandwiches. The herbs are optional if you plan to use the roast for cold deli slices. This roast is large (about 2.5 lbs.)

Sift together the following dry ingredients in a large mixing bowl:

- 2 cups vital wheat gluten
- 1/4 cup garbanzo bean (chickpea) flour
- 1 tsp cornstarch (preferably non-GMO), arrowroot powder or potato starch

For the liquid ingredients, mix the following in a separate bowl or measuring cup until the salt and sugar dissolves:

- 2 and 2/3 cups water
- 2 T vegetable oil
- 3 T nutritional yeast
- 2 tsp onion powder
- 1 and 1/2 tsp sea salt or kosher salt
- 1 tsp poultry seasoning
- 1 tsp garlic powder
- 1/2 tsp organic sugar
- 1/2 tsp ground white pepper

Additional ingredients (optional):

- 2 or 3 sprigs of fresh rosemary, tarragon or sage, stems removed and leaves finely chopped

For the pan-glaze, you will need:

- 2 T Savory Butter (pg. 29), Better Butter (pg. 62), vegan margarine or vegetable oil
- 2 T dry white wine or lemon juice
- a few pinches of coarse ground black pepper

Technique:

Add the liquid ingredients (not the pan-glaze ingredients) to the dry mixture. Mix well until combined. The mixture will be very wet, but this is desirable as the gluten needs to be at saturation. Keep mixing until the dough has absorbed as much liquid as possible.

Let the dough rest for 10 minutes (during this time the dough will become a bit firmer and easier to work with). While the dough is resting, preheat the oven to 350°F.

On a work surface, lay out a large sheet of heavy-duty aluminum foil (18-inch wide). Place the chopped herbs on the foil with a few pinches of ground black pepper, and lay the dough directly on top.

Continue to follow the instructions for wrapping, baking and pan-glazing on pages 27-28.

Island Roast

This tender seitan roast has a flavor that is reminiscent of pulled pork served at island luaus. Try slicing ultra-thin for amazing hot sandwiches. This is a large roast (about 2.5 lbs.)

Sift together the following dry ingredients in a large mixing bowl:

- 2 cups vital wheat gluten
- 2 T garbanzo bean (chickpea) flour
- 1 T garlic powder
- 2 tsp onion powder
- 1 and 1/2 tsp ground ginger
- 1 tsp cornstarch (preferably non-GMO), arrowroot powder or potato starch
- 1/2 tsp ground white pepper

For the liquid ingredients, mix the following in a separate bowl or measuring cup until the salt dissolves:

- 2 T nutritional yeast
- 2 and 1/2 cups water
- 2 T vegetable oil
- 1 T liquid smoke
- 1 and 1/2 tsp Hawaiian red sea salt (substitute with sea salt or kosher salt if you cannot find this ingredient)

For the pan-glaze, you will need:

- 2 T Savory Butter (pg. 29), Better Butter (pg. 62), vegan margarine or vegetable oil
- 1 T liquid smoke
- a few pinches of coarse ground black pepper

Technique:

Add the liquid ingredients (not the pan-glaze ingredients) to the dry mixture. Mix well for a few minutes until all ingredients are thoroughly combined and some elasticity begins to develop in the dough. Let the dough rest for 10 minutes (during this time the dough will become a bit firmer and easier to work with).

While the dough is resting, preheat the oven to 350°F. Continue to follow the instructions for wrapping, baking and pan-glazing on pages 27-28.

Thin slices of Island Roast are best served warm. If pan-glazing has not sufficiently reheated the roast, wrap in foil and gently re-heat in the oven; or briefly heat the slices in the microwave or in a warm skillet before serving.

To create an au jus for the roast, combine 2 cups prepared vegetable broth in a saucepan with 1 tablespoon liquid smoke, 2 crushed cloves garlic and 2 thick slices of ginger root. Simmer for about 20 minutes. Season with Hawaiian red salt or soy sauce to taste (the au jus should be somewhat salty). Strain the garlic and ginger. With a pair of tongs, dip the sliced roast in the hot au jus until heated through and serve with white sticky rice and macaroni salad (aka 'Hawaiian plate lunch').

Tip: Shaved slices of Island Roast slathered in tangy BBQ sauce makes awesome Island-style sandwiches! Try my own BBQ Sauce (pg. 208)

Carving Board Smoked Turk'y

Carving Board Smoked Turk'y has a mellow smoked flavor and can be served hot or cold. The real magic occurs during the final pan-glazing of the roast; the exterior becomes golden brown and lightly crisp, while the interior remains moist and tender. Carve ultra-thin slices for awesome deli-style sandwiches. This is a large roast (about 2.5 lbs.)

Sift together the following dry ingredients in a large mixing bowl:

- 2 cups vital wheat gluten
- 1/4 cup garbanzo bean (chickpea) flour
- 2 tsp onion powder
- 1 tsp poultry seasoning
- 1 tsp cornstarch (preferably non-GMO), arrowroot powder or potato starch
- 1/2 tsp garlic powder
- 1/2 tsp ground white pepper*

*For Peppered Turk'y, omit the white pepper and add 1 tablespoon coarsely ground black pepper to the pre-sifted dry ingredients (coarsely ground assorted peppercorns are wonderful too; try lightly toasting them in a dry skillet to add a unique dimension to their flavor).

For the liquid ingredients, mix the following in a separate bowl or measuring cup until the salt dissolves:

- 2 T nutritional yeast
- 2 and 1/2 cups water
- 2 T vegetable oil
- 1 T tamari, soy sauce or Bragg Liquid Aminos™
- 1 T liquid smoke
- 1 tsp sea salt or kosher salt

For the pan-glaze, you will need:

- 2 T Savory Butter (pg. 29), Better Butter (pg. 62), vegan margarine or vegetable oil
- a few pinches of smoked black pepper (or substitute with regular black pepper)

Technique:

Add the liquid ingredients (not the pan-glaze ingredients) to the dry mixture. Mix well for a few minutes until all ingredients are thoroughly combined and some elasticity begins to develop in the dough. Let the dough rest for 10 minutes (during this time the dough will become a bit firmer and easier to work with).

While the dough is resting, preheat the oven to 350°F.

Continue to follow the instructions for wrapping, baking and pan-glazing on pages 27-28.

Baked Hammy

Spiked with hints of allspice and clove, this seitan roast is reminiscent in flavor of baked ham. Ultra-thin slices taste wonderful on hot or cold sandwiches paired with a nice spicy brown or Dijon mustard. Sliced hammy is also perfect for Eggless Benedict (pg. 85). This is a large roast (about 2.5 lbs.)

Sift together the following dry ingredients in a large mixing bowl:

- 2 cups vital wheat gluten
- 2 T garbanzo bean (chickpea) flour
- 1 T onion powder
- 1 and 1/2 tsp ground ginger
- 1 tsp garlic powder
- 1/2 tsp paprika
- 1/2 tsp ground white pepper
- 1/4 tsp ground allspice

For the liquid ingredients, stir together the following in a separate bowl or large measuring cup until the yeast, brown sugar and salt is dissolved:

- 2 T nutritional yeast
- 2 and 1/2 cups water
- 2 T vegetable oil
- 1 T liquid smoke
- 1 T brown sugar
- 2 tsp sea salt or kosher salt

You will also need 1/2 tsp ground cloves to season the dough before wrapping in foil.

For the pan-glaze, you will need:

- 2 T Better Butter (pg. 62), vegan margarine or vegetable oil

And the following ingredients combined together in a small bowl:

- 1 T liquid smoke
- 1 T real maple syrup or brown sugar – optional
- 1/4 tsp coarse ground black pepper

Technique:

Add the liquid ingredients (not the pan-glaze ingredients) to the dry mixture. Mix well for a few minutes until all ingredients are thoroughly combined and some elasticity begins to develop in the dough. Let the dough rest for 10 minutes (during this time the dough will become a bit firmer and easier to work with).

While the dough is resting, preheat the oven to 350°F.

On a work surface, lay out a large sheet of heavy-duty aluminum foil (18-inch wide) and sprinkle the foil where you will place the dough with 1/4 tsp ground cloves. Place the dough on top of the ground cloves on the foil. With your hands, form the dough into a round mass. The dough will be very soft and somewhat difficult to shape, but don't worry, it will expand to conform to the shape of the foil package during baking. Sprinkle the top of the dough with the remaining 1/4 tsp ground cloves.

Continue to follow the instructions for wrapping, baking and pan-glazing on pages 27-28.

Roast Turk'y with Stuffing

This roast is perfect for holiday celebrations. The stuffing is very traditional and simple; however, you can add some chopped nuts or dried fruits (chopped dried apricots, dried cranberries, etc.) if you like - but don't add more than 1/2 cup or the roast will not roll properly. You can also add additional fresh ingredients to the stuffing (apple, leeks, mushrooms, shredded carrot, etc.), but once again, don't add more than 1/2 cup, and be sure to cook them down with the onions and celery to reduce as much moisture as possible. The roast is superb when served with Golden Gravy (pg. 205).

Ingredients for the stuffing:

- 3 slices whole grain bread, cubed and slightly stale
- 1/4 cup (4 T) Better Butter (pg. 62) or vegan margarine
- 1 small onion, finely diced
- 1 rib celery, finely diced
- 1 tsp dry rubbed sage
- 1/2 tsp poultry seasoning
- 1/4 tsp sea salt or kosher salt
- 1/4 tsp ground black pepper
- 1/2 cup fresh or dried stuffing ingredients of your choice - optional
- a few tablespoons chik'n broth (see pg. 121-122 for broth options), vegetable broth (see pg. 121 for broth options) or water, but only if necessary to moisten the stuffing

Technique:

Cube the bread, place into a bowl and let sit uncovered for a few hours until lightly stale.

In a skillet over medium heat, melt the butter or margarine and sauté the onions and celery (and any additional fresh ingredients) until the onions are translucent. Add the poultry seasoning, rubbed sage, salt and pepper and stir to combine.

Pour the skillet contents over the bread in the bowl and mix thoroughly. Add any chopped dried fruit or nuts at this time. The stuffing needs to be on the dry side for this recipe, but if it seems overly dry, add a few tablespoons of broth to moisten. Be careful not to add too much; the stuffing should be firm, not mushy. Set aside to cool.

For the Turk'y Roast, sift together the following dry ingredients in a large mixing bowl:

- 2 cups vital wheat gluten
- 1/4 cup garbanzo bean (chickpea) flour
- 2 tsp onion powder
- 1 tsp cornstarch (preferably non-GMO), arrowroot powder or potato starch
- 1 tsp poultry seasoning
- 1/2 tsp garlic powder
- 1/2 tsp ground white pepper

For the liquid ingredients, mix the following ingredients in a separate bowl or large measuring cup:

- 2 and 1/2 cups water
- 2 T nutritional yeast
- 2 T vegetable oil
- 1 T tamari, soy sauce or Bragg Liquid Aminos™
- 1 T liquid smoke
- 1 tsp sea salt or kosher salt

For the pan-glaze you will need:

- 2 T Savory Butter (pg. 29), Better Butter (pg. 62), vegan margarine or vegetable oil
- 2 T white wine (dry, not sweet) or lemon juice
- a few pinches of coarse ground black pepper

Technique:

Add the liquid ingredients (not the pan-glaze ingredients) to the dry mixture. Mix well until combined and until some elasticity begins to develop in the dough. Let the dough rest for 10 minutes (during this time the dough will become a bit firmer and easier to work with). While the dough is resting, preheat the oven to 350°F.

On a work surface, lay out a large sheet of aluminum foil. Spread the dough on the foil in an oval shape. Layer the stuffing over the dough, avoiding the edges by about 1-inch.

Use the edge of the foil to lift the dough over the stuffing, encasing it inside the dough.

Push the sides of the dough back in towards the center with the palms of your hands, as a thicker, more compact roast is ideal and will be easier to fit into a large skillet or grill pan. Begin to roll the dough inside the foil, pinching the ends closed simultaneously while rolling; twist the ends tightly.

Wrap with 2 additional sheets of foil to completely seal the dough, twisting the ends very tight.

Important! The seitan dough will expand under steam pressure while baking; therefore, it is crucial that the dough for this particular recipe be wrapped in three layers of heavy-duty foil and the ends twisted very tightly. If you fail to do so, the package may explosively burst open during baking.

Place into a shallow baking dish and roast for 2 hours, turning after 1 hour.

Remove from the oven and transfer the foil package to a plate or work surface. Let cool at room temperature for about 30 minutes before pan-glazing. If you plan to store the roast to serve at a future date, let the roast cool to room temperature, then refrigerate for up to 10 days or freeze up to 3 months in its foil wrapper until ready to pan-glaze.

Finishing the Roast:

With sharp kitchen shears, cut the ends off of the foil package to ease removal. Peel off the foil and recycle. The roast will be soft at this stage, so handle it carefully.

In a large, deep non-stick skillet, melt the butter or margarine over medium heat. Add the roast and roll it around to coat with the butter/margarine. Sauté until the roast begins to lightly brown. Add the white wine or lemon juice and a dash of black pepper. The mixture will sizzle and begin to caramelize, turning the roast a beautiful golden brown color. Continue to roll the roast in the mixture until lightly crispy.

Transfer to a serving platter. Let cool for 10 to 15 minutes before slicing. For the sake of presentation, discard the end pieces if you find them unappealing, as they sometimes become misshapen by the twisted foil. Slice into 1/2-inch thick medallions. Serve with gravy.

Store leftovers in an airtight container in the refrigerator and consume within 10 days. To reheat the roast, wrap it securely in foil and warm at 350°F until heated through.

Roast Beaf

Roast Beaf is superb when sliced ultra-thin and served hot or cold. The real magic occurs during the final pan-glazing of the roast; the exterior becomes golden brown and lightly crisp, while the interior remains moist and tender. Make Beaf Au Jus (pg. 38) for dipping or garnish with Creamy Horseradish Sauce (pg. 205), if you desire. This is a large roast (about 2.5 lbs.)

Sift together the following dry ingredients in a large mixing bowl:

- 2 cups vital wheat gluten
- 2 T garbanzo bean (chickpea) flour
- 2 tsp onion powder
- 2 tsp garlic powder
- 1 tsp cornstarch (preferably non-GMO), arrowroot powder or potato starch
- 1/2 tsp ground white pepper*

*For Pastrami (peppered beaf), omit the white pepper and add 1 tablespoon coarsely ground black pepper to the pre-sifted dry ingredients (coarsely ground assorted peppercorns are wonderful too; try lightly toasting them in a dry skillet to add a unique dimension to their flavor).

For the liquid ingredients, mix the following in a separate bowl or measuring cup:

- 1/4 cup nutritional yeast
- 2 and 1/3 cups water
- 2 T vegetable oil
- 2 T tamari, soy sauce or Bragg Liquid Aminos™
- 1 T homemade vegan Worcestershire Sauce (pg. 206) or commercial
- 2 tsp Gravy Master™ or other browning liquid

For the pan-glaze, you will need:

- 2 T Savory Butter (pg. 29), Better Butter (pg. 62), vegan margarine or vegetable oil
- 2 T dry red wine or dry sherry (optional)
- a few pinches of coarse ground black pepper

Technique:

Add the liquid ingredients (not the pan-glaze ingredients) to the dry mixture. Mix well for a few minutes until all ingredients are thoroughly combined and some elasticity begins to develop in the dough. Let the dough rest for 10 minutes (during this time the dough will become a bit firmer and easier to work with).

While the dough is resting, preheat the oven to 350°F.

Continue to follow the instructions for wrapping, baking and pan-glazing on pages 27-28.

For delectable BBQ Beaf sandwiches, follow the Roast Beaf recipe above, slice the beaf ultra-thin and then slather the slices with my own BBQ Sauce (pg. 208) or your favorite sauce. Heat the slices in the microwave or in a saucepan over low heat until hot. Serve on your favorite sandwich roll or bun (make sure it's vegan!)

French Dip Sandwich with Beaf Au Jus

Tender roast beaf slices are piled high on crusty toasted French bread and served with savory beaf au jus for dipping. The ultimate in vegan gastronomical hedonism and one of my best signature seitan roast and deli sandwich recipes.

Ingredients:

- Better Butter (pg. 62) or vegan margarine to "butter" the bread
- Roast Beaf (pg. 37), thinly sliced and brought to room temperature
- ground black pepper
- 1 loaf of crusty French bread cut into quarters and then split - or any other crusty bread (many varieties of crusty bread are vegan, but double check ingredients to be sure)

Technique:

Prepare the Beaf Au Jus (recipe below) and place on low heat to keep warm. Set out 4 small soup cups or ramekins for dipping and 4 large plates. Set the oven on "broil". Lightly "butter" the interior of each bread quarter and lay open, "buttered" side up, on a cookie sheet. Place under the broiler for a minute or two, or until lightly toasted.

To assemble the sandwiches, use a pair of kitchen tongs to dip the deli slices into the hot au jus and then pile onto four slices of bread. Season the beaf with a dash of black pepper and top with the remaining bread slices. Pour the au jus into cups or ramekins and serve alongside the sandwiches. *Très excellent!*

Beaf Au Jus

- 2 T Better Butter (pg. 62) or vegan margarine, plus more to "butter" the bread
- 1 shallot, minced or 2 T minced red onion
- 1 T flour (unbleached all-purpose wheat, rice or soy)
- 1 jigger dry sherry, optional
- 3 cups beaf broth (see pg. 123 for broth options)

Melt the butter or margarine in a large saucepan over medium heat. Add the shallot or red onion and sauté 2 minutes. Reduce heat to medium-low and whisk in the flour until a smooth paste is achieved (roux) and cook a minute longer.

Now, whisk in the broth in a slow stream (which helps avoid lumps) and continue to whisk until smooth. Add the optional sherry. Bring the sauce to a boil, stirring frequently and then reduce heat to low until ready to serve the sandwiches.

The Gentle Philly

Ingredients:

- 1/2 cup No-Eggy Mayo (pg. 105) or commercial vegan mayonnaise
- 1 clove garlic, minced
- 4 hoagie-style bread rolls, split
- 2 sweet yellow onions, sliced thin
- 2 T vegetable oil
- 1 lb Roast Beef (pg. 37), sliced very thin
- Easy Cheesy Sauce (pg. 215)

Technique:

In a small bowl, combine the mayo and minced garlic. Cover and refrigerate.

Preheat the oven or toaster oven to 400°F.

Make the Easy Cheesy Sauce and set aside on the lowest heat setting.

In a large skillet, heat the oil over medium heat. Add the onions and sauté until translucent. Add the roast beef to the onions in the skillet and continue to sauté until the onions begin to caramelize and the beef begins to lightly brown.

While the onions and beef are cooking in the skillet, place the split rolls on a baking sheet, split-side up, and toast in the oven for about 5 to 6 minutes.

Remove the rolls from the oven and spread some garlic mayo on each slice. Top four slices with the beef and onions and slather with the cheese sauce. Top with the remaining slices and serve immediately.

Tip: Homemade No-Eggy Mayo is much more economical than commercial vegan mayonnaise and tastes better too!

Classic Greek Gyro

Ingredients:

- Greek Gyro Roast (see following recipe)
- pita bread
- thinly sliced onion
- sliced or chopped tomatoes
- Tzatziki Sauce (pg. 209)

Technique:

Shave thin slices from the roast lengthwise with a sharp knife. Serve warm on pita bread with sliced onion, chopped tomatoes and Tzatziki sauce.

Greek Gyro Roast

Tender slices of seitan roast are generously seasoned with aromatic Mediterranean herbs and spices. Gyro (pronounced "year-ro") roast is the primary component of the Classic Greek Gyro pita pocket sandwich (recipe follows). This is a large roast (about 2.5 lbs.)

Thoroughly stir together the following dry ingredients in a large mixing bowl:

- 2 cups vital wheat gluten
- 1/4 cup nutritional yeast
- 2 T garbanzo bean (chickpea) flour
- 1 T dried minced onion
- 2 tsp onion powder

Process the following in a blender until the herbs and garlic are finely ground:

- 2 and 1/4 cups water
- 3 T tamari, soy sauce or Bragg Liquid Aminos™
- 4 cloves garlic (or 4 tsp minced garlic)
- 2 T extra-virgin olive oil
- 1 T liquid smoke
- 2 tsp Gravy Master™ or other browning liquid
- 2 tsp ground cumin
- 1 tsp dried oregano
- 1 tsp dried marjoram
- 1/2 tsp coarsely ground black pepper
- 1/2 tsp ground dried rosemary or 1 and 1/2 tsp dried rosemary needles

For the pan-glaze, you will need:

- 2 T Better Butter (pg. 62), vegan margarine or vegetable oil
- a few pinches of coarse ground black pepper

Technique:

Add the liquid ingredients (not the pan-glaze ingredients) to the dry mixture. Mix well for a few minutes until all ingredients are thoroughly combined and some elasticity begins to develop in the dough. Let the dough rest for 10 minutes (during this time the dough will become a bit firmer and easier to work with).

Continue to follow the instructions for wrapping, baking and pan-glazing on pages 27-28.

To serve, shave thin slices from the roast lengthwise with a sharp knife. If necessary, reheat slices wrapped in foil in the oven; gently pan-sear in a lightly oiled skillet (my favorite); or heat in a microwave safe container in the microwave.

Serve warm on pita bread with sliced onion, chopped tomatoes and Tzatziki Sauce (pg. 209).

Seitan Sausages

Seitan sausages are relatively easy to make. The gluten dough is rolled and sealed in aluminum foil and then steamed (the two exceptions are pepperoni and breakfast sausage patties, which are baked).

It is very important that you use heavy-duty aluminum foil when steaming or baking gluten. Regular foil is too thin and easily tears when twisting the ends of the foil wrappers. It can also easily rupture from expansion of the gluten as it cooks, and from steam pressure which builds up inside the foil. Always err on using too much foil rather than not enough and when in doubt, reroll with an additional sheet of foil.

The sausage recipes are formulated with as much liquid as possible. This liquid is necessary for creating a juicy and "meaty" sausage. However, this extra moisture will also make the sausage dough very soft (except for pepperoni, which has a drier, firmer texture) and this softness can make handling and rolling in foil a little tricky (at least initially). So be patient when learning to roll and wrap the sausages – it takes a little practice.

Meat-based sausages use a casing to give the sausage its shape. Vegan sausages, on the other hand, have no casing and since they are hand-rolled in foil, minor imperfections in their appearance are to be expected. However, these slight imperfections will not detract from their excellent taste and texture.

Steamed or baked sausages should be cooled to room temperature and then thoroughly chilled to optimize their texture. The sausages are rather fragile after cooking, so refrigerate them in their foil wrappers until they have firmed up.

For serving, the sausages are at their best when browned in the skillet (pepperoni being the exception, as it needs no browning) with a little Better Butter (pg. 62), vegan margarine or vegetable oil - but they can be successfully grilled on the BBQ too. Just be sure to brush them generously with vegetable oil to keep them from drying out. Do not grill over open flames – hot embers are best; and avoid overcooking as this will make the sausages dry.

Foil Wrap and Steam Technique for Sausages

The foil wrap and steam technique applies to all sausages and is described here to avoid repetition in each recipe (Pepperoni and Brown 'n' Serve Sausage Patties are foil wrapped, but are baked rather than steamed).

For steaming, you will need a large pot with a lid and a steamer insert. Add enough water to your cooking pot to just reach the bottom of the steamer insert.

Cut the HEAVY DUTY foil into individual square wrappers according to the recommended number and size in the recipe. The goal is to wrap the sausages in the foil and leave plenty of room on each end to twist the foil very tight. This is important, as you do not want the foil packages to burst open while steaming. Always err on too much foil rather than not enough.

Place a piece of dough onto a foil square, and with your fingers shape the dough into a sausage shape, about 6 inches long for sausages and 4 inches long for breakfast links (keep a wet paper towel on hand to wipe your fingers as you work). Don't worry about shaping perfection, as the dough will expand to conform to the shape of the foil package when cooked. Now roll the dough inside the foil like a "tootsie roll" while simultaneously pinching the ends of the foil closed with your fingers. Twist the ends very tightly to seal. If the foil tears a bit while twisting, wrap in an additional piece of foil. The dough needs to be securely sealed to prevent bursting while steaming. Repeat with the remaining pieces of dough and set aside.

Bring the water in the steamer to a rapid boil and add the foil packages. Cover and set the timer for the recommended time in the recipe. Check the pot at regular intervals (lift the lid with an oven mitt to avoid steam burns) and add some HOT water to replace water lost to steam evaporation. DO NOT let the pot boil dry. It's not unusual to need to replace 2 to 4 cups of water during steaming.

When the sausages are finished steaming, remove the foil packages from the pot and let them cool to room temperature. Leave them in their foil wrappers and refrigerate for a minimum of 8 hours before browning them in the skillet or on the grill. This will firm and optimize their texture. You can also store the sausages in their foil wrappers for up to 10 days in the refrigerator or in the freezer for up to 3 months. Refer to the specific recipe for finishing instructions.

German Bratwurst

Brats are perfect for celebrating Oktoberfest, but I enjoy them any time of the year. They're made with my own special blend of seasoning. I hope you enjoy them too! This recipe makes 6 sausages.

Thoroughly stir together the following dry ingredients in a large mixing bowl:

- 1 cup vital wheat gluten
- 1 T garbanzo bean (chickpea) flour
- 1 T nutritional yeast
- 1 T dried minced onion
- 1 tsp onion powder

Process the following ingredients in a blender until smooth (mini-blenders work great for this):

- 1 and 1/4 cup water
- 1 T vegetable oil
- 1 T brown sugar
- 1 tsp liquid smoke
- 3 cloves fresh garlic (1 T minced)
- 1 and 1/2 tsp fine sea salt or kosher salt
- 1 tsp finely grated lemon zest, loosely packed
- 1/2 tsp ground ginger
- 1/2 tsp grated nutmeg
- 1/2 tsp poultry seasoning
- 1/4 tsp ground allspice
- 1/4 tsp ground white pepper

Technique:

Add enough water to your cooking pot to just reach the bottom of the steamer insert.

Tear off three 10-inch long sheets from a roll of 18" wide HEAVY DUTY foil. Cut those sheets in half. This will make six 9" x 10" wrappers. Set aside.

Add the blender mixture to the dry ingredients and mix for several minutes to develop the gluten. The dough will be very soft - this is normal. Let the dough rest for 10 minutes (during this time the dough will become a bit firmer and easier to work with).

Flatten the dough evenly in the mixing bowl and divide into roughly 6 equal size pieces with the edge of a rubber spatula or butter knife (cut in half and then each half into thirds).

Wrap and steam the dough for 45 minutes according to the directions on page 42. After steaming, let the foil packages cool to room temperature. Leave the sausages in their foil wrappers and refrigerate for a minimum of 8 hours before browning them in the skillet or on the grill. This will firm and optimize their texture. You can also store the sausages in their foil wrappers for up to 10 days in the refrigerator or in the freezer for up to 3 months.

Browning the brats:

With sharp kitchen shears, cut the ends off of the foil packages to ease removal. Peel away the foil and recycle. In a well-heated skillet, brown the brats in a tablespoon or two of Better Butter (pg. 62), vegan margarine or vegetable oil. Transfer to a plate lined with paper towels to blot any excess oil. For grilling, brush the brats generously with vegetable oil and grill over hot embers – no flames! Do not overcook! The brats are ready to eat or use in your favorite recipe.

Italian Sausage

Italian seasonings give these sausages their wonderful flavor. This recipe makes 6 sausages.

Thoroughly stir together the following dry ingredients in a large mixing bowl:

- 1 cup vital wheat gluten
- 2 T nutritional yeast
- 1 T garbanzo bean (chickpea) flour
- 1 T dried minced onion
- 1 tsp onion powder

Process the following ingredients in a blender until the fennel seeds are finely ground (mini-blenders work great for this):

- 1 cup plus 3 T water
- 2 T soy sauce, tamari or Bragg Liquid Aminos™
- 1 T extra-virgin olive oil
- 1 T whole fennel seeds or 1 tsp ground fennel

- 1 tsp liquid smoke
- 3 cloves garlic (1 T minced)
- 1 tsp dried oregano
- 1 tsp dried basil
- 1/2 tsp crushed red pepper flakes - or more, depending on amount of "heat" desired

Technique:

Add enough water to your cooking pot to just reach the bottom of the steamer insert.

Tear off three 10-inch long sheets from a roll of 18" wide HEAVY DUTY foil. Cut those sheets in half. This will make six 9" x 10" wrappers. Set aside.

Add the blender mixture to the dry ingredients and mix for several minutes to develop the gluten. The dough will be very soft - this is normal. Let the dough rest for 10 minutes (during this time the dough will become a bit firmer and easier to work with).

Flatten the dough evenly in the mixing bowl and divide into roughly 6 equal size pieces with the edge of a rubber spatula or butter knife (cut in half and then each half into thirds).

Wrap and steam the dough for 45 minutes according to the directions on page 42. After steaming, let the foil packages cool to room temperature. Leave the sausages in their foil wrappers and refrigerate for a minimum of 8 hours before browning them in the skillet or on the grill. This will firm and optimize their texture. You can also store the sausages in their foil wrappers for up to 10 days in the refrigerator or in the freezer for up to 3 months.

Browning the sausages:

With sharp kitchen shears, cut the ends off of the foil packages to ease removal. Peel away the foil and recycle. In a well-heated skillet, brown the sausages in a tablespoon or two of Better Butter (pg. 62), vegan margarine or vegetable oil. Transfer to a plate lined with paper towels to blot any excess oil. For grilling, brush the sausages generously with vegetable oil and grill over hot embers – no flames! Do not overcook! The sausages are ready to eat or use in your favorite recipe.

Andouille Sausage

Andouille sausage is French in origin, and was later brought to Louisiana by French immigrants. In the United States, the sausage is most often associated with Cajun cooking. Andouille sausages, which are heavily seasoned with garlic and red pepper, are sometimes referred to as "hot link" sausages. I offer you a compassionate and healthier version of this flavorful sausage. This recipe makes 6 sausages. Bon appétit!

Thoroughly stir together the following dry ingredients in a large mixing bowl:

- 1 cup vital wheat gluten
- 2 T nutritional yeast
- 1 T garbanzo bean (chickpea) flour
- 1 T dried minced onion
- 1 tsp onion powder

Process the following ingredients in a blender (mini-blenders work great for this):

- 1 cup plus 2 T water
- 2 T soy sauce, tamari or Bragg Liquid Aminos™
- 6 cloves garlic (2 T minced)
- 1 T vegetable oil
- 1 tsp liquid smoke
- 1 tsp organic sugar
- 2 tsp red pepper flakes
- 1/2 tsp smoked paprika
- 1/2 tsp poultry seasoning

Technique:

Add enough water to your cooking pot to just reach the bottom of the steamer insert.

Tear off three 10-inch long sheets from a roll of 18" wide HEAVY DUTY foil. Cut those sheets in half. This will make six 9" x 10" wrappers. Set aside.

Add the blender mixture to the dry ingredients and mix well to develop the gluten. The dough will be very soft - this is normal. Let the dough rest for 10 minutes (during this time the dough will become a bit firmer and easier to work with).

Flatten the dough evenly in the mixing bowl and divide into roughly 6 equal size pieces with the edge of a rubber spatula or butter knife (cut in half and then each half into thirds).

Wrap and steam the dough for 45 minutes according to the directions on page 42. After steaming, let the foil packages cool to room temperature. Leave the sausages in their foil wrappers and refrigerate for a minimum of 8 hours before browning them in the skillet or on the grill. This will firm and optimize their texture. You can also store the sausages in their foil wrappers for up to 10 days in the refrigerator or in the freezer for up to 3 months.

Browning the sausages:

With sharp kitchen shears, cut the ends off of the foil packages to ease removal. Peel away the foil and recycle. In a well-heated skillet, brown the sausages in a tablespoon or two of Better Butter (pg. 62), vegan margarine or vegetable oil. Transfer to a plate lined with paper towels to blot any excess oil. For grilling, brush the sausages generously with vegetable oil and grill over hot embers – no flames! Do not overcook! The sausages are ready to eat or use in your favorite recipe.

"Bangers"

Bangers are a type of sausage common to the UK. They may sometimes be called British bangers, but this is somewhat inaccurate, since the Irish as well as the English enjoy bangers. Bangers are often an essential part of pub food, as they are quick to prepare. Bangers and Mash (pg. 169) is the traditional British Isles favorite. The term "bangers" is attributed to the fact that sausages, particularly the kind made during World War II under rationing, were made with water so they were more likely to explode under high heat if not cooked carefully. Ironically, all vegan sausages made with the foil wrap and steam method will also burst if not wrapped tightly - so please follow directions. This recipe makes 6 sausages.

Thoroughly stir together the following dry ingredients in a large mixing bowl:

- 1 cup vital wheat gluten
- 2 T nutritional yeast
- 1 T garbanzo bean (chickpea) flour
- 1 T dried minced onion
- 1 tsp onion powder

Process the following ingredients in a blender (mini-blenders work great for this):

- 1 and 1/4 cups water
- 2 T soy sauce, tamari or Bragg Liquid Aminos™
- 1 T vegetable oil
- 1 tsp liquid smoke
- 2 tsp dry rubbed sage
- 1 tsp finely grated lemon zest, loosely packed
- 1/2 tsp ground ginger
- 1/2 tsp grated nutmeg
- 1/2 tsp sea salt or kosher salt
- 1/4 tsp coarsely ground black pepper
- 1/4 tsp ground red or cayenne pepper

Technique:

Add enough water to your cooking pot to just reach the bottom of the steamer insert.

Tear off three 10-inch long sheets from a roll of 18" wide HEAVY DUTY foil. Cut those sheets in half. This will make six 9" x 10" wrappers. Set aside.

Add the blender mixture to the dry ingredients and mix well to develop the gluten. The dough will be very soft - this is normal. Let the dough rest for 10 minutes (during this time the dough will become a bit firmer and easier to work with).

Flatten the dough evenly in the mixing bowl and divide into roughly 6 equal size pieces with the edge of a rubber spatula or butter knife (cut in half and then each half into thirds).

Wrap and steam the dough for 45 minutes according to the directions on page 42. After steaming, let the foil packages cool to room temperature. Leave the sausages in their foil wrappers and refrigerate for a minimum of 8 hours before browning them in the skillet or on the grill. This will firm and optimize their texture. You can also store the sausages in their foil wrappers for up to 10 days in the refrigerator or in the freezer for up to 3 months.

Browning the sausages:

With sharp kitchen shears, cut the ends off of the foil packages to ease removal. Peel away the foil and recycle. In a well-heated skillet, brown the sausages in a tablespoon or two of Better Butter (pg. 62), vegan margarine or vegetable oil. Transfer to a plate lined with paper towels to blot any excess oil. For grilling, brush the sausages generously with vegetable oil and grill over hot embers – no flames! Do not overcook! The sausages are ready to eat or use in your favorite recipe.

Maple Sage Breakfast Sausage

The wonderful flavors of rubbed sage and maple syrup complement these tasty breakfast sausages. They're perfect served alongside scrambles, pancakes or French toast. This recipe makes 10 sausage links.

Thoroughly stir together the following dry ingredients in a large mixing bowl:

- 1 cup vital wheat gluten
- 2 T nutritional yeast
- 1 T garbanzo bean (chickpea) flour
- 1 T dried minced onion
- 1 tsp onion powder
- 1 tsp garlic powder

Process the following ingredients in a blender (mini-blenders work great for this):

- 1 and 1/4 cups water
- 2 T soy sauce, tamari or Bragg Liquid Aminos™
- 1 T real maple syrup
- 1 T vegetable oil
- 2 tsp dry rubbed sage
- 1 and 1/2 tsp poultry seasoning
- 1/2 tsp sweet paprika
- 1/2 tsp grated nutmeg (preferably fresh)
- 1/4 tsp coarsely ground black pepper
- 1/4 tsp ground red or cayenne pepper (optional)

Technique:

Add enough water to your cooking pot to just reach the bottom of the steamer insert.

Cut HEAVY DUTY foil into 10, roughly 6" by 8" squares. Set aside.

Add the blender mixture to the dry ingredients and mix well to develop the gluten. The dough will be very soft - this is normal. Let the dough rest for 10 minutes (during this time the dough will become a bit firmer and easier to work with).

Flatten the dough evenly in the mixing bowl and divide into roughly 10 equal size pieces with the edge of a rubber spatula or butter knife (cut in half and then each half into five pieces).

Wrap and steam the dough for 30 minutes according to the directions on page 42. After steaming, let the foil packages cool to room temperature. Leave the sausages in their foil wrappers and refrigerate for a minimum of 8 hours before browning them in the skillet. This will firm and optimize their texture. You can also store the sausages in their foil wrappers for up to 10 days in the refrigerator or in the freezer for up to 3 months.

Browning the sausages:

With sharp kitchen shears, cut the ends off of the foil packages to ease removal. Peel away the foil and recycle. In a well-heated skillet, brown the sausages in a tablespoon or two of Better Butter (pg. 62), vegan margarine or vegetable oil. Transfer to a plate lined with paper towels to blot any excess oil.

Brown 'n' Serve Sausage Patties

For this recipe, the sausage roll is baked rather than steamed, refrigerated for a minimum of 8 hours to firm its texture, and then sliced and browned in a skillet. You can also make Sausage Crumbles (pg. 50) with this recipe.

Preheat the oven to 350°F.

Thoroughly stir together the following dry ingredients in a large mixing bowl:

- 1 cup vital wheat gluten
- 2 T nutritional yeast
- 1 T garbanzo bean (chickpea) flour
- 1 T dried minced onion
- 1 tsp onion powder
- 1 tsp garlic powder

Process the following ingredients in a blender (mini-blenders work great for this):

- 1 cup plus 2 T water
- 2 T soy sauce, tamari or Bragg Liquid Aminos™
- 2 T vegetable oil
- 2 tsp dry rubbed sage
- 1 and 1/2 tsp poultry seasoning
- 1/2 tsp sweet paprika
- 1/2 tsp ground nutmeg (preferably fresh grated)
- 1/4 tsp coarsely ground black pepper
- 1/4 tsp ground red or cayenne pepper (optional)

Pour the blender ingredients into the dry ingredients and stir well. Make sure the ingredients are distributed thoroughly. Let the dough rest for 10 minutes (during this time the dough will become a bit firmer and easier to work with).

On a work surface, lay out a large sheet of heavy-duty aluminum foil (18-inch wide). Place the dough directly on top.

Shape the dough into a compact log shape. Don't worry too much about shaping perfection, as the dough will expand to conform to the shape of the foil package. Now, roll the dough inside the foil like a "tootsie-roll", simultaneously pinching the ends of the foil closed as you roll. Twist the ends tightly to seal. Repeat with an additional sheet of foil.

Important! The seitan dough will expand under steam pressure while baking; therefore, it is crucial that the dough be wrapped in a minimum of two layers of heavy-duty foil and the ends twisted very tightly. If you fail to do so, the package may explosively burst open during baking.

Place in a shallow casserole dish and bake for 1 hour and 30 minutes, turning over after 45 minutes. Remove from the oven and let rest until cooled to room temperature.

Leave the sausage roll in its foil wrapper and refrigerate for a minimum of 8 hours before slicing and browning in the skillet. This will firm and optimize the sausage texture. You can also store the sausage in its foil wrapper for up to 10 days in the refrigerator or in the freezer for up to 3 months.

Browning the Sausage Patties:

With sharp kitchen shears, cut the ends off of the foil package to ease removal. Peel away the foil and recycle. Slice into 1/4-inch thick patties. In a well-heated skillet, brown the sausage patties in a tablespoon or two of Better Butter (pg. 62), vegan margarine or vegetable oil. Transfer to a plate lined with paper towels to blot any excess oil before serving.

Sausage Crumbles

Prepare the Brown 'n' Serve Sausage Patties (see preceding recipe). Let the foil package cool to room temperature and refrigerate for a minimum of 8 hours or until ready to use (up to 10 days in the refrigerator or in the freezer for up to 3 months).

When thoroughly chilled, cut the ends off of the foil package with sharp kitchen shears to ease removal. Peel away the foil and recycle. Slice into 1/2-inch thick patties. Place into a food processor and pulse to grind to desired texture.

In a skillet over medium heat, lightly brown the sausage crumbles in two tablespoons of Better Butter (pg. 62), vegan margarine or vegetable oil. Use in your favorite recipe.

Pepperoni

I was a big fan of pepperoni before I embraced veganism, so my taste for it has never waned completely. I can say that the flavor of this vegan pepperoni rivals the best of its meat counterpart, without all that excess grease (and animal suffering). It took a few attempts to get the seasonings proportioned just right, but I feel this recipe is a huge success. Unlike my other sausage recipes which utilize steam for cooking, this recipe requires oven baking. Buono Appetito!

Thoroughly stir together the following dry ingredients in a large mixing bowl:

- 1 cup vital wheat gluten
- 2 T nutritional yeast
- 2 tsp onion powder
- 1 tsp paprika
- 1 tsp whole fennel seeds
- 1 tsp garlic powder
- 1 tsp ground mustard
- 1 tsp red pepper flakes (or more or less to taste)

Process the following ingredients in a blender until the fennel seeds are finely ground (mini-blenders work great for this):

- 2/3 cup water
- 2 T tamari, soy sauce or Bragg Liquid Aminos
- 2 T tomato paste
- 1 T organic sugar
- 1 T liquid smoke
- 2 T extra-virgin olive oil
- 2 tsp whole fennel seeds

Technique:

Preheat the oven to 350°F.

Pour the blender ingredients into the dry ingredients and stir well. Make sure ingredients are distributed thoroughly.

On a work surface, lay out a large sheet of heavy-duty aluminum foil (18-inch wide). Place the dough directly on top.

Shape the dough into a slender log shape, about 10 inches long. Don't worry too much about shaping it perfectly, as the dough will expand to conform to the shape of the foil package. Now, roll the dough inside the foil like a "tootsie-roll", simultaneously pinching the ends of the foil closed as you roll. Twist the ends tightly to seal. Repeat with an additional sheet of foil.

Important! The seitan dough will expand under steam pressure while baking; therefore, it is crucial that the dough be wrapped in a minimum of two layers of heavy-duty foil and the ends twisted very tightly. If you fail to do so, the package may explosively burst open during baking.

Place on a cookie sheet and bake for 90 minutes, turning over after 45 minutes. Remove from the oven and cool to room temperature, then place in the refrigerator for a minimum of 8 hours to firm its texture.

When thoroughly chilled, cut the ends off of the foil package with sharp kitchen shears to ease removal. Peel away the foil and recycle; slice the pepperoni as needed. The pepperoni does not require finishing with pan browning or glazing.

Store the pepperoni in an airtight container in the refrigerator and use within 10 days, or freeze for up to 3 months.

Tip: Seitan Pepperoni, Daiya Cheese™ and fresh veggies make a great vegan pizza!

Frankfurters

These tasty all-seitan franks are at their best when browned in the skillet but they're great for grilling on the BBQ too. My special blend of seasonings gives them their characteristic "hot dog" flavor. The franks need to refrigerate for a minimum of 8 hours to optimize their texture before browning and serving - so plan accordingly. This recipe makes 6 jumbo franks or 8 regular-size franks.

Sift together the following dry ingredients in a large mixing bowl:

- 1 cup vital wheat gluten
- 2 tsp onion powder
- 1/2 tsp ground coriander
- 1/2 tsp poultry seasoning
- 1/2 tsp paprika
- 1/2 tsp ground nutmeg
- 1/4 tsp ground white pepper

Process the following ingredients in a blender to purée the garlic and emulsify the ketchup:

- 1 cup water
- 3 cloves garlic (1 T minced)
- 2 T organic ketchup
- 2 T nutritional yeast
- 2 T tamari, soy sauce or Bragg Liquid Aminos™
- 1 T vegetable oil
- 1 T liquid smoke
- 1/2 tsp cornstarch (preferably non-GMO) or arrowroot powder

Technique:

First, tear off three10-inch long sheets (for jumbo franks) or four 10-inch long sheets (for regular-size franks) from a roll of 18" wide HEAVY DUTY foil. Cut those sheets in half. This will make six or eight 9" x 10" wrappers, respectively. Set aside.

Next, add enough water to your cooking pot to just reach the bottom of the steamer insert. Set aside.

Add the blender mixture to the dry ingredients and mix well to develop the gluten. The dough will be very soft - this is normal. Let the dough rest for 10 minutes (during this time the dough will become a bit firmer and easier to work with).

Flatten the dough evenly in the mixing bowl and divide into roughly 6 or 8 equal size pieces with the edge of a rubber spatula or butter knife (cut in half and then each half into thirds for jumbo franks or fourths for regular-size franks).

Wrap and steam the dough for 45 minutes for jumbo franks or 40 minutes for regular-size franks according to the directions on page 42. After steaming, let the foil packages cool to room temperature.

Leave the franks in their foil wrappers and refrigerate for a minimum of 8 hours before browning them in the skillet or on the grill. This will firm and optimize their texture. You can also store the franks in their foil wrappers for up to 10 days in the refrigerator or in the freezer for up to 3 months.

Heating the franks:

With sharp kitchen shears, cut the ends off of the foil packages to ease removal. Peel away the foil and recycle. The franks can be reheated by gently simmering them in water for 5 minutes; or for best results, brown the franks in a skillet very lightly coated with vegetable oil. For grilling, brush them generously with vegetable oil and grill until lightly browned and heated through. Do not grill them over flames on the BBQ - hot embers are best. Do not overcook!

How to make a Brava Dog:

Brown your franks in the skillet or on the grill. Mix a little hot red pepper sauce (Sriracha™ is my favorite) with some No-Eggy Mayo (pg. 105) or commercial vegan mayonnaise, to taste. Garnish the franks with the sauce and top with crushed potato chips. Different and delicious!

Chapter 2

Soy Proteins 101

What is Tofu?

Tofu, or bean curd, is produced by coagulating soymilk and then pressing the resulting curds into soft white blocks. It is of Chinese origin and is also a part of East Asian and Southeast Asian cuisine such as Chinese, Japanese, Korean, Indonesian, Vietnamese, and others.

Tofu is also considered a staple in vegan diets because of its high protein content, low content of calories and fat, high calcium and iron content and the ability to substitute for meat, eggs and dairy products in a variety of recipes.

There are many different varieties of tofu, including fresh tofu and tofu that has been processed in some way. Tofu has a subtle flavor and can be used in both savory and sweet dishes. It is often seasoned or marinated to suit the dish.

Calcium sulfate (gypsum) is the traditional and most widely used coagulant to produce Chinese-style block tofu. It produces a tofu that is tender yet firm in texture. The coagulant itself has no perceivable taste. Use of this coagulant also makes a tofu that is rich in calcium. The coagulant and soymilk are mixed together in large vats, allowed to curdle and the resulting curds are drained, pressed into blocks and then packaged.

Chinese-style block tofu is sold in plastic tub containers completely immersed in water to maintain its moisture content. It will always be found in the refrigerated section of the market. Soft to extra-firm Chinese-style block tofu are the varieties commonly used in vegan cooking to replicate eggs and replace meat. Please note that the package will not be labeled "Chinese-style" - this description is just used to differentiate block tofu from Japanese silken tofu.

Magnesium chloride and calcium chloride are the coagulants (called *nigari* in Japan) used to make "silken" tofu, which has a smooth and tender texture. These coagulants are added to soymilk and the mixture is then sealed in aseptic cartons. The resulting bean curd is produced inside its own package, rather than being drained and pressed into blocks.

Firm and extra-firm silken tofu are the varieties commonly used in vegan cooking to produce sauces, thick creams and custard-like textures. They can be found on store shelves and need no refrigeration until the carton is opened. This gives them an extended shelf life, compared to fresh block tofu sold in tub containers. Some cooks may recommend using silken tofu as an egg replacement in such dishes as eggless salad and breakfast scrambles; however I don't recommend this as it's much too delicate and soft to hold up in sandwich fillings or scrambles. Believe me, I've tried. Save it for sauces, dairy replacements and desserts, and use the firmer Chinese-style block tofu for these recipes instead.

Edible acids such as acetic acid (vinegar) and citric acid (such as lemon juice), can also be used to coagulate soymilk and produce tofu, though they can affect the taste of the tofu more, and vary in efficacy and texture. The tender curds resulting from the mixing of vinegar and soymilk are often used in vegan baking, as they replace buttermilk in recipes.

In my recipes I will specify whether to use a block of soft, firm or extra-firm tofu (Chinese-style) or whether to use a carton of Mori Nu™ firm or extra-firm silken tofu. It is essential to know the difference between the two, as the type of tofu used will definitely affect your cooking results.

Preparing Tofu for Recipes

There's not much preparation involved before using silken tofu. Simply open the carton with kitchen shears, drain any small amount of liquid inside and use as directed in your recipe.

Chinese-style block tofu, on the other hand, requires draining and usually "pressing" to remove the excess moisture content. This is simply accomplished by first removing the tofu from its container and draining the excess liquid into the sink. Place the tofu block (whole or sliced) on a plate lined with several layers of paper towels or a clean, smooth kitchen towel (do not use terry cloth because the tofu may pick up lint). Cover with additional towels and place a cutting board on top of the towels.

Now place something heavy (like a cast-iron skillet) on top of the cutting board. Allow to press for about 30 minutes. This should sufficiently remove the excess moisture and the tofu will be ready for your recipe.

Some recipes may call for mashed tofu that is more thoroughly dried. Simply wrap the tofu in 2 or 3 layers of cheesecloth (make sure there is enough to completely enclose the tofu), twist the top closed and keep twisting and squeezing to drain the liquid into the kitchen sink. Your tofu will now be sufficiently dry to use in your recipe.

Keep in mind that tofu, because of it inherent water content, does not readily absorb marinades; so the drier you can make it, the more easily it will absorb other liquids.

The Tofu Press

The tofu press is a spring-loaded device which presses water more effectively from a standard-size block of commercially made tofu, thus changing its texture dramatically without damaging its shape. Since more moisture is removed, the tofu can better absorb marinades and flavorings. No more excessive paper towel waste! The resulting pressed tofu is significantly denser, which gives it a "meatier" texture. Visit the TofuXpress.com website directly to learn more about their product.

What is Tempeh?

While exploring vegan cooking, you will sometimes come across recipes calling for tempeh. Tempeh is not related to tofu at all, other than the fact that both are produced from soybeans. Tempeh is actually a cultured food made by the controlled fermentation of cooked soybeans with a *Rhizopus oligosporus* culture (or tempeh "starter"). This fermentation binds the soybeans into a compact white cake. Tempeh has been a favorite food and staple source of protein in Indonesia for several hundred years.

Vegans may find it useful as a meat replacement, as it has a firm texture and a nutty mushroom flavor. Normally tempeh is sliced or cut in cubes and fried until the surface is crisp and golden brown. It can also be crumbled or grated. Tempeh can be used as ingredient in soups, spreads, salads and sandwiches. Tempeh is now commonly available in many supermarkets, as well as in Asian markets and health food stores.

Glazed Tofu

Block tofu is sliced or cubed, pan-fried in a small amount of vegetable oil and then glazed with your favorite sauce (my Teriyaki Sauce on pg. 206 works perfectly for this technique). The caramelizing of the sauce makes this tofu very flavorful. Try adding the tofu to vegetable stir-fry and serve with jasmine rice. Tempeh can also be used for this recipe.

Ingredients:

- vegetable oil for frying, about 2 T
- 1 block (about 14 oz) firm or extra-firm tofu (do not use silken tofu)
- 1/4 cup favorite sauce or glaze
- 1 tsp sesame oil (optional)

Technique:

Drain and press the tofu to remove as much water as possible (see Preparing Tofu for Recipes, pg. 56). Cut the tofu into slices or cubes. Add 2 tablespoons vegetable oil to a non-stick skillet and place over medium-high heat. Adding an additional teaspoon of sesame oil gives the tofu a nice authentic Asian flavor, but this is optional.

When the skillet is hot, add the tofu. Pan-sear the tofu, turning frequently but gently so as not to break it apart.

When the cubes are turning a light golden brown, add the sauce or glaze. The contents of the skillet will sizzle, the liquid portion of the sauce will eventually evaporate and any natural sugars in the sauce will caramelize on the exterior of the tofu.

Turn frequently to coat with the glaze. Transfer to a plate or a bowl and use in your favorite recipe.

Crispy Fried Tofu

Sliced tofu is dredged in a light, dry coating before frying in oil. I have heard some compare the flavor to fried chicken. Serve hot as an appetizer with your favorite dipping sauce. Try it with Soy Ginger Dipping Sauce (pg. 208) or Spicy Thai Peanut Sauce (pg. 211).

Ingredients:

- 1 block (about 14 oz) firm or extra-firm tofu (do not use silken tofu)
- 1/4 cup nutritional yeast
- 1 T cornstarch (preferably non-GMO), arrowroot powder or potato starch
- 1 tsp onion powder
- 1 tsp garlic powder
- 1/2 tsp sea salt
- 1/2 tsp pepper
- vegetable oil (peanut oil is the best for frying because it has a high smoking point, but any good quality vegetable oil will work fine)

Technique:

Drain and press the tofu to remove as much water as possible (see Preparing Tofu for Recipes, pg. 56). Cut the tofu into slices or cubes. Try cutting a slice in half and then again on the diagonal to form a triangle.

In a bowl, combine the remaining ingredients, except for the oil. Dredge the tofu on each side in the mixture and shake off any excess back into the bowl. Alternately, you can place the coating mixture and the tofu in a zip-lock bag or covered container and shake gently.

Pour a thin layer of oil in the bottom of a skillet and heat the oil over medium-high heat. Once the skillet is hot, add the tofu.

Cook for 4 to 6 minutes, turning occasionally, until golden brown and lightly crispy. Drain on a plate lined with paper towels.

Fried tofu is best eaten immediately; reheated leftovers tend to lose their crispness and have an excessively chewy texture.

What is TVP?

TVP, or textured vegetable protein, is a meat analogue made from defatted soy flour which is a by-product of the extraction of soybean oil. TVP is manufactured using an extrusion process, which causes a change in the structure of the soy protein. This results in a fibrous spongy material that is similar in texture to meat. This process is done using factory equipment and is not something that can be produced in a home kitchen.

TVP cooks quickly, contains no fat, and has a protein content equal to that of the meat. It requires rehydration before use, with seasoning added in the same step. In its granular form, it closely resembles the texture of ground beef. TVP can be found in natural food stores and occasionally in larger supermarket chains. It can also be ordered through the internet. It is a very economical and versatile source of protein for the vegan diet.

Seasoned Ground

Seasoned ground is a superior vegan substitute for any recipe calling for cooked and seasoned ground beef. Makes about 3 cups; refrigerate any unused portion and consume within 7 days.

Ingredients:

- 2 T vegetable oil
- 1 medium onion, finely diced
- 1 T minced garlic (3 cloves) or 1 tsp garlic powder
- 1 and 1/3 cup water
- 2 T tamari, soy sauce or Bragg Liquid Aminos™
  or 2 tsp Better Than Bouillon™ No Beef Base
- 1 tsp onion powder
- 1 tsp Gravy Master™ or other browning liquid - optional
- 1 cup dry TVP granules (textured vegetable protein)
- sea salt or kosher salt and ground black pepper to taste

Technique:

In a skillet over medium heat, sauté the onion in the oil until the onion is translucent, about 4 to 5 minutes. Add the minced garlic and sauté an additional minute.

Pour the water into the skillet and add all the ingredients except the TVP, stirring thoroughly to combine. Continue to heat until the mixture comes to a boil. Add the TVP and combine well. Reduce heat to low and cover the skillet. Let rest for 5 minutes.

Remove the cover and continue to cook over low heat, stirring frequently until the excess moisture begins to evaporate and the texture becomes firm, about 10 minutes. Use in your favorite recipe.

Tex-Mex Seasoned Ground

Tex-Mex Seasoned Ground is a fragrantly seasoned and amazingly realistic ground beef replacement for tacos, nachos, burritos, enchiladas and other Tex-Mex and Mexican cuisine. Makes about 3 cups; refrigerate any unused portion and consume within 7 days.

Ingredients:

- 2 T vegetable oil
- 1 medium onion, diced
- 1/2 bell pepper, diced
- 1 T minced garlic (3 cloves) or 1 tsp garlic powder
- 1 and 1/3 cup water
- 2 T tamari, soy sauce or Bragg Liquid Aminos™
  or 2 tsp Better Than Bouillon™ No Beef Base
- 2 tsp chili powder
- 1 tsp onion powder
- 1 tsp dried oregano
- 1/2 tsp ground cumin
- 1/4 tsp red pepper flakes, or more to taste
- 1 tsp Gravy Master™ or other browning liquid - optional
- 1 cup dry TVP granules (textured vegetable protein)
- sea salt or kosher salt, to taste

Technique:

In a skillet over medium heat, sauté the onion and bell pepper in the oil until the onion is translucent, about 4 to 5 minutes. Add the minced garlic and sauté an additional minute.

Pour the water into the skillet and add all ingredients except the TVP, stirring thoroughly to combine. Continue to heat until mixture comes to a boil. Add the TVP and combine well. Reduce heat to low and cover the skillet. Let rest for 5 minutes.

Remove the cover and continue to cook over low heat, stirring frequently until the excess moisture begins to evaporate and the texture becomes firm, about 10 minutes. Add additional salt to taste if needed. Use in your favorite recipe.

Chapter 3

Udderly Un-Dairy!

Abstaining from dairy products, especially cheese, seems to be the greatest obstacle for many wishing to transition to a vegan diet. However, dairy foods don't have to be such a sacrifice when so many excellent homemade and commercial non-dairy products are now available.

If you are serious about producing the best quality, homemade non-dairy products, you may want to invest in a high-powered blender, such as a Vitamix™.

Regular blenders simply don't have the power (torque) to churn through very thick mixtures, such as those used to make cremes and various vegan cheeses (or other foods like nut butters or hummus). Vitamix™ blenders also provide a "tamper tool" that fits through the lid. This helps keep mixtures turning in the blades, without having to start and stop the blender as frequently to stir.

Please note that the cheese recipes presented here are meant primarily for snacking. Although some will melt to varying degrees, they will not exhibit the "stretch" like some of the commercially produced vegan cheeses on the market, such as Daiya™, Teese™ and Sheese™. I'm still working on creating a homemade cheese that melts and stretches.

Whole raw cashew nuts are a common ingredient in many of my non-dairy recipes. If possible, avoid purchasing cashew halves and pieces because they are often poor quality and dried out. You can successfully substitute with the same weight measurement of whole raw macadamia nuts. For the best results, raw cashew nuts and macadamia nuts should be soaked in water to soften them before processing.

Agar Agar is the primary ingredient specified in several of the cheese recipes for creating firmness. Agar is a tasteless seaweed derivative and a vegetarian replacement for gelatin; it can be purchased in most health food and natural food stores or online through vegan retail websites. I specify flake agar in my recipes; however, if you can only obtain powdered agar, use this conversion:

1/4 cup (4 T) flake agar = 2 tsp powdered agar

My rule of thumb for refrigerated storage life of all perishable products is 10 days. This is a general food safety guideline. However, non-dairy foods may last somewhat longer if they are stored properly in an airtight container. You will have to judge for yourself by appearance, smell and taste. If in doubt, throw it out. Better Butter (pg. 62) can be stored in the freezer but I have never tried to freeze other non-dairy foods.

Better Butter

Better Butter is a superior tasting, PALM OIL FREE, buttery alternative to dairy butter and vegan margarine. This recipe produces a "butter" that looks, tastes and melts like real dairy butter. Just like its dairy counterpart, it should not be used for high-heat cooking in the skillet - it works best with low to medium heat. Two of its ingredients may be unfamiliar to some: soy lecithin and guar gum.

Soy lecithin, simply stated, is a mixture of phospholipids derived from the processing of soybeans and used in various food applications. One of the most popular uses of lecithin comes from its emulsifying properties, in other words, it binds oil and water together. It is thus used for promoting solidity in margarine, to give consistent textures to creams and dressings, and to avoid oil splattering during frying.

Guar gum, also called guaran, is a natural substance derived from the ground seeds of the guar plant which grows primarily in Pakistan and the northern regions of India. It is used as a thickener and stabilizer in food applications. This recipe makes about 2 cups of Better Butter.

Ingredients:

- 2/3 cup plain unsweetened soymilk, chilled
- 2 tsp raw apple cider vinegar
- 1 tsp organic sugar
- 1 cup refined coconut oil* (this can be found in some supermarkets but definitely in health food stores or natural markets)
- 1/3 cup sunflower, safflower or soybean oil
- 1 T plus 1 tsp (4 tsp total) liquid soy lecithin** (this can be found in most health food stores or natural markets)
- 3/4 tsp fine sea salt (for sweet creme butter, reduce salt to 1/4 tsp; this is ideal for baking)
- 1/2 tsp nutritional yeast
- 1/2 tsp guar gum (this can also be found in most health food stores or natural markets)

* There's a good deal of processing involved in the refinement of coconut oil. Organic unrefined (or "virgin") coconut oil is available for those who prefer a minimally processed product; however, unrefined coconut oil may impart a light coconut flavor to your butter. I have found that it is also significantly more expensive than the refined oil. Coconut oil is frowned upon by some nutritionists, and yet praised by others. It seems everyone has a different opinion. Research the subject yourself and draw your own conclusions but always remember the best advice for good health: "everything in moderation".

**Liquid soy lecithin is a syrupy, waxy substance that is difficult to remove from your measuring utensils. Coat the inside of your measuring spoons with a small amount of the melted coconut oil before measuring to reduce stickiness. You will need to wipe your measuring spoons with a paper towel and wash with hot, soapy water to completely remove any residue. The blender, and any other utensils used to make this recipe, will also need to be thoroughly washed in this manner as well.

Technique:

You will need a 2 cup minimum food storage container with a lid to store your spread. If you prefer, you can also shape the butter in a flexible silicone or plastic form, or divide it into several forms, and release it after hardening.

First, measure out the solid coconut oil into a non-metal bowl and microwave just until it is melted, about 30 to 60 seconds (you can also melt in a double-boiler over simmering water in a saucepan if you prefer). Try not to overheat the oil as it will take longer to cool. Pour into the blender and let cool to room temperature.

In a non-metal bowl, combine the vinegar and sugar with the chilled soymilk and let stand to curdle for about 30 minutes. About this time, the coconut oil should be sufficiently cooled.

Add the vegetable oil, lecithin, salt, yeast and guar gum to the coconut oil in the blender and process on high for about 30 seconds or until the lecithin is fully incorporated.

Reduce the speed of the blender to medium and pour in the curdled soymilk. As the mixture begins to thicken, increase the speed to high. Blend until the mixture becomes very thick. Stop the blender at this point as the ingredients are now fully emulsified. Total blending time should be no more than two minutes, usually less.

Pour the butter into your storage container or form and place in the freezer until completely hard. Freezing is important, as it prevents the mixture from separating. Once hardened, place in the refrigerator for use; or it can be stored in the freezer for extended periods of time. To release the butter from a form, simply wiggle the sides a bit to loosen and then press out onto a plate.

Heavy Creme

Heavy Creme is the perfect substitute for any recipe calling for heavy dairy cream. It's an essential ingredient for vegan "cream" soups (cream of mushroom, cream of broccoli, etc.) and ideal for adding creaminess to mashed potatoes. A high-powered blender (Vitamix™, for example) is very helpful in producing an ultra-smooth creme; otherwise you may notice a very fine "grit" in its texture. However, this can be reduced by straining the creme through a fine mesh sieve. The consistency can also be thinned with water to create a lighter creme or nut milk. Keep in mind that for best results, the nuts should be soaked in water for a minimum of 8 hours before processing - so plan ahead. This recipe makes about 2 cups heavy creme.

Ingredients:

- 1 cup (5 oz by weight) whole raw cashews
- pinch of sea salt
- 1 cup plus 2 T water

Technique:

Soak the nuts for a minimum of 8 hours in the refrigerator with enough water to cover; or if you're in a hurry, place them in a bowl, cover with near boiling water and let soak for about an hour.

Drain the nuts, discarding the soaking water. Add the nuts to a high-powered blender with a pinch of salt and 1 and 1/4 cups fresh water; process until completely smooth, about 1 to 2 minutes.

Strain the creme by pressing through a fine mesh sieve to eliminate any residual particles if necessary. Pour into an airtight container and refrigerate for up to 10 days. The creme will thicken a bit upon refrigeration. To lighten the creme, add more water, a tablespoon at a time to reach desired consistency.

Note: If you don't have any cashew nuts for making heavy creme, you can substitute with 5 oz macadamia nuts; 5 oz of blanched almonds, or 1 and 1/4 cup almond meal (5 oz by weight). After processing, strain the creme through a fine mesh sieve or cheesecloth to eliminate any "grit" before using.

For a soy-based creme, try blending equal parts extra-firm silken tofu and soymilk with a dash of organic sugar and a pinch of sea salt.

Sour Creme

Rich and velvety smooth; this recipe makes approximately 1 cup of superior vegan sour cream. A high-powered blender is essential for the best texture.

Ingredients:

- 1 cup (5 oz by weight) whole raw cashews
- 1/2 cup plain unsweetened soymilk (avoid substitution; other milks will not curdle as well)
- 2 T fresh lemon juice
- 2 T refined coconut oil, melted
- 1 tsp raw apple cider vinegar
- pinch of sea salt or kosher salt

Technique:

Soak the nuts for a minimum of 8 hours in the refrigerator with enough water to cover; or if you're in a hurry, place them in a bowl, cover with near boiling water and let soak for about an hour.

In a small dish, melt the coconut oil in the microwave for about 10 seconds.

Drain the nuts, discarding the soaking water. Add the nuts to a high-powered blender. Add the soymilk, the melted coconut oil and the additional ingredients. Blend for a minute or two until completely smooth, stopping to stir the contents or scrape down the sides of blender as necessary. Refrigerate to thicken before using.

Golden Parmesan

Golden Parmesan is a superior vegan replacement for dairy parmesan. The nutritional yeast imparts a light golden color to the parmesan. Because this parmesan is made with miso, a fermented product, it should stay fresh in the refrigerator for several weeks if stored in an airtight container. If you are allergic to soy, look for miso paste made from barley.

Combine in a food processor:

- 1 cup almond meal (Bob's Red Mill™ produces an excellent almond meal)
- 1 T mellow white miso paste
- 1 T nutritional yeast
- 1/2 tsp sea salt or kosher salt
- 1/4 tsp garlic powder
- 1/4 tsp onion powder

Process all ingredients until well blended and finely ground. Refrigerate in a covered container until ready to use.

Heavenly Whipped Creme

This heavenly whipped topping rivals its finest dairy counterpart. Smooth, creamy, lightly sweetened and flavored with a hint of vanilla, it's ideal for topping vegan desserts. Follow the instructions to the letter and you will have success every time. Enjoy, but consume moderately - this is not a low fat/calorie topping! This recipe makes about 2 to 2.5 cups of whipped creme if you use a good quality coconut milk.

Ingredients:

- 2 cans (about 13 oz each) premium quality, full fat organic coconut milk*
- 1/3 cup organic sugar (evaporated cane juice)
- 1/2 tsp real vanilla extract
- a pinch of freshly grated nutmeg (optional)

Special equipment needed:

- a ceramic or metal mixing bowl (ceramic is ideal because it stays cold longer, but metal will work fine too)
- an electric beater

* I have had the most consistent quality and best results using Native Forest™ organic coconut milk.

Technique:

Chill the cans of coconut milk towards the back of the refrigerator for a minimum of 24 hours. The cans must get as cold as possible without freezing. This will ensure that the cream is completely solidified and separated from the coconut water.

Place your mixing bowl and the metal beaters in the freezer to get VERY cold. Place 1/3 cup organic sugar in a dry, high-powered blender. Pulse process until the sugar is finely powdered.* Set aside.

*Why make your own powdered sugar? Non-vegan commercial powdered sugar is made from refined white sugar which has typically been filtered through bone char during the refining process.

Now open the top of the cans with a can opener, leaving a small hinge for the lids to stay attached. Scoop out the solidified cream into the mixing bowl until you reach the coconut water. If using a good quality coconut milk, there should be a substantial amount of cream. Close the lid and drain away the coconut water, reserving for another use if you desire (smoothies perhaps?) - DO NOT add the coconut water to the mixing bowl! Open the can and scoop out any remaining cream that has solidified near the bottom of the can and add to the mixing bowl.

Add the vanilla and powdered sugar to the cream and fold in to combine. Add the optional nutmeg if you desire.

Beat the mixture on high-speed for several minutes until the mixture is thick, smooth and peaks begin to form. Transfer to an air-tight container and refrigerate until ready to use. The whipped creme will stay firm as long as it is refrigerated.

Gentle Swiss

This smooth and mild snacking cheese can be made with either cashew nuts or tofu. It has an excellent Swiss cheese flavor that makes it ideal for slicing and serving on crackers or sandwiches; or for gently shredding and using in recipes. Keep in mind that although it does melt slightly, it lacks the "stretch" of some of the commercial vegan cheeses available.

First, you will need a container which will hold a minimum of 2 cups liquid, to act as the form to shape your block of cheese. A square, round or rectangular-shaped plastic food storage container works well for this purpose. A ceramic or glass bowl will also work; and dessert ramekins are perfect for making smaller portions of cheese. Spray the form(s) lightly with cooking oil spray. This will ease removal of the cheese.

Ingredients:

- 1 cup (5 oz by weight) whole raw cashews;
  or
  1/2 block (7 oz) firm or extra-firm tofu
  (do not use silken tofu)
- 1 cup water
- 1/4 cup (4 T) agar flakes
- 2 T nutritional yeast

- 2 T mellow white miso paste
- 1 T fresh lemon juice
- 1 tsp white wine vinegar
- 1 tsp dry ground mustard
- 1/2 tsp onion powder
- 1/4 tsp garlic powder
- 1 T vegetable oil (tofu base only)

Technique:

If using the nuts as a base, soak them for a minimum of 8 hours in the refrigerator with just enough water to cover; or if you're in a hurry, place them in a bowl, cover with near boiling water and let soak for about an hour.

If using tofu as a base, press the tofu until it is not releasing any more liquid (see Preparing Tofu for Recipes, pg. 56).

In a small saucepan, combine the agar flakes with 1 cup of water and bring the mixture to a brief boil. Reduce the heat and simmer, stirring often, until the agar dissolves and becomes gelatinous.

For the nut base: While the agar is dissolving in the saucepan, drain the nuts and discard the soaking water. Place the nuts in a high-powered blender with the remaining ingredients.

For the tofu base: While the agar is dissolving in the saucepan, crumble the tofu into a blender and add the remaining ingredients including the 1 tablespoon of vegetable oil.

Pour the hot agar/water mixture into the blender. Process the mixture at high-speed until completely smooth, about 1 to 2 minutes. Stop to scrape down the sides of the blender as necessary with a rubber spatula.

Transfer the mixture to the prepared container and smooth the top with back of a spoon or rubber spatula. Cover and chill for several hours until firm. To serve, run a sharp knife around the inside of the form to loosen the cheese; turn out of the container (tapping the container sharply if necessary to remove) and slice.

Crème Fraîche

Crème Fraîche is a slightly tangy, slightly nutty, thickened cream. This is a non-dairy version of course.

Ingredients:

- 2/3 cup plain unsweetened soymilk (sorry, no substitutions)
- 1 T raw apple cider vinegar
- 1/3 cup Sour Creme (pg. 65) or commercial vegan sour cream

I highly recommend Bragg™ Organic Raw Apple Cider Vinegar

Technique:

Mix the soymilk and vinegar together, cover and set aside un-refrigerated for several hours to curdle (up to 12 hours). Whisk in the sour creme until smooth and creamy. Refrigerate until ready to use. Herbs can be added prior to serving, if desired, to accommodate various ethnic cuisines (cilantro Crème Fraîche, for example, is an excellent topping for Tex-Mex Cuisine).

Tofu Ricotta

Tofu ricotta is superb for stuffed pasta shells or lasagna.

Ingredients:

- 1 block (about 14 oz) firm or extra-firm tofu (do not use silken tofu)
- 2 T extra-virgin olive oil
- 1 T fresh lemon juice
- 1 tsp onion powder
- 1 tsp nutritional yeast
- 1/2 tsp salt
- 1/4 tsp ground white pepper
- 1 tsp each of dried basil, parsley, and oregano (optional)
- plain unsweetened soymilk if necessary to thin to desired consistency

Technique:

Drain and press the tofu to remove excess moisture (see Preparing Tofu for Recipes, pg. 56). Mash the tofu with a fork; add the remaining ingredients and blend well. Use a scant amount of soymilk if necessary to thin to desired texture. Refrigerate in a covered container until ready to use. For spinach ricotta: Steam the spinach and press in a strainer (or tofu press) to remove excess moisture. Add about 1 cup pressed spinach to a food processor and pulse to puree. Add pureed spinach to the ricotta in a bowl and stir to blend. Delicious in stuffed pasta shells, manicotti and lasagna.

Creme Cheese

This recipe produces a superior tasting, firm yet creamy, PALM OIL FREE creme cheese with no soy undertaste (because it is also soy free). The creme cheese is extremely thick; therefore, you will need a high-powered blender, such as a Vitamix™, to produce the proper consistency. This recipe makes about 1 cup of creme cheese; for more, simply double the recipe.

Ingredients:

- 1 cup (5 oz by weight) whole raw cashews
- 1 T fresh lemon juice
- 1 and 1/2 tsp raw apple cider vinegar
- 2 T filtered water
- 1/4 tsp plus scant pinch fine sea salt or kosher salt
- 2 T refined coconut oil, melted

Technique:

Soak the nuts for a minimum of 8 hours in the refrigerator with just enough water to cover; or, if you're in a hurry, place them in a bowl, cover with near boiling water and let soak for about an hour.

In a small dish, warm the coconut oil in the microwave until just melted (about 15 to 30 seconds). You can also use a saucepan on low heat for melting, but the microwave is easier for such a small amount.

Drain the nuts and discard the soaking water. Place the nuts in a high-powered blender and add the remaining ingredients including the melted coconut oil. Process the mixture until completely smooth, stopping the blender as necessary to scrape the sides and stir the mixture back down into the blades. If using a blender with a tamper tool, insert it through the lid while processing to keep the mixture turning in the blades.

Transfer to a container, cover and chill overnight to firm completely.

For creme cheese with onion and chives, stir in 1 tsp onion powder (or more to taste) and 1 T fresh or freeze-dried minced chives before chilling.

For a fruit flavored creme cheese, mix 2 T all-fruit jam into the creme cheese after it has chilled and firmed.

Herbed Chevre

This creamy herbed cheese makes a wonderful spread for crackers or crusty bread. A high-powered blender is essential for this recipe. As an appetizer spread, this cheese will serve about 4 guests.

Ingredients:

- 1 cup (5 oz by weight) whole raw cashews
- 3 T refined coconut oil, gently melted
- 2 T water
- 2 T fresh lemon juice
- 1/2 tsp onion powder
- 1/2 tsp fine sea salt or kosher salt
- fresh minced tarragon and chives, about 1 T each (or other herbs of your choice)
- 1/2 tsp ground black pepper, or more to taste

Technique:

Soak the nuts for a minimum of 8 hours in the refrigerator with just enough water to cover; or if you're in a hurry, place them in a bowl, cover with near boiling water and let soak for about an hour.

Drain the nuts, discarding the soaking water. Place the nuts in a high-powered blender.

In a small dish, gently melt the coconut oil for about 15 seconds in the microwave and then add to the blender. Add the water, lemon juice, onion powder and salt.

Process until completely smooth, stopping the blender as needed to pack the mixture back down into the blades. If using a blender with a tamper tool, insert it through the lid while processing to keep the mixture turning in the blades. Transfer the mixture to a container with a lid. Cover and refrigerate overnight.

The next day, lay out a small sheet of aluminum foil. Lightly mist the foil with cooking oil spray; this will help prevent the cheese from sticking to the foil.

Sprinkle the foil with half of the chopped herbs and black pepper. Scoop the cheese mixture on top of the herbs and pepper on the sheet of foil.

With your fingers, gently form the cheese into a log shape. Don't worry about perfection; the foil will shape the log for you when rolled.

Sprinkle the remaining herbs and pepper on top of the cheese. Roll the mixture, like a tootsie roll, inside the foil, and twist the ends tightly. Place back in the refrigerator for a couple of hours to re-firm.

To serve, simply remove the foil wrapper and place on a serving plate.

Onion, Dill and Horseradish Cheese

This tangy semi-soft cheese makes a wonderful spread for crackers or crusty bread. A high-powered blender is essential for this recipe. As an appetizer spread, this cheese will serve about 4 guests.

Ingredients:

- 1 cup (5 oz by weight) whole raw cashews
- 3 T refined coconut oil, gently melted
- 2 T water
- 1 T fresh lemon juice
- 1 T prepared horseradish (not creamed)
- 1 tsp onion powder
- 1 tsp Dijon mustard
- 3/4 tsp fine sea salt or kosher salt
- 1/4 tsp garlic powder
- 1 T minced or flaked dried onion
- 2 T fresh dill, finely minced

Technique:

Soak the nuts for a minimum of 8 hours in the refrigerator with just enough water to cover; or if you're in a hurry, place them in a bowl, cover with near boiling water and let soak for about an hour. Drain the nuts, discarding the soaking water. Place the nuts in a high-powered blender.

In a small dish, gently melt the coconut oil for about 15 seconds in the microwave and then add to the blender. Add the remaining ingredients EXCEPT for the minced onion and dill.

Process until completely smooth, stopping the blender as needed to pack the mixture back down into the blades. If using a blender with a tamper tool, insert it through the lid while processing to keep the mixture turning in the blades.

Add the dried onion and dill and stir to combine. Transfer the mixture to a decorative serving container. Cover and refrigerate overnight to blend the flavors and firm the cheese before serving.

Garlic Pepper Havarti

This piquant and peppery snacking cheese can be made with either cashew nuts or tofu. It's ideal for slicing and serving on crackers or sandwiches; or for gently shredding and using in recipes. Keep in mind that although it does melt slightly, it lacks the "stretch" of some of the commercial vegan cheeses available.

First, you will need a container which will hold a minimum of 2 cups liquid, to act as the form to shape your block of cheese. A square, round or rectangular-shaped plastic food storage container works well for this purpose. A ceramic or glass bowl will also work; and dessert ramekins are perfect for making smaller portions of cheese. Spray the form(s) lightly with cooking oil spray. This will ease removal of the cheese.

Ingredients:

- 1 jalapeno or Serrano chili, seeded
- 1 cup (5 oz by weight) whole raw cashews; or
  1/2 block (7 oz) firm or extra-firm tofu (do not use silken tofu)
- 1 cup water
- 1/4 cup (4 T) agar flakes
- 1/4 cup nutritional yeast

- 1 T white wine vinegar
- 1 T fresh lemon juice
- 2 tsp Dijon mustard
- 1 tsp onion powder
- 3/4 tsp sea salt or kosher salt
- 2 cloves garlic or 2 tsp minced garlic
- crushed red pepper flakes
- 1 T vegetable oil (tofu base only)

Technique:

If using the nuts as a base, soak them for a minimum of 8 hours in the refrigerator with just enough water to cover; or, if you're in a hurry, place them in a bowl, cover with near boiling water and let soak for about an hour. If using tofu as a base, press the tofu until it is not releasing any more liquid (see Preparing Tofu for Recipes, pg. 56).

In a small saucepan, combine the agar flakes with 1 cup of water. Set aside.

Seed and finely mince the chili pepper. Wear gloves if you have sensitive skin or be sure to wash your hands thoroughly after handling. Spray a small skillet with a little cooking oil spray and sauté the pepper until lightly browned. Set aside to cool.

For the nut base: Drain the nuts and discard the soaking water. Place the nuts in a high-powered blender with the remaining ingredients including 1 tsp of crushed red pepper flakes. Set aside.

For the tofu base: Crumble the tofu into a blender and add the remaining ingredients including 1 tsp crushed red pepper flakes and the 1 tablespoon of vegetable oil. Set aside.

Now, bring the agar/water mixture to a brief boil. Reduce the heat and simmer, stirring often, until the agar dissolves and becomes gelatinous.

Pour the hot agar/water mixture into the blender. Process the mixture at high-speed until completely smooth, about 1 to 2 minutes. Stop to scrape down the sides of the blender as necessary with a rubber spatula.

With the blender off, add an additional 1/2 tsp crushed red pepper along with the sautéed jalapeno. Process for a few seconds until mixed but not liquefied, as you will want small flecks of pepper in the cheese. Transfer the mixture to the prepared container and smooth the top with the back of a spoon or rubber spatula. Cover and chill for several hours until completely firm. To serve, run a sharp knife around the inside of the form to loosen the cheese, turn out of the container (tapping the container sharply if necessary to remove) and slice.

Fresh Nut Mozzarella

This creamy and mild semi-firm cheese is ideal for slicing and serving on crackers or sandwiches. Try slices of this cheese with Insalata Caprese (pg. 112), a salad comprised of stewed tomatoes, sliced onions, basil and balsamic vinaigrette. It can also be gently shredded and used in recipes. Keep in mind that although it does melt slightly, it lacks the "stretch" of some of the commercial vegan cheeses available. A high-powered blender is essential for creating an ultra-smooth texture.

First, you will need a container which will hold a minimum of 2.5 cups liquid, to act as the form to shape your block of cheese. A square, round or rectangular-shaped plastic food storage container works well for this purpose. A ceramic or glass bowl will also work; and dessert ramekins are perfect for making smaller portions of cheese. Spray the form(s) lightly with cooking oil spray. This will ease removal of the cheese.

Technique:

Ingredients:

Soak the nuts for a minimum of 8 hours in the refrigerator with just enough water to cover; or if you're in a hurry, place them in a bowl, cover with near boiling water and let soak for about an hour.

- 1 cup (5 oz by weight) whole raw cashews
- 1 cup water
- 1/4 cup (4 T) agar flakes
- 1/2 cup plain unsweetened almond milk
- 2 T fresh lemon juice
- 1 tsp raw apple cider vinegar
- 1 tsp sea salt or kosher salt
- 1/2 tsp onion powder
- 2 T vegetable oil

In a small saucepan, combine the agar flakes with the water and bring the mixture to a brief boil. Reduce the heat and simmer, stirring often, until the agar dissolves and becomes gelatinous.

Drain the nuts, discarding the soaking water. Place the nuts in a high-powered blender with the remaining ingredients.

Pour the hot agar/water mixture into the blender and process at high-speed until completely smooth, about 1 to 2 minutes. Stop to scrape down the sides of the blender as necessary with a rubber spatula.

Transfer the mixture to the prepared container and smooth top with back of a spoon or rubber spatula. Cover and chill for several hours until completely firm. To serve, run a sharp knife around the inside of the form to loosen the cheese, turn out of the container (tapping the container sharply if necessary to remove) and slice.

Crumbly Block Feta

This vegan cheese is very simple to make and is very reminiscent of dairy feta cheese in taste and texture. It's very high in protein, yet low in fat and calories and is perfect for crumbling on salads. A tofu press is ideal, although not essential, for drying the tofu sufficiently for this recipe (see Tofu Press, pg. 56). Be sure to use EXTRA-FIRM block tofu for this recipe.

Ingredients:

- 1 block (about 14 oz) extra-firm tofu (do not use silken tofu)
- 2 T water
- 2 T fresh lemon juice
- 1 T white wine vinegar
- 2 tsp sea salt or kosher salt
- 1/2 tsp very fine onion powder
- optional: 2 T fresh finely chopped herbs such as oregano, marjoram or basil (or 2 tsp dry)

Technique:

Place the tofu into the tofu press and put the spring plate into place. Press for several hours in the refrigerator, draining occasionally, until the tofu is not releasing any more liquid. If you do not have a tofu press, place the tofu into a sieve over a large bowl to catch the liquid. Place a small plate or plastic wrap on top and then place a heavy weight on top of the plate or plastic. Allow to press until very dry as described previously.

In a small bowl, combine the remaining ingredients to make the brine. The onion powder is somewhat stubborn to disperse, but keep stirring until the salt is dissolved and the onion powder is completely incorporated (if you're using herbs, the herbs will help break up the onion powder easily).

Next, remove the tofu from the press and pierce repeatedly on both sides with a fork. This will create small holes to allow the brine to absorb evenly.

Place the tofu into a zip-lock bag and add the brine. Force as much air out of the bag as you can and seal.

Allow to marinate several hours or until most of the brine is absorbed. Your feta is now ready to crumble and use.

English Gloucester with Onion and Chives

This savory medium-sharp snacking cheese can be made with either cashew nuts or tofu. It's ideal for slicing and serving on crackers or sandwiches; or for gently shredding and using in recipes. Keep in mind that although it does melt slightly, it lacks the "stretch" of some of the commercial vegan cheeses available.

First, you will need a container which will hold a minimum of 2 cups liquid, to act as the form to shape your block of cheese. A square, round or rectangular-shaped plastic food storage container works well for this purpose. A ceramic or glass bowl will also work; and dessert ramekins are perfect for making smaller portions of cheese. Spray the form(s) lightly with cooking oil spray. This will ease removal of the cheese.

Ingredients:

- 1 cup (5 oz by weight) whole raw cashews; or
  1/2 block (7 oz) firm or extra-firm tofu (do not use silken tofu)
- 1 cup water
- 1/4 cup (4 T) agar flakes
- 1/4 cup nutritional yeast
- 2 T homemade vegan Worcestershire Sauce (pg. 206) or commercial

- 2 T raw apple cider vinegar
- 2 T tomato paste
- 2 tsp onion powder
- 3/4 tsp sea salt or kosher salt
- 1/2 tsp garlic powder
- 1/4 tsp turmeric
- 2 T fresh or freeze-dried minced chives
- 1 T dried minced or flaked onion

Technique:

If using the nuts as a base, soak them for a minimum of 8 hours in the refrigerator with just enough water to cover; or, if you're in a hurry, place them in a bowl, cover with near boiling water and let soak for about an hour. If using tofu as a base, press the tofu until it is not releasing any more liquid (see Preparing Tofu for Recipes, pg. 56).

In a small saucepan, combine the agar flakes with 1 cup water and bring the mixture to a brief boil. Reduce the heat and simmer, stirring often, until the agar dissolves and becomes gelatinous.

For the nut base: While the agar is dissolving in the saucepan, drain the nuts and discard the soaking water. Place the nuts in a high-powered blender with the remaining ingredients EXCEPT for the dried minced onion and chives.

For the tofu base: While the agar is dissolving in the saucepan, crumble the tofu into a blender and add the remaining ingredients EXCEPT for the dried minced onion and chives.

Pour the hot agar/water mixture into the blender. Process the mixture at high-speed until completely smooth, about 1 to 2 minutes. Stop to scrape down the sides of the blender as necessary with a rubber spatula. With the blender off, add the chives and minced onion. Stir to combine with the rubber spatula.

Transfer the mixture to the prepared container and smooth the top with the back of a spoon or rubber spatula. Cover and chill for several hours until completely firm. To serve, run a sharp knife around the inside of the form to loosen the cheese, turn out of the container (tapping the container sharply if necessary to remove) and slice.

Tangy Smoked Chedda'

This smoky medium-sharp snacking cheese can be made with either cashew nuts or tofu. It's ideal for slicing and serving on crackers or sandwiches; or for gently shredding and using in recipes. Keep in mind that although it does melt slightly, it lacks the "stretch" of some of the commercial vegan cheeses available.

First, you will need a container which will hold a minimum of 2 cups liquid, to act as the form to shape your block of cheese. A square, round or rectangular-shaped plastic food storage container works well for this purpose. A ceramic or glass bowl will also work; and dessert ramekins are perfect for making smaller portions of cheese. Spray the form(s) lightly with cooking oil spray. This will ease removal of the cheese.

Ingredients:

- 1 cup (5 oz by weight) whole raw cashews;
  or
  1/2 block (7 oz) firm or extra-firm tofu
  (do not use silken tofu)
- 1 cup water
- 1/4 cup (4 T) agar flakes
- 1/4 cup nutritional yeast
- 2 T tomato paste

- 2 T raw apple cider vinegar
- 1 T mellow white miso paste
- 1 T liquid smoke
- 2 tsp onion powder
- 3/4 tsp smoked sea salt (substitute with plain sea salt or kosher salt)
- 1/2 tsp garlic powder

Technique:

If using the nuts as a base, soak them for a minimum of 8 hours in the refrigerator with just enough water to cover; or, if you're in a hurry, place them in a bowl, cover with near boiling water and let soak for about an hour. If using tofu as a base, press the tofu until it is not releasing any more liquid (see Preparing Tofu for Recipes, pg. 56).

In a small saucepan, combine the agar flakes with 1 cup water and bring the mixture to a brief boil. Reduce the heat and simmer, stirring often, until the agar dissolves and becomes gelatinous.

For the nut base: While the agar is dissolving in the saucepan, drain the nuts and discard the soaking water. Place the nuts in a high-powered blender with the remaining ingredients.

For the tofu base: While the agar is dissolving in the saucepan, crumble the tofu into a blender and add the remaining ingredients.

Pour the hot agar/water mixture into the blender. Process the mixture at high-speed until completely smooth, about 1 to 2 minutes. Stop to scrape down the sides of the blender as necessary with a rubber spatula.

Transfer the mixture to the prepared container and smooth the top with back of a spoon or rubber spatula. Cover and chill for several hours until firm. To serve, run a sharp knife around the inside of the form to loosen the cheese; turn out of the container (tapping the container sharply if necessary to remove) and slice.

Smoked Gouda

This mild but flavorful snacking cheese can be made with either cashew nuts or tofu. It's ideal for slicing and serving on crackers or sandwiches; or for gently shredding and using in recipes. Keep in mind that although it does melt slightly, it lacks the "stretch" of some of the commercial vegan cheeses available.

First, you will need a container which will hold a minimum of 2 cups liquid, to act as the form to shape your block of cheese. A square, round or rectangular-shaped plastic food storage container works well for this purpose. A ceramic or glass bowl will also work; and dessert ramekins are perfect for making smaller portions of cheese. Spray the form(s) lightly with cooking oil spray. This will ease removal of the cheese.

Ingredients:

- 1 cup (5 oz by weight) whole raw cashews; or
- 1/2 block (7 oz) firm or extra-firm tofu (do not use silken tofu)
- 1 cup water
- 1/4 cup (4 T) agar flakes
- 1/4 cup nutritional yeast
- 1 T white wine vinegar

- 1 T liquid smoke
- 2 tsp onion powder
- 2 tsp homemade vegan Worcestershire Sauce (pg. 206) or commercial
- 3/4 tsp fine sea salt or kosher salt
- 1/2 tsp ground mustard
- 1/4 tsp garlic powder
- 1 T vegetable oil (tofu base only)

Technique:

If using the nuts as a base, soak them for a minimum of 8 hours in the refrigerator with just enough water to cover; or if you're in a hurry, place them in a bowl, cover with near boiling water and let soak for about an hour.

If using tofu as a base, press the tofu until it is not releasing any more liquid (see Preparing Tofu for Recipes, pg. 56)

In a small saucepan, combine the agar flakes with 1 cup water and bring the mixture to a brief boil. Reduce the heat and simmer, stirring often, until the agar dissolves and becomes gelatinous.

For the nut base: While the agar is dissolving in the saucepan, drain the nuts and discard the soaking water. Place the nuts in a high-powered blender with the remaining ingredients.

For the tofu base: While the agar is dissolving in the saucepan, crumble the tofu into a blender and add the remaining ingredients including the 1 tablespoon of vegetable oil.

Pour the hot agar/water mixture into the blender. Process the mixture at high-speed until completely smooth, about 1 to 2 minutes. Stop to scrape down the sides of the blender as necessary with a rubber spatula.

Transfer the mixture to the prepared container and smooth the top with back of a spoon or rubber spatula. Cover and chill for several hours until firm. To serve, run a sharp knife around the inside of the form to loosen the cheese; turn out of the container (tapping the container sharply if necessary to remove) and slice.

Chapter 4

Breakfast and Brunch

In this chapter, you will encounter an ingredient called "kala namak" (Himalayan or Indian black salt). It is useful in vegan cooking as it imparts a cooked egg taste to tofu, which is used as an alternative to eggs. Kala namak is mined from the Himalayan Mountains in Northern India. It has a high mineral concentration, most notably sulfur, which gives it its characteristic and pungent "hard-boiled egg" aroma. Interestingly, it is not black but pink in color.

Kala namak is considered a cooling spice in Ayurvedic medicine and is used as a digestive aid. It can be found in specialty food stores as well as online. I purchase mine through Amazon.com. Be advised, that if you detest the sulfurous smell of hard-boiled eggs, you probably will not care for this salt and will want to substitute with regular sea salt or kosher salt.

Ruddy Mary Cocktail

A Sunday brunch classic.

Salt and pepper the rim of a 16 oz glass (if desired). Coarse kosher salt or margarita salt works great for this, mixed with a little freshly ground black pepper. Moisten the rim of the glass with the lime before dipping in the salt and pepper.

Into the glass combine:

- 12 oz tomato juice or vegetable juice (such as V8™)
- 1 shot of premium vodka (optional)
- 2 tsp homemade vegan Worcestershire Sauce (pg. 206) or commercial
- juice of 1/2 a lime
- 2 tsp prepared horseradish, or more to taste (make sure you purchase fresh prepared horseradish from the refrigerated section of your market; creamed horseradish from store shelves almost always contains milk and believe or not - egg; always read labels)
- 1 T dill pickle brine or green olive brine
- dash of red hot sauce

Stir well and add ice. Garnish with vegetable of your choice: celery sticks, green olives, green onion, dill pickle spear, pickled green beans, pickled okra, pickled asparagus spears or lime wedges.

Blueberry Pancakes

Plump blueberries naturally sweeten these light and fluffy eggless pancakes.

Ingredients:

- 1 and 1/4 cups unbleached all-purpose wheat flour
- 2 tsp baking powder
- 1/2 tsp salt
- 1 and 1/4 cups non-dairy milk (almond milk works best)
- 1/4 cup water
- 2 T real maple syrup
- 2 T canola oil
- 1 tsp real vanilla extract
- 1 cup fresh blueberries (or thawed from frozen)

Technique:

If using frozen blueberries, thaw them and place on a paper towel to drain any excess liquid. Set aside.

Sift the flour, baking powder and salt into a large bowl. Mix the liquid ingredients together in a separate bowl.

Make a well in the center of the dry ingredients, and pour in the liquid ingredients. Stir thoroughly until no large lumps of flour remain (very small lumps are okay). The batter may seem a little thin – this is how it should be. Fold in the blueberries.

Heat a lightly oiled griddle over medium-high heat until very hot. Drop batter by the large spoonful onto the griddle, and cook until bubbles form and the edges are dry.

Flip, and cook until browned on the other side. Repeat with remaining batter.

Serve with Better Butter (pg. 62) or margarine and warm syrup.

Note: For plain pancakes, simply omit the berries.

Southwestern Eggless Scramble

Velvety tofu, vegan sausage and southwestern flavors come together in this favorite breakfast or brunch scramble.

Ingredients:

- 1 T vegetable oil
- 10 oz Sausage Crumbles (pg. 50) - or commercial vegan sausage, cooked and crumbled
- 2 T Better Butter (pg. 62) or vegan margarine
- 1 small onion, finely diced
- 1 small bell pepper, finely diced
- 1 block (about 14 oz) soft to firm tofu (do not use silken tofu)
- 2 T nutritional yeast
- 1 tsp onion powder
- a pinch of turmeric (turmeric adds a nice scrambled "egg" color to the tofu, but do not use too much or the scramble will look artificially yellow)
- 1/4 tsp kala namak (Himalayan black salt) - optional
- sea salt or kosher salt to taste
- pepper to taste
- vegan shredded cheese that melts - optional (i.e., Daiya™, etc.)
- salsa verde or red salsa

Drain, slice and lightly press the tofu with paper towels to remove excess moisture. The goal is to retain some moisture so the scramble has a velvety texture.

Lightly coat a skillet with a little vegetable oil and brown the sausage over medium heat. Transfer to a bowl and set aside.

In the same skillet, sauté the onions and bell pepper in the butter or margarine until tender. Add the crumbled tofu, nutritional yeast, onion powder, turmeric and salt and pepper to taste. "Scramble" for about 3 minutes until the seasonings are evenly combined and some of the excess moisture has been evaporated from the tofu.

Add the sausage back to the skillet, combine and heat through. Top the contents of the skillet with the shredded vegan cheese. Cover, reduce heat to low and let "steam" until the cheese melts a bit. Serve and top with salsa of your choice.

Corn Griddlecakes

In some regions this dish is called "fried mush", especially when served for breakfast/brunch with syrup; but somehow the word "mush" doesn't sound as appealing as "griddlecake". Whatever you wish to call it, it's satisfying, easy to make and inexpensive too. This recipe needs to be prepared and refrigerated the night before, to allow time for the cornmeal cake to firm up before slicing and frying. So plan accordingly.

Ingredients:

- 3 cups water
- Better Butter (pg. 62) or vegan margarine
- 1 T organic sugar
- 1/2 tsp sea salt or kosher salt
- 1 cup yellow cornmeal (preferably non-GMO)

Technique:

In a medium saucepan, bring the water and 1 tablespoon of the butter or margarine to a boil. Reduce heat to medium; add salt and sugar. Now add the cornmeal, SLOWLY pouring into the water while vigorously whisking the mixture – this is important so that the corn meal does not form solid lumps. If lumps form, keep whisking until they break apart.

Cook, stirring frequently, until the mixture is thick and begins to pull away from sides of saucepan. At this stage of cooking, the cornmeal is also known as *polenta*.

Spoon the cornmeal mixture into a lightly greased 9×5 inch loaf pan and smooth the top with the back of a spoon or rubber spatula. Place plastic wrap directly in contact with the surface and refrigerate overnight.

In the morning, lightly coat a griddle or skillet with a little vegetable oil and set over medium-high heat. Slice the corn cake into 1/4-inch thick slices. Fry until light golden brown on both sides. Serve with a little Better Butter (pg. 62) or margarine and warm syrup or all-fruit jam.

Shredding and Freezing Potatoes for Hash Browns

Peel and shred russet potatoes, one at a time, and immerse the shreds in a bowl of cold water until all the potatoes are shredded. Drain in a colander and then blanch in boiling water for 2 minutes. Drain, rinse in cold water, and then drain again.

Pat dry between layers of paper towels; or wrap in cheesecloth or a lint-free kitchen towel and squeeze. Pack into freezer containers or re-sealable bags. Store in the freezer for up to 1 year.

Thaw the shreds before making skillet hash browns or for using in any recipe calling for shredded potatoes, such as Potatoes Parmigiano (see following page).

Potatoes Parmigiano

Freshly shredded potatoes are blended with a creamy Béchamel sauce and vegan parmesan, and then baked until tender and golden on top. For cheesy potatoes, add 1/2 cup vegan cheese that melts (Daiya™, for example). I chose to use fresh potatoes because commercial frozen hash browns often contain numerous chemical additives.

Ingredients:

- 3 large russet potatoes
- 1/4 cup (4 T) Better Butter (pg. 62) or vegan margarine
- 1 medium onion, finely diced
- 1/4 cup flour (unbleached all-purpose wheat; rice or soy)
- 2 cups plain unsweetened non-dairy milk

- 2 T nutritional yeast
- 1 tsp sea salt or kosher salt
- 1 tsp onion powder
- 1/4 tsp black pepper, or more to taste
- 1/4 tsp garlic powder
- pinch of nutmeg, optional
- 1/2 cup Golden Parmesan (pg. 65) or commercial vegan parmesan

Technique:

Add about 2 quarts of water to a large stockpot and place over high heat to bring the water to a boil. Meanwhile, peel and shred the potatoes one at a time with a standard cheese/vegetable grater (or the shredding blade of a food processor) and immerse the potato shreds immediately in a large bowl of cold water; this will prevent oxidation (turning brown). Let the potatoes sit in the water until all of the potatoes are shredded. Agitate the water to remove excess starch and then drain in a colander.

Now, carefully add the shredded potatoes to the boiling water. This will halt the boiling action but that's okay; just give them a stir and set a timer for 2 minutes.

Drain the shreds in the colander and rinse thoroughly with cold water. Press the shredded potatoes with the back of a sturdy spoon to remove as much water as possible.

Pat the shreds as dry as possible between layers of paper towels or wrap them in cheesecloth or a lint-free kitchen towel and squeeze. Transfer to a large mixing bowl.

Oil a shallow baking dish with cooking oil spray; set aside. Preheat oven to 350°F.

In a saucepan over medium heat, melt the butter or margarine and sauté the onion until translucent. Add the flour and whisk together into a thick paste. Slowly whisk in the non-dairy milk until smooth. Add the nutritional yeast, salt, onion powder, black pepper, garlic powder and optional nutmeg. Continue stirring until the mixture is bubbling and thickened.

Remove from the heat and stir in the parmesan. Pour the sauce over the potatoes in the bowl and mix well. Turn the potato mixture into the prepared baking dish, sprinkle with additional black pepper if desired, and bake uncovered for 1 hour and 15 minutes. Serve piping hot.

French Toast

Vegan French toast can be a bit tricky because there is no egg to "set up" the batter when cooking; but this recipe has worked well for me. The toast tends to take a bit longer to cook, so don't get your skillet too hot – this will scorch the exterior before the batter is cooked through.

You will need:

- 4 to 6 slices whole grain bread (slightly stale is best - leave fresh bread out overnight; whole grain bread also holds up better to the batter and is better for you too)
- Better Butter (pg. 62) or vegan margarine
- toppings of your choice, such as real maple syrup, coconut syrup, fruit syrup or jam; or top with fruit compote and dust with Organic Powdered Sugar (pg. 232)

And for the batter:

- 1 cup plain or vanilla non-dairy milk
- 1/2 banana
- 2 T organic sugar
- 2 T flour (unbleached all-purpose wheat; rice or soy)
- 2 tsp nutritional yeast
- 1 tsp real vanilla extract
- 1/2 tsp cinnamon (optional; or you can use pumpkin pie spice)

Technique:

Combine the batter ingredients in a blender. Blend until smooth. Pour the mixture into a pie plate or wide dish. Gently and briefly dip the bread slices into the mixture, coating both sides. DO NOT leave the bread to soak.

In a NON-STICK skillet, melt 2 tablespoons of the butter or margarine. Add the bread slices and fry until golden brown on each side. Test each piece in the center with the tip of the spatula to make sure the batter is cooked through and toast has firmed up.

Add more butter or margarine to the skillet as necessary for cooking additional slices. Serve hot with toppings of your choice.

Country Frittata

This hearty breakfast/brunch casserole is a complete meal in itself. Serve with some fresh fruit on the side.

Ingredients:

- 1 block (about 14 oz) soft to firm tofu (do not use silken tofu)
- vegetable oil
- 10 oz Sausage Crumbles (pg. 50) or 1 pkg commercial vegan sausage, cooked and crumbled
- 4 slices whole grain bread
- Better Butter (pg. 62) or vegan margarine, brought to room temperature
- 1 medium onion, diced
- 2 cups sliced mushrooms
- 1 cup vegan shredded cheddar cheese that melts (Daiya™, for example)
- 2 T nutritional yeast
- 1 tsp onion powder
- 1/2 tsp garlic powder
- pinch of turmeric (turmeric adds a nice scrambled "egg" color to the tofu, but do not use too much or the scramble will look artificially yellow)
- 1/4 tsp kala namak (Himalayan black salt) - optional
- sea salt or kosher salt to taste
- coarse ground black pepper to taste

Technique:

Drain, slice and lightly press the tofu with paper towels to remove excess moisture. The goal is to retain some moisture so the scramble has a velvety texture. Lightly coat a skillet with a little vegetable oil and crumble and cook the sausage over medium heat until lightly browned. Transfer to a bowl and set aside.

Preheat the oven to 350°F. "Butter" the bread with the butter or margarine and cover the bottom of an 8" square baking pan, buttered side down (overlapping the slices will be necessary).

In the same skillet over medium heat, melt 2 tablespoons of the butter or margarine and sauté the onions and mushrooms until they begin to lightly brown.

Add the sausage to the vegetables and mix well. Layer the sausage and vegetables over the bread in the baking pan. Sprinkle 1/2 cup of the shredded vegan cheese over the mixture in the baking pan.

Add 2 tablespoons of the butter or margarine to the skillet and melt over medium/low heat. Crumble the tofu into the skillet and add the nutritional yeast, onion powder, garlic powder, turmeric and salt and pepper to taste. "Scramble" for about 3 minutes until the seasonings are evenly combined and some of the excess moisture has been evaporated.

Layer the tofu scramble over the casserole contents, sprinkle with the remaining 1/2 cup of cheese and cover with foil. Bake for 30 minutes. Uncover and bake an additional 15 minutes.

Eggless Benedict

This is my version of the classic brunch favorite, vegan-style; serves 4.

Ingredients:

- 4 whole grain English muffins
- 1 block (about 14 oz) firm tofu (do not use silken tofu)
- sliced Baked Hammy (pg. 33) or commercial vegan ham slices
- asparagus spears or tomato slices (optional)
- Hollandaise Sauce (pg. 216)

Tofu marinade:

- 1/4 cup vegetable oil
- 2 T fresh lemon juice (about 1 lemon)
- 2 T tamari, soy sauce or Bragg Liquid Aminos™
- 1/4 tsp kala namak (Himalayan black salt) - optional

Technique:

Drain the tofu, slice into 8 pieces and then press to remove the excess water (see Preparing Tofu for Recipes, pg. 56). If using a tofu press, press the block first and then slice. You can cut rounds from each of the slices using a large cookie cutter or similar object, but this isn't essential. Place into a container with the marinade and refrigerate for a minimum of 1 hour.

Prepare your hollandaise sauce and set aside.

If using tomatoes, slice and set aside. For asparagus, brush spears with a little extra-virgin olive oil and season with salt and pepper. Place on a baking sheet and bake at 425°F until bright green and crisp, about 15 to 20 minutes.

While the asparagus is roasting, lightly coat a grill pan or skillet with vegetable oil and place over medium-high heat. Pan-sear the vegan ham until it is lightly browned and crispy on the edges. Remove and set aside.

When the asparagus spears are almost done, add a little more vegetable oil to the grill pan or skillet, heat on medium-high and pan-sear the tofu slices until lightly golden. While the tofu is grilling, toast your English muffins. Gently re-warm your hollandaise sauce if necessary.

To assemble: Place a slice or two of vegan ham on each slice of the English muffins. Top with a slice of tofu and top that with a slice of tomato or roasted asparagus spears. Spoon the hollandaise sauce on top and sprinkle with a little paprika and black pepper. Serve immediately.

Variation: For Eggless Florentine, place crisp Bacun (pg. 23) or commercial vegan bacon on English muffins and top with the tofu slices. Layer with tomato slices, sautéed spinach and top with Béarnaise Sauce (pg. 214).

Sunburst Quiche

A colorful sunburst pattern tops this mushroom, onion, spinach and bell pepper quiche. The combination of block tofu and silken tofu produces a velvety egg-like texture.

Ingredients:

- 1 homemade or pre-packaged vegan pie crust
- 1 block (about 14 oz) firm tofu
- 1 carton (about 12 oz) firm or extra-firm Mori-Nu™ silken tofu, drained
- 1/3 cup nutritional yeast
- 2 tsp onion powder
- 2 T Better Butter (pg. 62) or vegan margarine
- 1 medium onion, finely chopped
- 2 cups sliced mushrooms
- 2 packed cups chopped baby spinach leaves

- 2 tsp minced garlic (2 cloves)
- 1/2 tsp dried thyme
- 1/2 tsp ground black pepper
- 3/4 tsp sea salt or kosher salt
- 1/4 tsp kala namak (Himalayan black salt) - optional (substitute with sea salt or kosher salt)
- 1/2 cup shredded vegan cheese that melts – optional (Daiya™, for example)
- thin slices of yellow, orange or red bell pepper (or any combination)

Technique:

Drain and press the block tofu (not the silken tofu) for about 10 minutes to remove excess water (see Preparing Tofu for Recipes, pg. 56). Remove the silken tofu from its carton, draining away excess water and place on a plate lined with a few paper towels.

Crumble the block tofu and silken tofu into a bowl. Mash together with a fork but leave a little texture. Add the nutritional yeast, onion powder and salt(s) and thoroughly mix together. Set aside.

Preheat the oven to 400°F.

Pre-bake your pie shell for 15 minutes. Remove and let cool but leave the oven on.

Melt the butter or margarine in a large skillet over medium heat. Add the onions, mushrooms and spinach and cook, stirring often, until the mushrooms and spinach have released most of their liquid. Add the garlic, thyme and black pepper and cook until the vegetables begin to lightly brown.

Now, remove the skillet from the heat and fold the mashed tofu into the cooked vegetables. Replace the skillet over the heat and cook, stirring occasionally, for about 5 minutes. The goal is to remove some of the excess moisture from the tofu, as well as blend the flavors.

Spoon the mixture into the pie shell, packing firmly. Gently smooth the surface. Top with the optional shredded vegan cheese, if desired.

Arrange the bell pepper slices decoratively on top and bake for 50 minutes. Let cool for at least 20 minutes to allow it to set before slicing and serving. In my experience, vegan quiche is actually better after being refrigerated and then reheated the next day.

Chapter 5

Appetizers, Dips and Spreads

Deli Roll-ups

These roll-ups make a festive and delicious appetizer for lunch or dinner parties.

Ingredients:

- plain, spinach or sun-dried tomato wraps (tortillas or lavash)
- assorted homemade deli slices (see Seitan Roasts, pg. 27) or commercial vegan sandwich slices
- assorted spreads such as Hummus (pg. 88); Baba Ghannouj (pg. 90); Herbed Chevre (pg. 70); Onion, Dill and Horseradish Cheese (pg. 71); Creme Cheese (pg. 69) or commercial vegan cream cheese, etc.
- assorted fillings such as roasted red pepper, chopped fresh baby spinach, blanched asparagus, shredded carrot, zucchini or cucumber cut into thin strips, chopped lettuces, chopped herbs or anything your creativity can conjure up!

Technique:

Spread each lavash or tortilla with a thin layer of spreadable cheese (or other spreads). Make sure the cheese or spread comes into contact with the outer edges. This will help the roll-up adhere to itself. Add a layer of deli slices and assorted fillings of your choice in the center. Roll up the lavash or tortilla tightly and cut into 3/4 to 1 inch segments with a very sharp knife. Arrange on a serving platter.

Gazpacho Shots

A cold, refreshing appetizer perfect for a party or vegan BBQ on a hot Summer day!

Ingredients:

- several large cucumbers for creating "shot glasses"
- Gazpacho (pg. 124)
- optional garnish: chopped fresh cilantro

Technique:

To prepare the "shot glasses", peel the cucumbers and cut into 2-inch long pieces. Scoop out the interior, leaving 1/4-inch on the sides and bottom, to create a cup. Spoon the gazpacho into the cucumber cups. Garnish with chopped cilantro if desired and serve immediately; or refrigerate for up to several hours prior to serving.

Hummus

Hummus is a classic Middle Eastern dish and is excellent served as an appetizer or sandwich spread. This recipe is my personal variation.

Process in a high-powered blender until very smooth:

- 1 can (16 oz) garbanzo beans, rinsed well
- 2/3 cup water
- 1/4 cup sesame tahini
- 1/4 cup extra-virgin olive oil
- 2 cloves fresh garlic, chopped (or 2 tsp minced)
- 2 T fresh lemon juice (about 1 average-size lemon)
- 3/4 tsp sea salt or kosher salt, or more to taste
- 1/2 tsp ground cumin
- 1/4 tsp ground white pepper
- garnish: extra-virgin olive oil; chopped fresh parsley and/or paprika

Try also adding some roasted red pepper as a variation. For a mellower garlic flavor, use roasted garlic. The hummus will thicken upon refrigeration; if it becomes too thick after refrigeration, simply incorporate a little water.

Black Olive Tapenade

If you love olives, as I do, then you will love this spread. Serve on pita wedges, crostini, bruschetta or crackers.

Pulse in a food processor (but do not over-process; the tapenade should retain some texture):

- 2 cups pitted black olives, drained
  (or try brine-cured olives, such as pitted Kalamata or Gaeta olives, drained)
- 2 T capers, drained
- 2 tsp minced garlic
- 1 tsp dried oregano
- juice of 1/2 lemon
- 1/4 tsp sea salt (no salt necessary for brine cured olives)
- 1/4 tsp ground black pepper
- 2 T extra-virgin olive oil
- chopped fresh parsley for garnish (optional)

Taste and adjust the seasonings. The tapenade will keep well for a week or two, stored tightly covered in the refrigerator.

Tempura Jalapeno Poppers

Tempura Jalapeno Poppers are a delicious, yet fiery appetizer. Warning! These pack some heat and are not for the faint of heart.

Ingredients:

- canola or peanut oil for frying
- fresh or canned whole jalapenos (as many as you like - the canned jalapenos seem to pack less heat than the fresh)
- commercial vegan cream cheese, cheddar, Monterey jack or mozzarella
- "Buttermilk" Ranch Dressing (pg. 111) - optional

Batter ingredients – whisk together:

- 1/2 cup flour (unbleached all-purpose wheat; rice or soy)
- 2/3 cup beer (alcoholic or non-alcoholic)-a few pinches of sea salt or kosher salt
- a few pinches of black pepper

Technique:

Wear gloves if you have sensitive skin, as raw jalapenos can be irritating to some people. Cut the jalapenos lengthwise to open and remove seeds. Leave stem intact. Stuff the peppers with your favorite vegan cheese.

Heat the oil in a skillet over medium-high heat. The oil will be ready for frying when a drop of the batter sizzles and pops when added to the oil.

Dip the stuffed jalapenos into the batter and carefully drop into the hot oil. Fry until golden and remove with a slotted spoon to a plate lined with paper towels. Serve with vegan ranch dressing if desired. Enjoy, but keep some tortilla chips or bread on hand to help reduce the fire in your mouth!

Pepper-Garlic Edamame

Pepper-Garlic Edamame (soybeans) are wonderful as an appetizer or nutritious snack. Eat by holding a pod by one end, placing in your mouth and squeezing the beans out of the pod with your fingertips.

Technique:

Cook 1 pound frozen edamame (soybeans) in pods in salted boiling water until tender, about 5 minutes; drain. Heat 1 T vegetable oil, 1/4 tsp red pepper flakes and 2 or 3 minced garlic cloves in a skillet over medium heat for 1 to 2 minutes. Stir in the edamame and juice of 1 lime. Toss to coat thoroughly and salt to taste.

Baba Ghannouj

Baba Ghannouj is a Middle Eastern dish of cooked eggplant puréed and mixed with sesame tahini and various seasonings. This is my version of the classic dish. Eggplant is a nutritional powerhouse. It's high in dietary fiber and contains folate, potassium, manganese, vitamin C, vitamin K, thiamin, niacin, vitamin B6, pantothenic acid, magnesium, phosphorus and copper.

Ingredients:

- 1 large eggplant
- 1/4 cup sesame tahini
- 2 cloves fresh garlic, chopped (or 2 tsp minced)
- juice of 1 small lemon (about 2 T)
- 1 tsp liquid smoke (optional)
- 1/2 tsp sea salt or kosher salt, or to taste
- 1/2 tsp ground cumin
- 1/4 tsp ground white pepper
- 1 T extra-virgin olive oil
- garnish: chopped fresh parsley, smoked paprika

Technique:

There are 3 methods to cook the eggplant but for the most authentic smoky taste, grilling over charcoal briquettes on the BBQ is the best. For the BBQ method, slice the eggplant lengthwise, brush with some extra-virgin olive oil and sprinkle with salt on the cut sides and lay on the grill, cut sides up until the skins begin to blister. Turn the eggplant over and grill until the flesh begins to brown and char slightly. Let cool.

For the microwave method, pierce the eggplant several times with a sharp knife and microwave on high for about 5 minutes. Remove and wrap in foil. Let cool (the eggplant will continue to steam in the foil).

For the oven method, slice the eggplant lengthwise, brush with some extra-virgin olive oil and sprinkle with salt on the cut sides and lay each half cut-side down on a cookie sheet. Broil until the skin begins to blister. Turn the slices over and continue to broil until the flesh begins to brown and char slightly. Let cool.

When cool, scrape the pulp (discarding the skin) into a high powered blender or food processor and add additional ingredients, except for the garnish. Process the mixture until completely smooth. If necessary, add a scant amount of water to thin the mixture to preferred consistency, keeping in mind that it will thicken substantially after refrigeration.

Taste and adjust salt if necessary. Transfer to a serving dish and serve immediately or refrigerate.

When ready to serve, form a small "well" in the center to drizzle the extra-virgin olive oil. Garnish with parsley and smoked paprika, if desired, before serving.

Stuffed Potato Poppers

A delicious vegan alternative to deviled eggs!

Ingredients:

- 6 baby red or new potatoes, halved
- 2 T vegetable oil
- 1/4 cup (4 T) No-Eggy Mayo (pg. 105) or commercial vegan mayonnaise
- 2 T finely minced yellow or red onion, or snipped fresh chives
- 1 to 2 tsp Dijon mustard, or more to taste
- dash hot pepper sauce
- pinch garlic powder
- salt and pepper, to taste
- dash turmeric, optional, for yellow color
- paprika, capers or snipped chives for garnish

Technique:

Preheat oven to 350°F, and oil a baking sheet. Coat all sides of each potato with vegetable oil. Place potatoes face down on prepared baking sheet and bake for about 45 minutes, or until soft (but not mushy). When the potatoes are done, allow to cool a bit.

With a teaspoon, scoop out the flat side of the potato, adding the removed portion of the potato to a bowl - you are trying to create a little potato cup to hold the filling. Set the potato cups aside.

Add the remaining ingredients to the bowl with the potato filling and blend well. Add a little more mayonnaise if necessary and adjust seasonings to taste.

Fill the hollowed out potato shells with the mixture (you can pipe it in with a cake decorating bag, or use a teaspoon to carefully fill the cups). Chill before serving. Garnish as desired.

Swedish Seitan Meatballs

Seasoned seitan meatballs are smothered in velvety gravy flavored with a hint of nutmeg. For optimum texture, the meatballs need to be prepared and refrigerated for a minimum of 8 hours prior to preparing this dish, so plan accordingly. This recipe makes plenty of gravy, which is excellent served over toast, mashed potatoes or eggless noodles as an entrée. To serve individually as an appetizer, insert toothpicks into each meatball.

Ingredients:

- 1 T vegetable oil
- 1 recipe Seitan Meatballs (pg. 18) - use the Swedish meatball variation
- 1/4 cup (4 T) Better Butter (pg. 62) or vegan margarine
- 1/4 cup flour (unbleached all-purpose wheat; rice or soy)
- 3 cups beaf broth (see pg. 123 for broth options)
- 1/4 teaspoon black pepper, or more to taste
- 1/2 teaspoon freshly grated nutmeg
- 1/4 cup Heavy Creme (pg. 64) or commercial vegan cream substitute

Technique:

Prepare seitan meatballs according to directions. Refrigerate for a minimum of 8 hours to firm the meatballs prior to preparation of this recipe. In a skillet over medium heat, sauté the meatballs in 1 T vegetable oil until browned. Remove the meatballs and set aside.

Melt the butter or margarine in the same skillet over medium-low heat. Whisk in the flour until a smooth paste (roux) develops. Cook for several minutes until the roux begins to brown lightly.

Now slowly whisk in the beaf broth until smooth. Bring the mixture to a boil and add the black pepper and nutmeg. Reduce heat to a simmer and cook until the mixture thickens.

Slowly whisk in the heavy creme until smooth and add the meatballs. Simmer for a few minutes until the meatballs are heated through. Add additional pepper as desired.

Garlic Herb Croutons

Thickly sliced or cubed Italian or French bread is brushed with garlic herb "butter" and baked until crispy and golden. The sliced croutons are perfect as a foundation for appetizer spreads and vegan cheeses and the cubed croutons are excellent as a topping for soups and salads.

Ingredients:

- 1 loaf Italian or French bread
- 1/4 cup vegetable oil
- 1/4 cup Better Butter (pg. 62) or vegan margarine
- 2 tsp garlic powder
- 1 tsp onion powder
- 1 tsp dried basil
- 1 tsp dried parsley flakes
- 1/4 tsp fine sea salt or kosher salt
- 1/4 tsp ground black pepper
- 1/4 tsp paprika

Technique:

For sliced croutons, cut the bread in 1/2-inch slices and cut each slice in half. For cubed croutons, cut the bread in 1/2-inch slices and cut each slice into 3/4-inch cubes. Set aside.

In a microwave safe dish, heat all of the other ingredients in the microwave until the butter or margarine is melted, about 30 to 45 seconds. Stir well to combine. You can also do this in a small saucepan over low heat if you prefer. Preheat the oven to 300°F.

For sliced croutons, brush each side of the slices with the melted herb/butter mixture and lightly brown on both sides in a skillet over medium heat.

For cubed croutons, add 1/3 of the herb/butter mixture to the skillet over medium heat; add the cubed bread and toss to coat. Add a little more of the mixture, tossing well and then add the remainder of the mixture. Toss occasionally until the cubes are lightly browned.

Transfer the slices or cubes to a baking sheet and bake until the bread is dry and crisp (this will depend upon the moisture content of the bread). This can take upwards of 30 minutes. Let cool and store in an airtight container until ready to use. Use within 2 or 3 days or freeze and re-warm in the oven.

Salsa non Queso

Salsa non Queso can be eaten with tortillas or tortilla chips. It can also be used as a topping for burritos, enchiladas, tostadas or any other Tex-Mex dish.

Ingredients:

- 1/4 cup (4T) Better Butter (pg. 62) or vegan margarine
- 1/4 cup flour (unbleached all-purpose wheat; rice or soy)
- 1/2 cup nutritional yeast
- 1 and 1/4 cup unsweetened non-dairy milk
  (I use almond milk for this recipe because of its richness)
- 1 tsp onion powder
- 1/2 tsp paprika
- 1/2 tsp sea salt or kosher salt
- 1/2 tsp garlic powder
- 1 cup of your favorite red salsa

Technique:

In a saucepan, melt the butter or margarine over medium-low heat. Whisk in the flour and stir to form a smooth paste (roux). Cook for about a minute, stirring constantly, but do not brown. Reduce the heat to low and slowly but vigorously whisk in the milk until the mixture is smooth.

Add the nutritional yeast, paprika, salt, onion powder and garlic powder. Increase the heat to medium and simmer the mixture until thickened, stirring frequently.

Stir in the salsa and continue to cook until the non Queso is heated through. Reduce the heat to low to keep warm until ready to serve.

Indian Curry Samosas

A samosa is a baked or fried Indian pastry with a savory filling that is traditionally served with chutney. For this version, I used puff pastry dough and then baked them until light, airy and golden brown. This recipe makes ample filling for 18 samosas.

Ingredients:

- 2 T vegetable oil
- 1 tsp Indian curry powder
- 1/2 tsp Skye's Garam Masala (pg. 187) or commercial garam masala
- 2 tsp fresh grated ginger root
- 1/4 tsp ground red pepper, or more to taste
- 1 T minced garlic (3 cloves)
- 1 large sweet yellow onion
- 2 large russet potatoes (about 1.5 lbs), peeled and cut into small chunks
- 1/2 tsp sea salt or kosher salt, or more to taste
- 1/2 cup canned baby peas; or frozen baby peas, thawed
- 1 box (2 sheets) puff pastry, such as Pepperidge Farms™, thawed from frozen
- 2 T Better Butter (pg. 62) or vegan margarine, melted

Technique:

In a large skillet over medium heat, stir the curry powder, garam masala, ginger and red pepper together with the vegetable oil. Add the onion and cook for about 2 minutes and then add the garlic and cook for an additional minute.

Add the potatoes and season with the salt. Toss thoroughly to coat the potatoes with the vegetable oil and spices. Cover and reduce heat to medium-low and cook, stirring occasionally until the potatoes are just beginning to break apart (about 25 to 30 minutes).

Transfer the potato mixture to a bowl and mash to a coarse texture. Gently fold the peas into the potatoes. Taste and add additional salt as desired. Preheat the oven to 375°F.

Lightly flour a work surface and cut a sheet of pastry dough along the folds into 3 strips; then cut each strip crosswise into thirds. Place a spoonful of curry potato mixture in the center and fold in half to form a triangle (avoid using too much filling, or the pastry will be difficult to seal). Pinch with water moistened fingertips to close the edges. Repeat with the other sheet of pastry dough.

Spray a baking sheet(s) with vegetable oil spray (or use parchment paper) to prevent sticking and arrange the pastries on the sheet(s). Brush the pastries with a little melted butter or margarine. Bake for about 25 to 30 minutes or until golden brown. Cool 5 minutes and serve.

Hot Spinach Artichoke Dip

Ingredients:

- 2 T vegetable oil
- 1 medium onion, chopped
- 1 T minced garlic (3 cloves)
- 1 pkg (about 10 oz) fresh baby spinach* (pre-packaged spinach can be found in the produce department with the lettuce and salad mixes)
- 2 cans (about 14 oz each) artichoke hearts, rinsed and drained well
- 1/4 cup No-Eggy Mayo (pg. 105) or commercial vegan mayonnaise
- 1/4 cup Golden Parmesan (pg. 65) or commercial vegan parmesan
- 1/4 cup Sour Creme (pg. 65) or commercial vegan sour cream
- 1/4 cup vegan shredded white cheese that melts** (i.e., Daiya™ mozzarella) - optional
- 1/2 tsp sea salt or kosher salt, or more to taste
- 1/4 tsp ground black pepper, or more to taste

*You can also use a 10 oz package of frozen spinach. Thaw and then press the spinach to remove as much liquid as possible.

**If you choose not to use shredded vegan cheese, add an additional 1/4 cup vegan sour cream

Technique:

Preheat the oven to 350°F and lightly oil a shallow baking dish.

In a skillet over medium heat, sauté the onion in the vegetable oil until the onion is translucent. Add the garlic and spinach. Sauté until the onion begins to lightly brown and the spinach is not releasing any more liquid. This will take several minutes. Transfer to a food processor. Add the artichoke hearts to the food processor with the spinach/onion/garlic mixture. Pulse a few times to coarsely chop but do not purée.

Transfer to a mixing bowl and add the mayonnaise, parmesan, sour cream, shredded vegan white cheese, salt and pepper; stir thoroughly to combine. Taste the mixture and add additional salt and pepper as desired. Transfer to the baking dish and bake uncovered for 40 minutes.

Now, set the oven on "broil" and broil for an additional 3 or 4 minutes or until lightly brown on top.

Serve hot with crackers, bread or crudités. To keep warm for a dinner party, transfer to a chafing dish and heat over a low flame. This recipe makes about 4 cups of dip.

Fried Green Tomatoes with Red Pepper Aioli

Fried green tomatoes evoke wonderful childhood memories of my father frying them in our kitchen. And now, I always crave them when watching the movie of the same name. Green tomatoes are difficult to find in most supermarkets but can be found in farmer's markets during the Summer season. Or you can grow and harvest your own from your garden. If you've never had them, I highly recommend this appetizer - the coating is crispy and the tomato is tender, tangy and slightly tart. The red pepper aioli pairs beautifully with this dish.

Ingredients for the red pepper aioli:

- 2 tsp minced garlic (2 cloves)
- 1 large red bell pepper or sweet Hungarian red wax pepper
- salt and freshly ground black pepper
- 1/3 cup No-Eggy Mayo (pg. 105) or commercial vegan mayonnaise
- 2 T extra-virgin olive oil

Technique:

Split the red pepper in half and remove the membrane and seeds. Lay cut-side down on a baking sheet, mist with a little vegetable oil spray and broil until skin begins to blacken. Remove from broiler and cover sheet with foil to hold in steam. Let cool for 15 minutes and then remove the skin; pat dry with a paper towel. Add the cooked red pepper, garlic, mayonnaise and extra-virgin olive oil to a food processor or mini-blender and process until smooth. Season the aioli, to taste, with salt and pepper. Transfer the aioli to a small bowl or applicator bottle. Cover and refrigerate. (The aioli can be made up to 2 days ahead.)

Ingredients for the fried green tomatoes:

- 3 large or 4 to 5 medium-sized green tomatoes
- 1 cup unsweetened soymilk
- 2 tsp raw apple cider vinegar
- 1/2 cup fine non-GMO cornmeal
- 3/4 cup flour (unbleached all-purpose wheat; rice or soy)
- 1 T Cajun seasoning (optional)
- 1 cup flour (unbleached all-purpose wheat; rice or soy) in a separate bowl
- vegetable oil for frying
- sea salt or kosher salt and ground black pepper to taste

Technique:

Combine the soymilk and vinegar in a non-metallic bowl, cover and set aside to thicken for a minimum of 15 minutes. Slice the tomatoes in 1/4-inch slices. Combine the cornmeal, 3/4 cup flour and optional Cajun seasoning in a bowl. Mix well.

In a large skillet, heat a thin layer of vegetable oil (about a 1/4-inch) over medium-high heat. Dip the tomato slices first in the plain flour, then in the soymilk mixture and then dredge in the cornmeal/flour blend. Carefully place into the hot oil. Fry until golden brown on each side. Remove to a plate lined with paper towels and season with salt and pepper. While still hot, arrange the fried tomatoes on a plate and garnish with the red pepper aioli. Serve immediately. To reheat: Bake uncovered in the oven or toaster oven at 350°F until heated through - do not microwave.

Wholly Guacamole!

Ingredients:

- 4 ripe avocados
- 2 limes, juiced
- 1/2 small onion, chopped
- 1 small garlic clove, minced
- 1 Serrano chili, chopped
- a handful of fresh cilantro leaves, roughly chopped
- sea salt or kosher salt and freshly ground black pepper
- drizzle of extra-virgin olive oil
- optional additional ingredients: chopped tomato; red salsa or salsa verde

Technique:

Halve and pit the avocados. With a tablespoon, scoop out the flesh into a mixing bowl. Mash the avocados with a fork, leaving them still a bit chunky. Add all of the rest of the ingredients, and fold everything together.

Lay a piece of plastic wrap directly on the surface of the guacamole so it doesn't brown and refrigerate for at least 1 hour before serving.

Savory Onion Dip

An easy-to-make dip that is wonderful served with crudités, chips or crackers.

Ingredients:

- 1 cup Sour Creme (pg. 65) or commercial vegan sour cream
- 1 T soy sauce, tamari or Bragg Liquid Aminos™ or 1/2 tsp Better Than Bouillon™ No Beef Base - or more to taste
- 1/2 tsp homemade vegan Worcestershire Sauce (pg. 206) or commercial
- 1 T dried minced or flaked onions
- 1 tsp onion powder, or more to taste
- 1/4 tsp garlic powder
- sea salt or kosher salt to taste, if needed

Technique:

Combine the ingredients in a bowl. Taste and adjust seasonings to your liking. Refrigerate for several hours to rehydrate the onions and blend the flavors.

Deviled Eggless

This is my vegan version of deviled eggs. Tofu is used to replace the egg whites and a purée of white beans and seasonings is used to replace the yolk filling. Himalayan black salt is essential to impart that familiar egg-like taste to these savory bites.

Ingredients:

- 1 block (about 14 oz) firm tofu (do not use silken tofu)
- 1 can (about 15 oz) cooked white beans (such as cannellini, white navy or great northern), rinsed and drained very well
- 2 T No-Eggy Mayo (pg. 105) or commercial vegan mayonnaise
- 2 T nutritional yeast
- 2 tsp Dijon mustard
- 1/4 tsp kala namak* (Himalayan black salt), plus more for sprinkling on "egg whites"
- 1/4 tsp turmeric
- 1 T dill pickle relish
- 1 T onion, very finely minced
- ground black pepper, to taste
- paprika, for garnish
- fresh snipped chives (optional, for garnish)

*Kala namak, or Himalayan black salt, is an Indian salt with a high mineral concentration, most notably sulfur, which gives it its characteristic and pungent "hard-boiled egg" smell. It is useful in vegan cooking as it imparts a cooked egg taste to recipes. Interestingly, it is not black but rather pink in color. Be advised, that if you detest the sulfurous smell of hard-boiled eggs, you probably will not care for this salt. Kala namak is considered a cooling spice in Ayurvedic medicine and is used as a digestive aid. It can be found in specialty food stores as well as online. I purchase mine through Amazon.com.

Technique:

Drain and press the tofu to remove excess water (see Preparing Tofu for Recipes, pg. 56). After pressing the tofu, cut into six even slices. Then cut each slice into four quadrants.

Place the beans, mayonnaise, nutritional yeast, mustard, turmeric, and 1/4 teaspoon black salt into a food processor. Process about one minute or until smooth. Transfer to a mixing bowl and stir in the relish, onion, and black pepper. Taste and season with additional black salt if needed. Set aside.

Now, pour a teaspoon or two of black salt into a small bowl. Using your fingertip, rub a small amount of the black salt on each tofu bite. Top each bite with a dollop (about one teaspoon) of the bean mixture. You can also use a pastry bag to pipe the bean mixture decoratively onto the tofu bites, if desired. You may have extra filling left over - just save and enjoy later with crackers.

Sprinkle with paprika and garnish with fresh snipped chives if desired.

Crispy Vegetable Pakoras

Pakoras are the Indian version of the Japanese tempura. Serve with Indian Raita (pg. 219) or chutney as a condiment.

Ingredients:

- 1 cup garbanzo bean (chickpea) flour
- 1/2 teaspoon ground coriander
- 1 teaspoon salt
- 1/2 teaspoon ground turmeric
- 1/2 teaspoon chili powder
- 1/2 teaspoon garam masala*
- 2 cloves garlic, crushed
- 2 chopped green chilies
- 2 T chopped cilantro
- 3/4 cup water
- soybean, canola or peanut oil for deep frying
- assorted vegetables of your choice (sliced onion, sliced potato, sliced eggplant, cauliflower florets and sliced zucchini)

*Garam masala is a blend of ground spices common in North Indian cuisine. It can be found in ethnic food stores, as well as online; or you can blend your own using Skye's Garam Masala recipe (pg. 187).

Technique:

Sift the garbanzo bean (chickpea) flour into a medium bowl. Mix in the coriander, salt, turmeric, chili powder, garam masala and garlic.

Make a well in the center of the flour. Gradually pour the water into the well and mix to form a thick, smooth batter. The batter should resemble the consistency of pancake batter, so add a scant more water if necessary.

Over medium high heat in a large, heavy saucepan, heat the oil until hot (360°F to 375°F is ideal).

Coat the vegetables in the batter and fry them in small batches until golden brown, about 4 to 5 minutes. Drain on paper towels before serving.

Faux Gras

An ultra smooth and rich mushroom pâté flavored with thyme, cognac and white truffle oil.

Ingredients:

- 1 cup raw cashews, soaked for a minimum of 8 hours in water and then drained
- 1/2 lb (8 oz) white mushrooms, sliced
- 2 T Better Butter (pg. 62) or vegan margarine
- 1/2 cup chopped shallots (or red onion)
- 3 cloves garlic, chopped
- 2 T cognac (i.e., Courvoisier) - or you can substitute with 2 T dry white wine
- 1 and 1/2 tsp fresh thyme leaves or 1/2 tsp dried
- 1 cup water
- 3 T agar flakes*
- 1 T tamari, soy sauce or Bragg Liquid Aminos™
- 1/4 tsp ground black pepper, or more to taste
- 1 T white truffle oil
- sea salt or kosher salt, if necessary, to taste

*Agar is a tasteless seaweed derivative and a vegetarian replacement for gelatin; it can be purchased in most health food and natural food stores or online through vegan retail websites or through Amazon.com.

Technique:

Lightly coat a plastic container (which will act as your form for the pâté) with some cooking oil spray and set aside.

Place the soaked and drained raw cashews in a high-powered blender and set aside.

In a skillet over medium heat, melt the butter or margarine. Add the shallots (or onions) and mushrooms and sauté until the shallots are softened and translucent. Add the garlic, thyme and cognac and sauté another minute or two, until the shallots are golden, the cognac has evaporated and the mushrooms have released most of their liquid. Do not brown the contents of the skillet.

While the skillet ingredients are cooking, bring the water and agar flakes to a simmer in a small saucepan. Stir frequently until the agar flakes are completely dissolved.

Add the contents of the skillet to the blender with the raw cashews. Pour in the water/agar mixture and add the tamari, pepper and white truffle oil. Process the mixture until completely smooth. Adjust salt and pepper to taste.

Pour the mixture into the lightly oiled container, cover and refrigerate for several hours until firm. When firm, turn out onto a plate. Trim the edges with a very sharp knife, if desired, to create a perfect square block of pâté; or use a biscuit cutter to create a round shape; or mash pate with a fork until light and fluffy and serve in a decorative bowl. To serve, let soften at room temperature for about 20 minutes and spread on hors-d'oeuvre toast or crackers.

Chik'n Salad in Fillo Cups

Savory Chik'n Salad makes a lovely and elegant appetizer when served in miniature fillo (Greek pastry) cups.

Ingredients:

- 1 recipe Tarragon Chik'n Salad (pg. 109) or Chik'n Nirvana Salad (pg. 110)
- 2 pkgs frozen mini fillo shells (15 per pkg; 30 count total)

Technique:

With a teaspoon, fill the frozen mini fillo (phyllo) shells. They will quickly thaw at room temperature. Serve immediately.

Zesty Ranch Dip

A thick and tangy ranch-style dip that is perfect for chips or crudités (bite-size fresh vegetables). This recipe makes about 1 and 1/2 cups.

Ingredients:

- 1 cup No-Eggy Mayo (pg. 105) or commercial vegan mayonnaise
- 1/2 cup Sour Creme (pg. 65) or commercial vegan sour cream
- 1 T fresh lemon juice
- 1 tsp white wine vinegar or white balsamic vinegar
- 1 tsp onion powder
- 1 tsp Dijon mustard
- 1/2 tsp garlic powder

- 1/4 tsp sea salt or kosher salt or more to taste
- 1/4 tsp ground black pepper or more to taste
- 1/4 tsp homemade vegan Worcestershire Sauce (pg. 206) or commercial - optional
- 1 T chopped fresh chives or 1 tsp dried
- 1 T chopped fresh parsley or 1 tsp dried
- 1 and 1/2 tsp chopped fresh dill or 1/2 tsp dry

Technique:

Place all of the ingredients except for the herbs into a food processor and process until smooth. Taste and add additional salt or pepper, as desired. Add the chopped herbs and pulse a few times to incorporate. Transfer to a container with a lid and refrigerate for a few hours to blend flavors. Use the dip within 7 days.

Tip: Homemade No-Eggy Mayo is much more economical than commercial vegan mayonnaise and tastes better too!

Dolmas (Stuffed Grape Leaves)

Grape leaves are stuffed with a mixture of delicately seasoned rice and chickpeas, steamed and then garnished with fresh lemon juice and extra-virgin olive oil. Excellent served as an hors d'oeuvre or with other Mediterranean favorites such as falafel, Tzatziki Sauce (pg. 209), Hummus (pg. 88), Baba Ghannouj (pg. 90), Crumbly Block Feta (pg. 74) and pita bread. You will need a large pot with a steamer insert for this recipe. This recipe makes 20 to 25 dolmas.

Ingredients:

- 1 jar grape leaves in brine (dry weight 8 oz or about 28 leaves), drained and rinsed
- extra-virgin olive oil
- 1/2 cup uncooked basmati rice*
- 1 cup water
- 1 can (about 16 oz) cooked chickpeas (garbanzo beans), drained and thoroughly rinsed
- 1/2 medium-sized onion
- 3 T fresh lemon juice
- 1 T finely minced garlic (3 cloves)
- 1/2 tsp ground cumin, or more to taste
- 1 tsp sea salt or kosher salt, or more to taste
- 1/4 tsp coarse ground black pepper, or more to taste
- 2 T finely chopped fresh Italian parsley (or 2 tsp dried parsley)

*This recipe will make 2 cups cooked basmati rice. You can substitute with 2 cups cooked rice of your choice, white or brown.

Technique:

Place the steamer insert into a large cooking pot and fill with just enough water to reach the bottom of the insert. Set aside.

Rinse the grape leaves and place into a colander to drain. With a pair of kitchen shears, snip off the tough stem at the bottom of the leaves. Set aside.

In a small saucepan, bring 1 cup of water to a boil with 1 T extra-virgin olive oil. Add the rice, stir and cover. Reduce heat to low and cook for 20 minutes. When done cooking, set the saucepan aside with the lid in place to cool for a bit.

Next, into a food processor add the chickpeas and onion. Process them almost to a paste but leave a little bit of texture. Transfer to a mixing bowl.

Add the rice to the chickpea mixture along with the garlic, cumin, salt, pepper, 1 T lemon juice, 2 T extra-virgin olive oil and chopped parsley. Stir thoroughly or mash with your hands until the mixture holds together a bit when squeezed in your hand. If the mixture seems dry, add a little water a tablespoon at a time to moisten. The mixture should be moist but not soggy. Taste and adjust seasonings to your liking.

Now place about 2 T filling onto the grape leaf. Fold the bottom of the leaf over the filling. Fold the sides in and roll up tightly.

Line the steamer insert with a few unused leaves. Lay the dolmas on top, seam side down, and cover the pot. Place over high heat and bring to a boil. Set the timer for 45 minutes. Check the pot at regular intervals, about every 15 minutes (lift the lid with an oven mitt to avoid steam burns) and add some HOT water to replace water lost to steam evaporation, as necessary. DO NOT let the pot boil dry.

After cooking, remove from the heat to cool. When cool enough to handle, transfer the dolmas to a container with a lid or zip-lock bag (handle them carefully because they are rather delicate until chilled). Drizzle with 2 tablespoons extra-virgin olive oil, 2 tablespoons fresh lemon juice and a generous sprinkle of coarse salt.

Chill in the refrigerator for several hours to overnight to marinate. Gentle invert the container or zip-lock bag occasionally, so that all of the dolmas are evenly marinated. Serve cold.

Chapter 6

Salads and Dressings

No-Eggy Mayo

This recipe produces a superior eggless mayonnaise that rivals real egg mayonnaise in both taste and texture and is much less expensive than commercial vegan mayonnaise. The ingredients are readily available in most markets and the food processor makes this a nearly foolproof method for making mayonnaise. This is my own signature blend. Makes about 2 cups; measurements for 1 cup of mayonnaise can be found on the following page.

Ingredients:

- 1/2 cup plain unsweetened soymilk
- 1 T plus 1 tsp fresh lemon juice
- 1 tsp apple cider vinegar, preferably raw organic
- 2 tsp organic sugar
- 1 tsp dry ground mustard*
- 1 tsp fine sea salt
- pinch of ground white pepper
- pinch of paprika - optional
- pinch of kala namak (Himalayan black salt) - optional (for an "egg" mayonnaise taste)
- 1 and 3/4 cup soybean or canola oil (you can also use sunflower or safflower, but they're expensive when using this amount of oil)

*Do not omit this ingredient; it contains a small amount of natural lecithin which is essential for emulsification of the oil and soymilk.

Tip: For garlic mayo, add 1 tsp minced garlic (1 clove) to the soymilk mixture and blend as instructed.

Technique:

Measure the oil into a liquid measuring cup (it should have a "lip" for pouring). Set aside.

Place all of the ingredients EXCEPT for the oil into a food processor and pulse once to blend. Let the mixture sit for 5 to 10 minutes until the soymilk curdles and thickens.

Turn the food processor on continuous run (if you have speed settings, run on high speed) and SLOWLY drizzle the oil into the mixture through the food chute. The addition of the oil will take several minutes, so be patient and don't rush. You should begin to note a change in the consistency of the mixture after about 1 and 1/4 cup of oil has been added. Continue to SLOWLY add the remainder of the oil. As soon as all of the oil has been incorporated, turn the processor off - the mayonnaise is finished. Transfer to a glass jar or plastic container and refrigerate.

Note: I cannot emphasize enough the importance of adding the oil slowly. If you add it too fast, the emulsion may break down and revert back to a liquid.

For 1 cup of mayonnaise, use these measurements and follow the same instructions:

- 1/4 cup plain unsweetened soymilk (sorry, no substitutions)
- 2 tsp fresh lemon juice
- 1/2 tsp apple cider vinegar, preferably raw organic
- 1 tsp organic sugar
- 1/2 tsp dry ground mustard (do not omit this ingredient)
- 1/2 tsp fine sea salt
- scant pinch of ground white pepper
- scant pinch of paprika, optional
- scant pinch of kala namak (Himalayan black salt) - optional (for an "egg" mayonnaise taste)
- 3/4 cup plus 2 T soybean or canola oil

Chunky Blue Cheese Dressing

This incredible vegan dressing tastes remarkably like restaurant-style dairy blue cheese dressing. The secret ingredient is the Sheese™ blue cheese, which is made by a vegan company in Scotland and imported to the United States. Depending on your location, you may be able to find it locally. I cannot find it locally, so I purchase it through either veganessentials.com or veganstore.com and have it cold-shipped to my door. It's a wonderful treat now and then. If you were a lover of dairy blue cheese (like myself), this will definitely satisfy your craving. This dressing is also excellent as a dip for crudités.

Ingredients:

- 4 oz (1/2 wheel) Sheese™ blue cheese, crumbled
- 1 cup No-Eggy Mayo (pg. 105) or commercial vegan mayonnaise
- 3 T Sour Creme (pg. 65) or commercial vegan sour creme
- 2 T non-dairy milk
- 1 T fresh lemon juice
- 1/4 tsp coarse ground black pepper, or more to taste
- 1/4 tsp sea salt or kosher salt, or more to taste
- 1/4 tsp homemade vegan Worcestershire Sauce (pg. 206) or commercial

Technique:

Into a food processor add 1/2 (2 oz) of the crumbled blue cheese and the remaining ingredients; process until smooth, about 30 seconds. If you wish to thin the consistency, add more non-dairy milk, a tablespoon at a time, until the desired consistency is reached. Add the remaining crumbled blue cheese and pulse once or twice to combine but not liquefy (you want to keep it a bit chunky). Season with salt and pepper to taste; transfer to a covered container and refrigerate until ready to use for up to 10 days.

Tip: Homemade No-Eggy Mayo is much more economical than commercial vegan mayonnaise and tastes better too!

Macaroni Picnic Salad

Ingredients:

- 4 cups uncooked elbow macaroni
- 1 cup No-Eggy Mayo (pg. 105) or commercial vegan mayonnaise
- 1/4 cup dill pickle brine or raw apple cider vinegar (or other vinegar of your choice)
- 2 T organic sugar
- 2 T prepared yellow or Dijon mustard
- 1 tsp sea salt or kosher salt, or to taste
- 1/2 tsp ground black pepper
- 1 onion, chopped
- 2 ribs of celery, chopped
- 1 green or red bell pepper, or half each, seeded and chopped
- 1 carrot, shredded

Technique:

Bring a large pot of lightly salted water to a boil. Add the macaroni, and cook according to directions or until tender. Rinse under cold water and drain.

In a large bowl, mix together the vegan mayonnaise, vinegar, sugar, mustard, salt and pepper. Mix in the onion, celery, green and/or red pepper, carrot and macaroni. Refrigerate for at least 4 hours, but preferably overnight. Add a little more vegan mayonnaise if necessary to remoisten before serving.

Russian Dressing

Whisk together:

- 1/2 cup No-Eggy Mayo (pg. 105) or commercial vegan mayonnaise
- 3 T organic ketchup
- 2 T chopped capers
- 1 T prepared horseradish (not creamed)

Thousand Island Dressing

Whisk together:

- 1 cup No-Eggy Mayo (pg. 105) or commercial vegan mayonnaise
- 1/3 cup organic ketchup
- 1/2 tsp onion powder
- dash of sea salt or kosher salt
- 3 T sweet pickle relish

Tip: Homemade No-Eggy Mayo is much more economical than commercial vegan mayonnaise and tastes better too!

Tarragon Chik'n Salad

A light and fresh salad with a hint of tarragon; this recipe calls for Chik'n Seitan, but you can also use leftover Herb Roasted Chik'n (pg. 30) or commercial vegan chicken such as Gardein™.

Ingredients:

- 10 oz Chik'n Seitan (pg. 11) or commercial vegan chicken, sliced into strips
- 1 cup diced celery
- 1/4 cup diced red onion
- No-Eggy Mayo (pg. 105) or commercial vegan mayonnaise
- 2 T chopped fresh tarragon
- 1 T fresh lemon juice (about 1/2 a lemon)
- 1 T chopped fresh parsley
- 1/2 tsp sea salt or kosher salt, or more to taste
- 1/4 tsp freshly ground black pepper, or more to taste
- 1/3 cup unsalted cashew pieces, coarsely chopped

Technique:

Coat a skillet with a little cooking oil spray and sauté the chik'n strips over medium-low heat, about 3 minutes. Avoid over-browning. Remove from heat and let cool.

Dice the chik'n and transfer to a large bowl. Add the remaining ingredients and incorporate about 1/4 cup vegan mayonnaise. Stir well to combine. Add more mayo as necessary for a moist and creamy consistency and adjust salt and pepper to taste.

Cover and refrigerate a minimum of 1 to 2 hours to blend flavors.

Tip: Homemade No-Eggy Mayo is much more economical than commercial vegan mayonnaise and tastes better too!

Chik'n Nirvana Salad

The special combination of ingredients makes a delightful and savory appetizer filling with a hint of sweetness. This recipe calls for Chik'n Seitan, but you can also use leftover Herb Roasted Chik'n (pg. 30) or commercial vegan chicken such as Gardein™.

Ingredients:

- 10 oz Chik'n Seitan (pg. 11) or commercial vegan chicken, sliced into strips
- 1/3 cup raisins or dried cranberries, coarsely chopped
- 1/3 cup unsalted walnut pieces, coarsely chopped
- No-Eggy Mayo (pg. 105) or commercial vegan mayonnaise
- 2 tsp Dijon mustard
- 1/2 cup thinly sliced celery
- 1 small crisp green apple, finely diced
- 1/4 cup diced sweet onion, or more to taste
- 1/2 tsp sea salt or kosher salt, or more to taste
- 1/4 tsp ground white pepper, or more to taste

Technique:

Coat a skillet with a little cooking oil spray and sauté the chik'n strips over medium-low heat, about 3 minutes. Avoid over-browning. Remove from heat and let cool.

Dice the chik'n and transfer to a large bowl. Add the remaining ingredients and incorporate about 1/4 cup mayo. Stir well to combine. Add more mayo as necessary for a moist and creamy consistency and adjust salt and pepper to taste.

Cover and refrigerate a minimum of 1 to 2 hours to blend flavors.

Variations: For curry chik'n salad, add 1/2 tsp curry powder. For ginger chik'n salad, add 1 and 1/2 tsp fresh grated ginger root or 1/2 tsp ground ginger.

Tip: Homemade No-Eggy Mayo is much more economical than commercial vegan mayonnaise and tastes better too!

"Buttermilk" Ranch Dressing

Creamy, tangy, and delicious! This recipe makes about 1 and 1/2 cups.

Ingredients:

- 1 cup (4 T) No-Eggy Mayo (pg. 105) or commercial vegan mayonnaise
- 1/2 cup Heavy Creme (pg. 64) or commercial vegan cream substitute
- 1 T fresh lemon juice
- 1 tsp white wine vinegar or white balsamic vinegar
- 1 tsp onion powder
- 1 tsp Dijon mustard
- 1/2 tsp garlic powder
- 1/4 tsp sea salt or kosher salt, or more to taste
- 1/4 tsp ground black pepper, or more to taste
- 1/4 tsp homemade vegan Worcestershire Sauce (pg. 206) or commercial - optional
- 1 T chopped fresh chives or 1 tsp dried
- 1 T chopped fresh parsley or 1 tsp dried
- 1 and 1/2 tsp chopped fresh dill or a 1/2 tsp dry

Technique:

Process all of the ingredients EXCEPT for the herbs in a blender or food processor until smooth. Taste and add additional salt or pepper, as desired. Add the herbs and pulse a few times. Pour into a container with a lid and refrigerate for a few hours to blend flavors. Use the dressing within 7 days.

Tip: Homemade No-Eggy Mayo is much more economical than commercial vegan mayonnaise and tastes better too!

Insalata Caprese

This is a vegan variation of the popular Caprese Salad, which is traditionally made with vine-ripened tomatoes, fresh dairy mozzarella, basil and extra-virgin olive oil. Here I've combined stewed tomatoes with sliced onions, fresh basil, homemade vegan mozzarella, optional capers and balsamic vinaigrette for a cool and refreshing salad. This is one of my favorites and I think you'll enjoy it too. This salad needs to be prepared a day ahead to allow time for the mozzarella to firm completely and for the salad ingredients to marinate, so plan accordingly.

Ingredients:

- 2 cans (28 oz each) stewed tomatoes with the juice
- 1 small onion, sliced very thin
- a generous handful of fresh basil chiffonade (sliced into ribbons)
- 2 T capers, drained (optional)
- 2/3 cup homemade Balsamic Vinaigrette (pg. 119)
  or your favorite commercial balsamic vinaigrette
- Fresh Nut Mozzarella (pg. 73)
- sea salt or kosher salt and coarse ground black pepper to taste

Technique:

Prepare your mozzarella and refrigerate.

In a large bowl or food storage container with a lid, combine all of the ingredients except the mozzarella. Cover and refrigerate overnight.

To serve, spoon the salad into a serving bowl and top with slices of the mozzarella. Garnish with additional fresh basil if desired.

Tip: Try serving Insalata Caprese over toasted crusty bread rounds or croutons; the crisp bread soaks up the flavorful juice and is absolutely delicious!

Creamy Caesar Dressing

This is my version of the classic dressing, vegan-style. The nori seaweed and green olives replace the "bite" of the anchovy paste and the nutritional yeast replaces the parmesan flavor. The white bean base not only adds creaminess but makes this dressing a good source of protein. This recipe makes about 2 cups.

Ingredients:

- 1 can (about 15 to 16 oz) cooked white beans, such as great northern, white navy or cannellini
- 3/4 cup extra-virgin olive oil
- 1/4 cup white balsamic vinegar or white wine vinegar
- 1/4 cup water
- 5 large garlic stuffed green olives
- 1/4 sheet sushi nori seaweed, torn into pieces (optional)
- 1 T Dijon mustard
- 1 T nutritional yeast
- 2 tsp organic sugar
- 1 tsp homemade vegan Worcestershire Sauce (pg. 206) or commercial
- 1/2 tsp sea salt or kosher salt, or more to taste
- 1/4 tsp coarse ground black pepper, or more to taste

Technique:

Process all ingredients in the blender until smooth. Adjust salt and pepper to taste. Chill before serving.

Mock Tuna Salad

Mock tuna salad makes a tasty, nutritious and satisfying sandwich filling. Nori seaweed contains high proportions of iodine, carotene, vitamins A, B and C, as well as significant amounts of calcium and iron.

Ingredients:

- 1 can garbanzo beans (16 oz) drained and rinsed well
- 1/2 sheet nori seaweed - optional
- 2 T minced red or sweet yellow onion
- 1 rib of celery, finely chopped
- 1 small dill or sweet pickle, finely chopped - or 2 T pickle relish
- 1 T fresh flat-leaf parsley, finely chopped - optional
- sea salt or kosher salt to taste
- ground black pepper to taste
- 1/4 cup (or more) No-Eggy Mayo (pg. 105) or commercial vegan mayonnaise

Technique:

Place the garbanzo beans in the food processor. Tear the optional seaweed into small pieces and add to the processor. Briefly pulse the processor several times to achieve a flake consistency. Do not over-process or you will end up with a paste.

Transfer to a bowl and add the remaining ingredients. Add a little more mayo if necessary for a moist and creamy texture and adjust seasonings.

Refrigerate for a few hours to blend flavors.

Eggless Salad

This sandwich filling amazingly resembles real egg salad in both taste and texture, but without the cholesterol (or animal cruelty).

Ingredients:

- 1 block (about 14 oz) firm or extra-firm tofu (do not use silken tofu)
- No-Eggy Mayo (pg. 105) or commercial vegan mayonnaise, to taste
- 2 tsp Dijon or spicy golden mustard
- 2 T nutritional yeast
- a pinch or two of turmeric
- 1 rib of celery, diced
- 2 T onion, minced
- pinch of Himalayan black crystal salt*
- sea salt, kosher salt to taste
- ground black pepper to taste
- optional ingredients: sliced black olives, capers, or diced pickle

*Kala namak, or Himalayan black salt, is an Indian salt with a high mineral concentration, most notably sulfur, which gives it its characteristic and pungent "hard-boiled egg" smell. It is useful in vegan cooking as it imparts a cooked egg taste to recipes. Interestingly, it is not black but rather pink in color. Be advised, that if you detest the sulfurous smell of hard-boiled eggs, you probably will not care for this salt. Kala namak is considered a cooling spice in Ayurvedic medicine and is used as a digestive aid. It can be found in specialty food stores as well as online.

Technique:

Drain and press the tofu to remove as much water as possible (see Preparing Tofu for Recipes, pg. 56).

Crumble the tofu into a bowl. Incorporate all other ingredients and mix well. Add enough vegan mayonnaise to thoroughly moisten the mixture.

Taste and adjust seasonings. Refrigerate for at least 30 minutes to combine flavors. This salad will last about 7 days refrigerated.

Tip: Homemade No-Eggy Mayo is much more economical than commercial vegan mayonnaise and tastes better too!

Refrigerator Pickles

These easy-to-make pickles are fresh, crisp, tangy and nicely seasoned.

Ingredients:

- cucumbers, any variety
- 1 large onion, thinly sliced
- 3 cups filtered water
- 1/2 cup white vinegar
- 3 T sea salt or kosher salt
- 1 T organic sugar
- 2 T minced garlic (6 cloves)
- 2 T fresh minced dill or 1 T freeze-dried
- 2 bay leaves

Technique:

Dissolve the salt and sugar in the vinegar and water to create the brine. Add the garlic, bay leaves and dill.

For smaller cucumbers, such as pickling cucumbers, leave unpeeled and slice in half or quarter lengthwise. For larger cucumbers which have tougher skins: use a vegetable peeler to cut strips of peel away, leaving some of the peel intact. This gives the cucumbers a nice variegated appearance; then cut into 1/4 to 1/2-inch crosswise slices.

Place the onions into a large plastic container with a lid and layer the sliced cucumbers on top. If using mason jars, divide the onions among the jars and layer the sliced cucumbers on top or stand the spears upright.

Pour the brine over the cucumbers, submerging them completely. Cover tightly. Refrigerate for a minimum of 48 hours, but the longer they "pickle", the better.

Quinoa Salad

This refreshing salad is a variation of Middle Eastern tabbouleh, which is traditionally made with bulgur wheat. Quinoa (pronounced keen-wah) is an ancient food that has been cultivated in the South American Andes since at least 3,000 B.C. The ancient Incas called quinoa the "mother grain" and revered it as sacred. Technically quinoa is not a true grain, but is the seed of the Chenopodium or Goosefoot plant.

Ingredients:

- 1 cup quinoa
- 2 cups water or vegetable broth (see pg. 121 for broth options)
- 1/3 cup extra-virgin olive oil
- 1/4 cup pine nuts
- juice of 2 lemons (about 1/4 cup); or try 1/4 cup white balsamic vinegar
- 1/2 tsp sea salt or kosher salt, or more to taste
- 1 large cucumber, (peeled if desired) seeded and diced
- 2 tomatoes, seeded and diced
- 1 small onion, diced
- 2 cloves garlic, minced (about 2 tsp)
- 1/2 cup fresh chopped parsley (curly or flat-leaf)
- fresh ground black pepper

Technique:

Place the quinoa and the water (or broth) in a medium-sized saucepan and bring to a boil. Reduce heat to a simmer, cover and cook until all water is absorbed, about 10 to 15 minutes. When done, the grain will appear soft and translucent and the germ ring will be visible along the side of the grain.

While the quinoa is cooking, heat a dry skillet over medium-heat, add the pine nuts and stir frequently until lightly toasted. Remove from heat and set aside to cool.

When the quinoa is done cooking, remove from the heat, stir in the extra-virgin olive oil and set aside to cool to room temperature. Once the quinoa has cooled, stir in the remaining ingredients including the pine nuts; taste and adjust with salt and fresh ground black pepper if desired.

Refrigerate at least a few hours prior to serving to blend flavors.

Asian Ginger Dressing (Restaurant-Style)

*If you've ever raved about the ginger salad dressing served
in Japanese restaurants, then this dressing is for you.*

Into a blender add:

- 1/2 cup diced onion
- 1/2 cup vegetable oil
- 1/3 cup rice vinegar
- 2 T fresh grated ginger root
- 1 rib of celery, chopped
- 1 large carrot, chopped
- 3 T tamari or soy sauce, or to taste
- 2 T organic ketchup or 1 T tomato paste
- 2 tsp organic sugar
- 1 tsp sesame oil (optional)
- 1 clove garlic (1 tsp minced)
- 1/4 teaspoon ground white pepper

Pulse process to combine, but try not to over-process as a little texture is desirable. Refrigerate in an airtight container for a few hours to blend flavors. The recipe will make about 2 cups of dressing.

Garlic Herb Vinaigrette

*Garlicky with a hint of sweetness, this herbal vinaigrette
will brighten the flavor of your favorite garden salads.*

Into a blender add:

- 1 cup extra-virgin olive oil
- 1/3 cup white wine vinegar or white balsamic vinegar
- 1 T fresh lemon juice (about 1/2 a lemon)
- 1/4 cup chopped fresh herbs (1 T each parsley, basil, marjoram, oregano; or 1 tsp each dried)
- 2 T chopped garlic (6 cloves)
- 2 T organic sugar
- 2 tsp Dijon mustard
- 1/2 tsp sea salt or kosher salt (or to taste)
- freshly ground black pepper to taste

Blend to emulsify. Bottle and refrigerate to blend flavors.

German Hot Potato Salad

Ingredients:

- 2 pounds small Yukon gold or red potatoes, unpeeled
- 1 white or yellow onion, finely chopped
- 1/3 cup white vinegar
- 3 T organic sugar
- 1 T Dijon mustard
- 1 tsp sea salt or kosher salt
- 1/4 cup chopped fresh parsley
- optional: garnish with cooked and crumbled Bacun (pg. 23) or tempeh bacon

Technique:

Place the potatoes in a cooking pot and cover them with enough water to extend 2 inches above the surface of the potatoes. Salt the water and bring to boil over medium-high heat. Continue cooking until potatoes are tender when pierced with a fork, about 15 to 20 minutes. Drain and slice into 1/4-inch rounds.

In a large skillet over medium heat, heat 2 T vegetable oil; add the onion. Cook until translucent and just beginning to brown, about 4 to 5 minutes.

Whisk in the vinegar, sugar, mustard, liquid smoke and salt and stir until bubbly. Add the sliced, cooked potatoes and parsley and toss to coat. Top with cooked and crumbled vegan bacon if desired. Serve warm.

Balsamic Vinaigrette

The classic dressing; simple and easy to prepare!

Ingredients:

- 1/4 cup balsamic vinegar
- 2 tsp organic sugar
- 1 T minced garlic (3 cloves)
- 1/2 tsp salt
- 1/2 tsp ground black pepper
- 3/4 cup extra-virgin olive oil

Technique:

Whisk the vinegar in a bowl with the sugar, garlic, salt and pepper until sugar and salt dissolves. Then slowly whisk in the oil. Or place all the ingredients in a screw-top jar and shake to combine. Taste and adjust the seasonings.

Gretchen's Favorite Potato Salad

Every time I make this potato salad for our vegan potlucks, my best friend Gretchen always raves about it. So, I named it after her. I hope you enjoy this salad too.

Ingredients:

- 3 lbs. red skinned potatoes, unpeeled
- 1/2 cup sweet yellow onion, finely diced
- 2 ribs celery, diced
- 1/4 cup chopped fresh parsley
- 2 T minced fresh chives
- No-Eggy Mayo (pg. 105) or commercial vegan mayonnaise
- 2 T dill pickle brine or red wine vinegar, or more to taste
- 1 T Dijon mustard (you can also use golden brown or yellow mustard, your choice)
- dash of homemade vegan Worcestershire Sauce (pg. 206) or commercial - optional
- 1/2 tsp coarse ground black pepper, or to taste
- sea salt or kosher salt to taste

Technique:

Cut the unpeeled red potatoes in half and then into quarters (no bigger than 1-inch) and place in a large cooking pot. Add enough water to cover by 1-inch. Add 1 T sea salt or kosher salt and bring to boil. Start testing for fork tenderness at about 6 minutes and every minute or two thereafter. Do not overcook! The potatoes should be fork tender but not mushy.

Drain into a colander and rinse well with cold water to stop the cooking process. Let drain thoroughly and chill in a covered mixing bowl until completely cool.

After cooling the potatoes, add the chopped vegetables and herbs and stir to combine.

In a separate bowl mix together 1/2 cup mayonnaise with the mustard, pickle brine (or vinegar), 1 tsp coarse pepper, 1/2 tsp salt and optional vegan Worcestershire. Stir thoroughly into the potato/vegetable/herb mixture (stir well but avoid mashing the potatoes; the potatoes should still retain some texture).

Add more mayonnaise as necessary, a tablespoon at a time, until the salad has a nice creamy texture and season with salt and pepper to taste. Chill well to blend flavors before serving.

Tip: Homemade No-Eggy Mayo is much more economical than commercial vegan mayonnaise and tastes better too!

Chapter 7

Soups, Broths and Stews

Quick Vegetable Broth

A quick vegetable broth can be made with Better Than Bouillon™ Organic Vegetable Base (1 tsp for each cup water) or other commercial vegetable broth cubes (1/2 cube for each cup water) - or more or less to taste. Pre-prepared commercial vegetable broths are also available in aseptic cartons from most markets.

Quick Chik'n Broth

A quick chik'n broth can be made with Better Than Bouillon™ Vegetarian No Chicken Base (1 tsp for each cup water) or other commercial no-chicken broth cubes (1/2 cube for each cup water) - or more or less to taste. For an instant broth, use 2 tsp to 1 level tablespoon Chik'n Broth Powder (pg. 122) for each cup of water.

Savory Chik'n Broth

I like to keep this stocked in my refrigerator for use in various recipes. It can be used to simmer seitan, and then saved again to be used for other recipes. It's excellent as a replacement for plain water when cooking rice, couscous or quinoa. Makes about 6 cups prepared broth.

Ingredients:
- 6 and 1/2 cups water
- 1/3 cup nutritional yeast
- 1 large onion, chopped
- 1 rib (stalk) celery, chopped
- 1 carrot, chopped
- 2 T sunflower oil (or other light-tasting oil)
- 2 cloves garlic, minced (2 tsp)
- 1/4 cup dry white wine (optional)
- 2 and 1/2 tsp sea salt or kosher salt, or more to taste
- 2 tsp organic sugar
- 1/2 tsp poultry seasoning
- 1 bay leaf
- 1/4 tsp ground black pepper

Technique:

Simmer the ingredients in a stockpot for 1 hour. Add salt if needed, to taste. Strain and use immediately or refrigerate in a covered container until ready to use.

Chik'n Broth Powder

This flavorful broth powder is ideal for creating a quick broth for soup, or simply for a soothing cup of hot bouillon. You can also use the broth for cooking rice, couscous or quinoa to add wonderful flavor. This recipe will make 32 cups of broth.

Blend in a food processor until finely powdered:

- 2 cups nutritional yeast flakes
- 1/4 cup onion powder
- 1/4 cup fine sea salt or kosher salt
- 2 T organic sugar
- 1 T poultry seasoning
- 1 T dried celery flakes or parsley flakes
- 2 tsp garlic powder
- 1 tsp paprika
- 1/2 tsp ground white pepper

Store in an airtight container and use 2 teaspoons to 1 level tablespoon per cup of piping hot water, or more or less to taste. Stir well and let the broth sit for a few minutes to let the sediment settle to the bottom. Pour off the clear portion of broth into another cup or container. Discard the sediment.

Quick Beaf Broth

A quick beaf broth can be made with Better Than Bouillon™ Organic Vegetable Base, 1/2 tsp for each cup water plus 2 tsp tamari, soy sauce or Bragg Liquid Aminos™ for each cup of broth - or more or less to taste.

A quick beaf broth can also be made with any commercially prepared vegetable broth, plus 2 tsp tamari, soy sauce or Bragg Liquid Aminos™ for each cup of broth - or more or less to taste.

Or, a quick beaf broth can be made with Better Than Bouillon™ Vegetarian No Beef Base (1 tsp for each cup water) - or more or less to taste. For some reason, this product has become increasingly more difficult to find. You can purchase it directly from the manufacturer, SuperiorTouch.com, if you cannot locate it anywhere else.

Savory Beaf Broth

I like to keep this stocked in my refrigerator for use in various recipes. It can be used to simmer seitan, and then saved again to be used for other recipes. It's excellent as a replacement for plain water when cooking rice, couscous or quinoa. It's also wonderful as a base for French Onion Soup (pg. 133). Makes about 6 cups prepared broth.

Ingredients:

- 6 and 1/2 cups water
- 1/4 cup tamari, soy sauce or Bragg Liquid Aminos™
- 2 T homemade vegan Worcestershire Sauce (pg. 206) or commercial
- 1 small onion, chopped
- 1 rib (stalk) celery, chopped
- 1 carrot, chopped
- 2 cloves garlic, chopped (or 2 tsp minced)
- 2 T extra-virgin olive oil
- 2 tsp organic sugar
- 1 tsp Gravy Master™ - optional (a natural meat-free product that enhances color; it can be found in most supermarkets where jar gravy is located)
- 1 bay leaf
- 1/2 tsp dried thyme or 1 and 1/2 tsp fresh thyme leaves
- 1/4 tsp ground black pepper
- 1/4 cup dry red wine or dry sherry (optional)
- sea salt or kosher salt to taste

Simmer ingredients in a stockpot for 1 hour. Add salt to taste. Strain and use immediately or refrigerate in covered container until ready to use.

Gazpacho

Bursting with fresh vegetables, this favorite cold soup is nutritious and refreshing on a hot Summer day! Optionally garnish with chopped fresh cilantro, diced avocado, a dollop of vegan sour cream or Crème Fraîche.

Ingredients:

- 1 large cucumber, peeled, halved and then seeded
- 1 red bell pepper, cored and seeded
- 1 green bell pepper, cored and seeded
- 1 large can (28 oz) whole or diced tomatoes with juice
- 1 small red onion
- 3 garlic cloves, minced
- 1 jalapeno pepper, seeded and finely minced (optional)
- 2 cups tomato juice
- 1/4 cup red wine vinegar or raw apple cider vinegar
- 1/4 cup extra-virgin olive oil
- 1 tsp sea salt, or to taste
- 1/2 tsp freshly ground black pepper, or to taste
- optional garnishes: chopped fresh cilantro, diced avocado or a dollop of Sour Creme (pg. 65) or Crème Fraîche (pg. 68).

Technique:

Roughly chop the cucumber, bell peppers and red onion into 1-inch cubes and place into a food processor; pulse once or twice.

Add the canned tomatoes. Pulse once or twice more but don't over-process, as the soup should retain some texture. If you prefer a smoother gazpacho however, simply process longer.

Transfer the mixture to a large bowl and add the garlic, tomato juice, vinegar, extra-virgin olive oil, optional jalapeno pepper, salt, and black pepper. Mix well and chill before serving. The longer gazpacho refrigerates, the more the flavors develop.

Ladle into serving bowls and garnish if desired.

Potato Leek Soup

This creamy, elegant soup can be served hot or cold. When served cold it is referred to as Vichyssoise. The traditional recipe calls for heavy dairy cream or Crème Fraîche, but I've substituted with several vegan options. The soup is wonderful without the addition of the creme, so it's really up to you whether to include it or not. Bon appétit!

Ingredients:

- 1/4 cup (4 T) Better Butter (pg. 62) or vegan margarine
- 1 large or 2 small leeks, about 1 pound
- 1 onion, chopped
- 1/2 tsp white pepper
- 1 and 1/2 tsp fresh thyme leaves or 1/2 tsp dry thyme
- 1/2 cup dry white wine
- 6 cups chik'n broth (see pg. 121-122 for broth options)
- 1 bay leaf
- 3 large russet potatoes, peeled and diced
- 1/2 cup Crème Fraîche (pg. 68), Sour Creme (pg. 65), Heavy Creme (pg. 64) or commercial non-dairy cream or sour cream
- sea salt or kosher salt to taste
- 2 tablespoons snipped chives for garnish (optional)

Technique:

Peel and dice the potatoes and set aside in a container with the chik'n broth (room temperature or chilled). Immersion in liquid prevents the potatoes from oxidizing (turning brown).

Using a sharp knife, remove the ends and the top leaf portion of the leek just where the dark leaves meet the light green. Discard or compost the leaves. Halve the white and light green part of the leek lengthwise and rinse well under cold running water to rid the leek of any sand (if there is any). Chop thinly crosswise and set aside.

In a large soup pot over medium heat, melt the butter or margarine and add the leeks and onions. Sauté until the leeks are wilted, about 5 minutes. Add the wine and thyme; bring to a boil. Add the chik'n broth, potatoes, bay leaf and white pepper; bring to a boil.

Reduce the heat to a simmer and cook for 45 minutes, or until the potatoes are falling apart and the soup is very flavorful.

Remove the bay leaf and, working in batches if necessary, purée the soup in a blender (if you own an immersion blender, you can purée the soup directly in the pot).

Stir in the Crème Fraîche, sour creme, or heavy creme and adjust the seasoning, if necessary. Garnish with the snipped chives and serve immediately.

African Peanut Soup

Various peanut soups are common throughout Africa. A delightful flavor combination of peanut butter, onion, tomatoes and spice make this soup an ethnic favorite.

Ingredients:

- 2 T extra-virgin vegetable oil
- 1 large onion, finely chopped
- 1 large red bell pepper, finely chopped
- 1 T finely minced garlic (3 cloves)
- 1 T fresh grated ginger root
- 1 large can (28 oz) crushed tomatoes, with liquid
- 6 cups chik'n broth (see pg. 121-122 for broth options)
- 1/4 tsp cayenne pepper
- 1 tsp chili powder
- 1 cup peanut butter (creamy or chunky - your preference)
- 1/2 cup uncooked brown or white rice

Technique:

Heat the oil in a large soup pot over medium high heat. Sauté the onions and bell peppers until lightly browned and tender, stirring in the garlic and ginger when almost done to prevent burning. Stir in the tomatoes, broth, cayenne pepper, and chili powder. Reduce heat to low and simmer, uncovered, for 30 minutes.

Carefully ladle 2/3 of the soup into a blender, and pulse to blend. Be careful, hot liquids tend to expand when blended, so keep the lid on tight by holding down with a dish towel. Return the mixture to the soup pot.

Stir in the rice, cover, and simmer until the rice is tender (about 50 minutes for brown rice and 20 minutes for white). Stir in the peanut butter until well blended, and serve.

Hawaiian Chik'n Long Rice

This dish is frequently served at luaus (Hawaiian feasts). Long rice is actually a clear noodle made from rice flour. The flavors of ginger and coconut milk bring back fond memories of my time spent on the islands of Hawaii. Ohoiho! (That's "enjoy!" in Hawaiian)

Ingredients:

- 2 T vegetable oil
- 10 oz thinly sliced Chik'n Seitan (pg. 11) or commercial vegan chicken
- 1 T finely minced garlic (3 cloves)
- 5 cups chik'n broth (see pg. 121-122 for broth options)
- 1 can (14 oz) unsweetened coconut milk (regular or lite)*
- 2 T fresh grated ginger root
- 1/2 tsp cayenne pepper (or to taste)
- 8 oz long rice (cellophane noodles)
- 1 can (15oz) straw mushrooms or 2 cups sliced white or brown mushrooms
- 1/2 cup chopped green onions

*Do not use Coconut Milk Beverage; it lacks the distinct coconut flavor essential for this recipe.

Technique:

In a skillet, heat the oil over medium-high heat. Add the chik'n and sauté until lightly browned. Add the garlic and sauté for another minute or two.

Transfer to a cooking pot and add the chik'n broth, coconut milk and the fresh ginger. Bring to a boil, lower heat and simmer for 15 minutes.

Add the long rice (noodles) and mushrooms and cook for another 10 to 15 minutes only, or until the long rice is clear in color. Long rice requires very little cooking time. It absorbs liquid very easily and can easily break down if cooked too long. Garnish with chopped green onions and serve immediately.

Moroccan Tagine (Stew)

This fragrant and spicy meatball stew is even better reheated the next day.

Ingredients:

- 1 large onion, sliced
- 2 T extra-virgin olive oil
- Seitan Meatballs (pg. 18) - use the Moroccan variation
- 1 large can (28 oz) diced or crushed tomatoes with juice
- 4 cups vegetable or beaf broth (see pg. 121-122 for broth options)
- 2 tsp paprika
- 2 tsp cumin
- 1/2 tsp cayenne pepper, or to taste
- 3 T chopped fresh parsley or 1 T dried
- 1 T minced garlic (3 cloves)
- sea salt and freshly ground black pepper, to taste

Technique:

In a non-stick skillet over medium-heat, sauté the onion in extra-virgin olive oil until lightly browned. Transfer to a large cooking pot. In the same skillet, brown the meatballs. Remove from the heat and set aside.

Add the remaining ingredients, except for the meatballs, to the onion in the cooking pot. Bring the mixture to a simmer and cook for a minimum of 30 minutes. During the last 10 minutes of cooking time, add the meatballs to the stew.

Serve in a soup bowl with a side of flatbread or pita bread, if desired, to soak up the fragrant sauce.

Tom Kha Kai (Thai Coconut Chik'n Soup)

This flavorful and deliciously fragrant soup is one of my all time favorites. Traditionally this soup is made with exotic ingredients such as lemongrass, galangal and kaffir lime leaves, but I have made substitutions with ingredients most cooks keep stocked in their pantry.

Ingredients:

- 2 cups chik'n broth (see pg. 121-122 for broth options)
- 2 cans (14oz each) unsweetened coconut milk (full-fat or lite)*
- 1 three-inch piece fresh ginger root, sliced
- 10 oz Chik'n Seitan (pg. 11) or commercial cooked vegan chicken (or substitute with extra-firm tofu)
- 1 can (15oz) straw mushrooms, drained (from the Asian food aisle or market) - or canned button mushrooms
- juice of 2 limes or to taste
- 1 T organic sugar, or to taste
- 1 piece (about 6-inch square) dashi kombu (dried kelp) - optional (this replaces the fish sauce flavor, a common ingredient in Thai cooking)
- 1/2 tsp Thai red chili paste (or more to taste)
- sea salt or kosher salt, to taste
- cilantro leaves for garnish
- Serrano chilies, sliced for garnish (optional)

*Do not use Coconut Milk Beverage; it lacks the distinct coconut flavor essential for this recipe.

Technique:

Add a tablespoon of oil to a skillet and sauté the chik'n (or tofu) over medium heat until lightly browned. Remove from the heat and set aside.

Combine the chik'n broth, coconut milk and sliced ginger in a large saucepan. Bring to a simmer and add the lime juice, sugar, kombu (optional) and chili paste. Simmer for at least 30 minutes so the ginger can infuse flavor into the soup.

Taste and adjust flavor by adding salt and a little more lime juice for tartness or a little more sugar for sweetness if desired.

With a slotted spoon, remove the ginger slices and seaweed and discard. Add the chik'n and mushrooms. Continue to simmer for 10 to 15 minutes.

Ladle the soup into individual bowls and top each with cilantro leaves. For a spicier experience, top with sliced Serrano chilies if desired.

Not Your Grandmother's Chik'n Noodle Soup

This soup is a classic in American comfort cuisine and much kinder to chickens than your grandmother's version.

Ingredients:

- 2 T vegetable oil
- 1 medium onion, chopped
- 3 garlic cloves, minced (1 T)
- 2 medium carrots, cut diagonally into 1/2-inch-thick slices
- 2 celery ribs, halved lengthwise, and cut into 1/2-inch-thick slices
- 4 fresh thyme sprigs or 1 tsp dried thyme
- 1 bay leaf

- 8 cups chik'n broth (see pg. 121-122 for broth options)
- 8 ounces wide eggless noodles
- 1 and 1/2 cups diced Chik'n Seitan (pg. 11) or commercial cooked vegan chicken
- sea salt or kosher salt and freshly ground black pepper to taste
- 1 handful fresh flat-leaf parsley, finely chopped

Technique:

Warm the oil in a soup pot over medium heat. Add the onion, garlic, carrots, celery, thyme and bay leaf. Cook and stir for about 6 minutes, until the vegetables are softened but not browned. Pour in the chik'n broth and bring the liquid to a boil. Add the noodles and simmer for 5 minutes until tender. Fold in the chik'n, and continue to simmer for another couple of minutes to heat through; season with salt and pepper to taste. Garnish with chopped parsley before serving.

Spicy Ginger Carrot Soup

Ingredients:

- 2 T vegetable oil
- 1 large onion, chopped
- 3 cups sliced carrots
- 4 cloves garlic, chopped
- 2 tsp fresh grated ginger root
- 4 cups vegetable broth (see pg. 121 for broth options)
- 1 tsp red pepper sauce, or to taste
- 1/2 tsp ground cumin
- sea salt or kosher salt to taste
- garnish with Heavy Creme (pg. 64) or commercial vegan cream substitute

Technique:

In a large soup pot over medium heat, sauté the onion and carrots in 2 tablespoons vegetable oil until soft.

Add the garlic and ginger and sauté an additional minute or two.

Add the broth, cumin and red pepper sauce and simmer until the vegetables are tender. Purée the soup in a blender; return to the pot to warm over low heat.

Add salt to taste. Serve and garnish with a swirl of heavy creme.

Cold Beet Borscht

Borscht is a soup of Ukrainian origin and is a staple part of the local culinary heritage of many other Eastern and Central European nations. Borscht is served cold in many different culinary traditions, including Lithuanian, Belarusian, Polish, Ukrainian and Russian.

Ingredients:

- 6 fresh red beets, peeled and quartered*
- 1/2 tsp sea salt or kosher salt
- 1 T light-tasting vegetable oil, such as sunflower or safflower
- 1 small red onion, chopped
- 2 cloves garlic, chopped (about 2 tsp minced)
- 1 rib celery, diced
- 1 carrot, diced
- 3 cups vegetable broth (see pg. 121 for broth options)
- 2 T raw apple cider vinegar
- 2 tsp organic sugar
- salt and pepper to taste
- 2 tsp minced fresh dill
- Sour Creme (pg. 65) or Crème Fraîche (pg. 68) or commercial vegan sour cream

*Fresh beets are essential for borscht because canned beets have lost a great deal of their vibrancy during the canning process.

Technique:

Boil the beets in 3 cups of salted water for about 20 minutes until they are fork-tender. Strain the beets and reserve the liquid in a bowl. Dice the beets once they are cool enough to handle.

Heat the vegetable oil in the same pot. Sauté the onion and garlic for about 4 minutes; add the carrot and celery and cook until tender, about 6-8 minutes.

Add the beet cooking liquid, broth, vinegar and sugar to the pot. Simmer for about 30 minutes.

Add salt, pepper and dill. Ladle the soup into a blender along with half of the diced beets and process until smooth. Return the puréed mixture to a container with a lid and add the remaining diced beets.

Chill well and serve with a dollop of commercial or homemade vegan sour cream or homemade Crème Fraîche. Garnish with a sprig of fresh dill if desired.

Beaf Bourguignon

This dish originates from the Burgundy region (in French, Bourgogne) which is in the east of present-day France. It is a stew prepared with red wine, traditionally burgundy wine, but any good quality dry red wine will work nicely. This dish is wonderful served over eggless noodles or garlic bread.

Ingredients:

- 1/3 cup extra-virgin olive oil
- 1 recipe (about 20 oz) Beaf Seitan (pg. 9), sliced thin
- 2 carrots, sliced
- 2 medium yellow onions, chopped in large pieces or 1 bag frozen pearl onions, thawed
- 1 lb mushrooms (any kind), thickly sliced
- 1 T minced garlic (3 cloves)
- 3 T flour (unbleached all-purpose wheat; rice or soy)
- 2 cups beaf broth (see pg. 123 for broth options)
- 3 cups dry red wine
- 1 T tomato paste
- 1/2 tsp dried thyme
- 1 bay leaf
- sea salt or kosher salt and ground black pepper to taste
- chopped flat-leaf parsley as a garnish (optional)

Technique:

In a large soup pot, heat 2 tablespoons of the extra-virgin olive oil and brown the seitan. Remove and set aside.

Heat the remaining extra-virgin olive oil in the same soup pot and add the carrot, onions and mushrooms. Sauté until the onions are transparent and lightly browned.

Add the garlic and sauté an additional minute. Sprinkle in the flour and stir well to combine. Cook until the flour mixture is a light golden brown, about 2 to 3 minutes.

Slowly stir in the broth, stirring vigorously to prevent lumps in the flour mixture.

Stir in the wine and tomato paste. Add the thyme and bay leaf and season with salt and pepper to taste.

Simmer on low, partially covered for 1 hour.

Add the seitan the last 20 minutes of cooking time. Serve and garnish with parsley, if desired.

French Onion Soup

Ingredients:

- 1/4 cup (4 T) Better Butter (pg. 62), vegan margarine or extra-virgin olive oil
- 3 large sweet yellow onions, thinly sliced
- 1 tsp organic sugar
- 1 T flour (unbleached all-purpose wheat; rice or soy)
- 6 cups beaf broth (see pg. 123 for broth options)
- 1 French baguette (make sure it's vegan!)
- shredded white vegan cheese that melts (Daiya™ mozzarella, for example)

Technique:

Melt the butter or margarine or heat the oil in a large soup pot. Stir in the sugar. Add the onions and sauté over medium heat for 10 minutes, or until caramelized.

Whisk in the flour until well blended with the onions and pan juices. Add the broth ingredients; heat to boiling. Reduce heat to low. Cover soup, and simmer for 30 minutes.

Cut 1 inch thick slices of bread from the loaf. Toast the bread slices at 325°F just until browned, about 10 minutes. Remove from the oven.

Increase the oven temp to 425°F.

Ladle soup into oven-safe soup bowls. Place 1 slice toasted bread on top of the soup in each bowl. Place shredded vegan cheese onto toasted bread slices. Place soup bowls on a cookie sheet for easier handling.

Bake uncovered at 425°F for 10 minutes, or just until cheese is melted. Serve with a nice tossed salad and additional bread if desired.

Creme of Broccoli Soup

No one would ever suspect this luscious soup to be non-dairy!

Ingredients:

- 1/4 cup (4 T) Better Butter (pg. 62), or vegan margarine
- 1 onion, chopped
- 1 rib (stalk) celery, chopped
- 5 cups chik'n broth
  (see pg. 121-122 for broth options)
- 1/2 cup nutritional yeast
- 1/2 tsp garlic powder
- 2 tsp onion powder
- 4 cups steamed broccoli florets
- 1 T cornstarch (preferably non-GMO) dissolved in 1 T water
- 1 cup Heavy Creme (pg. 64) or commercial vegan cream substitute
- salt and ground black pepper to taste
- snipped chives (optional)

Technique:

In a skillet over medium heat, sauté the onion and celery in the butter or margarine until translucent.

In a blender, combine contents of skillet, water, yeast, onion and garlic powder and steamed broccoli florets. Pulse blend a few times to desired consistency. Pour the contents into a saucepan and heat over medium heat.

Whisk in the cornstarch mixture and heavy creme. Cook until piping hot and thickened nicely. Salt if necessary and pepper, to taste. Garnish with snipped chives if desired.

Sweet and Sour Cabbage Soup

Ingredients:

- 1 onion, finely chopped
- 1 rib celery
- 1 carrot, diced
- 1 T chopped garlic (3 cloves)
- 2 T extra-virgin olive oil
- 4 cups beaf broth (see pg. 123 for broth options)
- 1 tsp crushed caraway seeds
- 1 large can (28 oz) crushed tomatoes with juice
- 2 T light brown sugar, or to taste
- 2 T raw apple cider vinegar, or to taste
- 1 small head green cabbage, chopped
- 10 oz diced Beef Seitan (pg. 9) or sliced Corned Beef (pg. 20) - optional
- salt and pepper to taste

Technique:

In a stock pot, sauté the onion, celery and carrot in oil until the onion is translucent.

Add the garlic and sauté for 1 or 2 minutes more.

Add all other ingredients except for the seitan. Gently simmer until the cabbage is very tender, 90 minutes or more (the longer, the better).

About 15 minutes before serving, add the optional seitan to the soup. Add salt and pepper to taste.

Vietnamese Phở Soup

In Vietnamese cuisine, phở (pronounced "fuh") noodle soup is a classic. In fact, it's practically the national dish of Vietnam. This is my vegan version of the fragrant soup.

Ingredients:

For the broth:
- 1 cinnamon stick
- 2 star anise pods or 1 tsp fennel seeds
- 4 whole cloves
- 6 cups beaf broth (see pg. 123 for broth options)
- 1 large unpeeled white or yellow onion, quartered
- 6 garlic cloves, halved or 2 T minced garlic
- 1 piece ginger root (about 2-inch), sliced
- 1 piece (about 6-inch square) dashi kombu (dried kelp) - optional
- 2 T tamari, soy sauce or Bragg Liquid Aminos™
- 1 T organic sugar
- juice of 1 lime
- sea salt or kosher salt, to taste

For the soup:
- 1 pkg rice noodles
- 10 oz Basic or Beaf Seitan (pg. 9), very thinly sliced
- 6 scallions, thinly sliced lengthwise (both green and white parts)
- 1 and 1/2 cups bean sprouts
- fresh chopped basil or cilantro (for garnish)
- red chili sauce (for garnish)

Technique:

To make the broth, heat a large pot over medium-high heat. Add the cinnamon stick, star anise (or fennel seeds) and cloves and dry-roast for 1 to 2 minutes, stirring occasionally, until the spices have released their aromatics. Add the broth, onion, garlic, ginger, tamari or soy sauce (or Bragg Liquid Aminos™), dashi kombu, sugar and lime juice and bring to a boil over high heat. Turn the heat down to medium-low, cover, and simmer for about 45 minutes.

While the broth is simmering, prepare the rice noodles. Place the noodles in a large bowl. Pour boiling water over the noodles to cover and soak for 20 minutes.

Now, strain the broth into a clean pot and discard the solids. Taste the broth and add salt or a little more sugar if necessary. Keep piping hot over medium-low heat.

When you are ready to assemble the soup, add the thinly sliced seitan to the hot broth and allow to heat through. Drain the softened rice noodles and divide evenly among 4 to 6 large bowls. Top with bean sprouts and scallions.

Using a slotted spoon, scoop the seitan out of the broth and distribute among the bowls. Ladle the hot broth over the contents of the bowl.

Garnish with the chopped basil or cilantro and a dash of red chili sauce, or more to taste.

Potato Corn Chowder

This deliciously satisfying chowder is sweetened with Summer corn and made extra-creamy by adding the milky starch from the cobs.

Ingredients:

- 3 ears fresh organic corn, shucked
- 4 cups vegetable broth or chik'n broth (see pg. 121-122 for broth options)
- 2 large russet potatoes, cut into 1/2-inch cubes
- 1 large onion, finely chopped
- 2 ribs celery, halved lengthwise, then diced
- 2 tsp minced garlic (2 cloves)
- 1 T vegetable oil
- 1 tsp thyme
- 2 bay leaves
- 1/2 teaspoon white pepper
- pinch of cayenne pepper
- 1 cup Heavy Creme (pg. 64) or commercial vegan cream substitute
- salt to taste
- garnish: chopped scallions or snipped chives

Technique:

Cut the corn from each cob, then hold the cob upright in a bowl and scrape with the blunt end of the knife to extract the "milk". Bring the broth and potatoes to a boil in a large covered pot, and then simmer stirring occasionally until the potatoes are tender, about 15 to 20 minutes.

Meanwhile, cook the onion and celery in oil in a skillet over medium heat, stirring occasionally, until onion is golden, about 10 minutes. Add the garlic and sauté for an additional minute. Do not let the garlic burn.

Add the contents of the skillet to the potatoes and broth along with the corn and its "milk". Stir thoroughly to combine and ladle half the contents of the soup pot into a blender. Blend until smooth and return to soup pot.

Add the thyme, bay leaves, white pepper and cayenne. Stir in the heavy creme. Salt to taste and continue low-simmering for about 30 minutes. Ladle into serving bowls and garnish with scallions or chives.

Creamy Tomato Bisque

Ingredients:

- 1/4 cup (4 T) Better Butter (pg. 62) or vegan margarine
- 1 medium onion, finely chopped
- 1 medium carrot, finely chopped
- 1 celery rib, finely chopped
- 2 garlic cloves, finely chopped (or 2 tsp minced garlic)
- 6 leaves fresh basil, chopped or 2 tsp dried
- 3 T flour (unbleached all-purpose wheat; rice or soy)
- 4 cups chik'n broth (see pg. 121-122 for broth options)
- 2 lbs. fresh tomatoes, preferably organic
- 3 T tomato paste
- 2 tsp organic sugar
- 1/2 cup Heavy Creme (pg. 64) or commercial vegan cream substitute
- 1/2 tsp sea salt or kosher salt, or more to taste
- 1/4 tsp ground white pepper, or more to taste

Technique:

Wash the tomatoes and remove the cores. Broil the tomatoes until the skins begin to blister and blacken. Remove the skins and coarsely chop the tomatoes. Set aside.

In a medium saucepan, melt the butter or margarine. Add the chopped onion, carrot, celery and garlic. Cover and cook over moderately high heat, stirring occasionally, until the vegetables are just beginning to brown, about 5 minutes.

Sprinkle the flour over the vegetables and stir over low heat for 1 minute, or until the flour is fully incorporated. Slowly whisk in the chik'n broth until smooth.

Add the tomatoes, tomato paste, salt, white pepper, basil, and sugar and bring to a boil. Cover partially and cook the soup over moderate heat, stirring occasionally, until the vegetables are tender.

Add the heavy creme; transfer the soup to a blender and purée until smooth. Return the purée to the saucepan, and adjust salt and pepper as needed.

Ladle the soup into bowls, garnish with drops of heavy creme, croutons, additional chopped fresh basil, cracked black pepper, etc.

Slow-Cooker Bean Barley Soup

This easy-to-make soup is prepared early in the day and left to cook until dinner time. The potatoes cook down, creating a thick, hearty and satisfying meal. This recipe makes a substantial amount of soup, so freeze any leftovers that will not be consumed within a few days.

Into a slow-cooker (crock pot) add:

- 8 cups vegetable broth or chik'n broth (see pg. 121-122 for broth options)
- 1/2 cup dry pearled barley
- 2 cans (about 15oz each) white beans (white navy, cannellini, or great northern) drained and rinsed well
- 1/4 cup nutritional yeast
- 2 T Better Butter (pg. 62) or vegan margarine
- 1 large onion, chopped
- 2 ribs celery, chopped
- 2 carrots, chopped
- 2 medium sized russet potatoes, cubed
- 1 T minced garlic (3 cloves)
- 1/2 tsp ground black pepper
- 1/2 tsp dried thyme
- 1 bay leaf
- sea salt or kosher salt to taste

Slow cook all day on low until the potatoes have cooked down and the vegetables are very tender. Add additional salt and pepper to taste.

Slow-Cooker Mexican Posole (Mexican Stew)

This easy-to-make, fragrant and mildly spiced soup is prepared early in the day and left to cook until dinner time. Hominy is made from dried maize (Indian corn) that has been treated with alkali to remove the hull and seed germ. This recipe makes a substantial amount of soup, so freeze any leftovers that will not be consumed within a few days.

Into a slow cooker (crock pot) add:

- 2 T Better Butter (pg. 62), vegan margarine or vegetable oil
- 8 cups chik'n broth (see pg. 121-122 for broth options)
- 1 T minced garlic (3 cloves)
- juice of 1 lime
- 1 T ground cumin
- 2 tsp chili powder
- 2 tsp dried oregano
- 1 jalapeno pepper, seeded and minced
- 1 large onion, chopped
- 2 cans (about 15oz each) hominy (golden, white or both)
- 2 cups shredded green cabbage
- 10 oz pan-seared and chopped Chik'n Seitan (pg. 11) or commercial vegan chicken
- sea salt or kosher salt and ground red pepper to taste
- chopped cilantro and sliced red radishes for garnish

Slow cook all day on low until the soup is fragrant and the vegetables are tender. Add the chik'n a half-hour before serving. Garnish with cilantro and sliced red radishes if desired.

Creamy Parsnip, Potato and Cauliflower Soup

Parsnips lend a subtle carrot flavor to this simple yet rich soup.

Ingredients:

- 5 cups vegetable broth or chik'n broth (see pg. 121-122 for broth options)
- 6 parsnips, peeled and sliced
- 2 russet potatoes, peeled and cubed
- 1/2 head of cauliflower
- 2 ribs (stalks) celery
- sea salt or kosher salt to taste, but only if necessary
- cracked black pepper, for garnish and to taste
- 1 cup Heavy Creme (pg. 64) or commercial vegan cream substitute

Technique:

Simmer the parsnips, potatoes, cauliflower and celery in the broth until very tender, about 30 to 45 minutes. Let cool for about 30 minutes.

Transfer to a blender (in portions if necessary) and process until very smooth.

Transfer the purée back to the soup pot and gently reheat. Stir in the heavy creme and season with salt to taste. Ladle into soup bowls and garnish with black pepper.

Chik'n Pot Pie Soup

This soup is a new twist on an American comfort food classic.

Ingredients:

- 1/4 cup (4 T) Better Butter (pg. 62) or vegan margarine
- 1/4 cup flour (unbleached all-purpose wheat; rice or soy)
- 1 yellow onion, finely chopped
- 2 ribs celery, chopped
- 1 carrot, chopped
- 2 cloves garlic, minced (about 2 tsp)
- 2 cups unsweetened non-dairy milk
- 4 cups chik'n broth (see pg. 121-122 for broth options)
- 1 and 1/2 cups diced Chik'n Seitan (pg. 11) or cooked commercial vegan chicken
- 2 russet potatoes, diced
- 1/2 cup canned peas (or fresh or thawed from frozen)
- 1/2 teaspoon dried thyme
- 1 vegan pie crust (preferably whole wheat)

Note: If you're using frozen pie crust, be sure to thaw before baking.

Technique:

Melt the butter or margarine in a large soup pot over medium heat and sauté the onions, celery and carrots until soft. Add the garlic and cook for 1 minute.

Whisk in the flour and let the mixture cook for an additional minute. Slowly whisk in the non-dairy milk until smooth. Add the chik'n broth. Stir continuously until the soup reaches a simmer.

Stir in the potatoes, corn, peas and thyme. Allow the soup to simmer, covered, stirring occasionally for 30 minutes. The soup will thicken as it cooks. Add the chik'n and simmer an additional 10 minutes.

To make the crust while your soup is cooking, preheat the oven to 400°F and break the pie crust into pieces. Bake the pieces for approximately 10 minutes, or until the edges brown. Serve some crust on the bottom and/or sides of each bowl of soup.

Mulligatawny Soup (Curry Chik'n Soup)

The name Mulligatawny comes from 2 Indian words meaning 'pepper water'. Curry is the particular ingredient that gives this incredible soup such a delicious flavor.

Ingredients:

- 1 onion, chopped
- 2 ribs celery, chopped
- 1 carrot, diced
- 2 cloves garlic, minced
- 1/4 cup (4 T) Better Butter (pg. 62) or vegan margarine
- 2 T flour (unbleached all-purpose wheat; rice or soy)
- 2 tsp Indian curry powder
- 4 cups chik'n broth (see pg. 121-122 for broth options)
- 1 T lemon juice (about 1/2 a lemon) or more to taste
- 1 small apple, peeled, cored and chopped
- 1/4 cup basmati rice
- 1 and 1/2 cups diced Chik'n Seitan (pg. 11) or cooked commercial vegan chicken
- sea salt or kosher salt to taste
- ground black pepper to taste
- 1/2 tsp dried thyme
- 1/2 cup Heavy Creme (pg. 64) or commercial vegan cream substitute

Technique:

Melt the butter or margarine in a soup pot over medium heat and sauté the onions, celery and carrot until tender, about 5 minutes. Add the flour, garlic and curry, and cook 5 more minutes, stirring frequently.

Whisk in the chik'n broth and lemon juice and bring to a boil. Reduce heat to medium-low and simmer about 30 minutes.

Add the apple, rice, chik'n seitan, salt, pepper, and thyme. Simmer 20 minutes, or until rice is tender. Adjust seasonings to taste. Blend in the heavy creme just before serving.

Creme of Mushroom Soup

Ingredients:

- 1 lb (16 oz) fresh white mushrooms
- 1/4 cup (4 T) Better Butter (pg. 62) or vegan margarine
- 2 T vegetable oil
- 1 large sweet yellow onion, chopped
- 1 and 1/2 tsp minced thyme leaves or 1/2 tsp dried thyme
- 1/4 cup flour (unbleached all-purpose wheat; rice or soy)
- 4 cups vegetable broth (see pg. 121 for broth options)
  or commercial or homemade mushroom broth
- 1 cup dry white wine (or substitute with additional broth)
- 1 cup Heavy Creme (pg. 64) or commercial vegan cream substitute
- sea salt or kosher salt, to taste
- freshly ground black pepper
- 1/4 cup minced fresh flat-leaf parsley

Technique:

Clean the mushrooms by wiping them with a dry paper towel. Slice the mushrooms 1/4-inch thick and if they are big, cut them into bite-sized pieces. Set aside.

In a large pot over medium heat, sauté the mushrooms in 2 tablespoons of vegetable oil until the mushrooms have released their liquid and are beginning to lightly brown. Remove to a bowl and set aside.

In the same pot over medium heat, melt the butter or margarine. Add the onions and sauté until caramelized. Sprinkle in the flour, stir until blended and cook for 1 minute. Slowly whisk in the chik'n or vegetable broth and stir until smooth.

Add back half of the cooked mushrooms to the pot along with the white wine and minced thyme leaves. Bring to a boil. Reduce the heat and simmer for 20 minutes.

Transfer the soup to a blender and purée until smooth. Return to the cooking pot.

Stir in the remaining cooked mushrooms, the heavy creme and parsley until well blended. Season with salt and pepper to taste, and heat through but do not boil. Serve hot.

Mock Lobster Bisque

Mock Lobster Bisque is a creamy, mushroom-based soup flavored with cognac and sherry. Lobster mushrooms stand in for the lobster and kombu seaweed imparts a delicate "seafood" flavor. It's an elegant first course which is sure to impress your dinner guests. Kombu seaweed is often labeled "dashi kombu" and can be found in Asian markets and some gourmet food stores. Fresh lobster mushrooms are sometimes difficult to obtain but they usually can be found at Fresh Market™, Whole Foods Market™ or gourmet food stores in dry form.

Ingredients:

- 1/4 cup dry sherry or dry white wine
- 3 T vegetable oil
- 1 oz dried lobster mushrooms
  or 1/2 lb (8 oz) fresh
- 1/2 lb (8 oz) fresh white mushrooms, sliced
- 1 medium-sized sweet yellow onion, chopped
- 2 ribs celery, chopped
- 1/4 cup cognac (i.e., Courvoisier)
- 3 T tomato paste
- 1/4 cup (4 T) Better Butter (pg. 62) or vegan margarine
- 1/4 cup flour (unbleached all-purpose wheat; rice or soy)

- 4 cups vegetable broth or chik'n broth (see pg. 121-122 for broth options)
- 1 tsp Old Bay™ or Chesapeake Bay™ seasoning
- 1 and 1/2 tsp minced thyme leaves or 1/2 tsp dried thyme
- 1/4 tsp white pepper
- 1 piece (about 6-inch) dashi kombu (dried kelp) - optional; this imparts a mild seafood flavor
- 2 cups Heavy Creme (pg. 64), strained or commercial vegan cream substitute
- sea salt or kosher salt to taste
- fresh snipped chives for garnish

Technique:

If using dried lobster mushrooms, rinse them with water to remove any debris. Place in saucepan with 2 cups of the broth. Bring to a boil, and then remove from heat. Set aside for a minimum of 15 minutes to let the lobster mushrooms reconstitute. Remove from the broth with a slotted spoon (reserve the broth for the soup) and coarsely chop. If using fresh lobster mushrooms, brush off any loose dirt with a paper towel and coarsely chop.

Sauté the lobster mushrooms in 1 tablespoon of vegetable oil in a skillet over medium heat until most of their liquid has been released, about 2 minutes. Remove the pan from the heat and add the cognac. Place back over the heat and cook for another minute or two until the alcohol has evaporated.

In the same skillet over medium heat, sauté the sliced white mushrooms, onions and the celery in 2 tablespoons of vegetable oil. Sauté until the onions and celery are tender and the onions are just beginning to caramelize. Now, whisk in the tomato paste, remove from the heat and set aside.

Next, in a large soup pot melt the butter or margarine over medium heat. Sprinkle in the flour and stir until smooth to create a roux. Cook for 1 minute or until golden with a nutty aroma. Slowly whisk in the 4 cups broth (including the reserved broth from reconstituting the dried mushrooms) and stir vigorously until smooth. Bring to a boil and then reduce to a simmer.

Add the contents of the skillet, 1/2 of the lobster mushrooms, the Old Bay™ or Chesapeake Bay™ seasoning, minced thyme leaves, white pepper and kombu to the broth. Gently simmer for about 30 minutes. Remove the kombu and discard. Stir in the dry sherry (or white wine).

Transfer the mixture to a blender and purée until smooth. Strain the mixture through a mesh sieve back into the soup pot and bring to a simmer for 10 minutes.

Stir in the heavy creme and the remaining lobster mushrooms until blended. Season with salt to taste and heat through but do not boil. Garnish with chopped parsley or snipped chives. Serve hot.

White Bean Kale Soup

This soup is perfect for a cold Winter's night as well as a cool Summer evening. Chock full of nutritious vegetables and bean protein, it makes a hearty meal in itself.

Ingredients:

- 3 T vegetable oil
- 6 cloves garlic, crushed or minced
- 1 large yellow onion, chopped
- 2 carrots, diced
- 2 ribs celery, diced
- 8 loosely packed cups chopped raw kale, tough stems removed
- 4 cups chik'n broth (see pg. 121-122 for broth options)
- 2 cans (15 oz each) cooked white beans (white navy, cannellini or great northern) drained and thoroughly rinsed
- 6 sprigs fresh thyme leaves or 1 tsp dried thyme
- 2 T minced fresh basil or 2 teaspoons dried basil
- 1/2 tsp ground black pepper or more to taste
- sea salt or kosher salt to taste
- optional garnish: 1/2 cup chopped flat-leaf parsley

Technique:

Place half of the beans into a blender with enough chik'n broth to completely purée. Process until smooth and set aside.

In a large soup pot, heat the vegetable oil. Add the onion, carrots and celery and sauté until the onions become slightly translucent. Add the garlic and kale and sauté, tossing well until the kale is wilted.

Add the broth and the bean/broth purée, the remaining whole beans, the thyme, basil and black pepper. Bring to a simmer and cook for about 30 minutes or until the vegetables are tender. Adjust salt and pepper to taste, if needed. Ladle into bowls and sprinkle with chopped parsley.

Chapter 8

Entrees and Accompaniments

Classic Americana

Beaf Mushroom Stroganoff

Ingredients:

- 3 T Better Butter (pg. 62) or vegan margarine
- 10 oz thinly sliced Beaf Seitan (pg. 9) or commercial vegan "steak" strips
- 1 medium onion, chopped
- 1 leek, white and light green part only, halved lengthwise and then chopped
- 2 cups sliced fresh mushrooms
- 2 T flour (unbleached all-purpose wheat; rice or soy)
- 2 cups beaf broth (see pg. 123 for broth options)
- 2 tsp Dijon mustard
- 1/2 cup Sour Creme (pg. 65) or commercial vegan sour cream
- salt and pepper to taste
- cooked eggless wide noodles
- chopped fresh parsley for garnish

Technique:

Spray a non-stick skillet with cooking oil spray and then place over medium-high heat. Pan-sear the seitan slices until lightly browned. Remove to a bowl and set aside.

In the same skillet over medium heat, melt 1 tablespoon of the butter or margarine. Add the onions, leek and mushrooms and sauté until the onions are golden and the mushrooms have released most of their moisture. Transfer to the bowl with the seitan.

In the same skillet, melt 2 tablespoons of the butter or margarine over medium heat. Add the flour and cook for about 1 minute. Slowly whisk in the beaf broth and add the mustard. Bring to a rapid simmer and stir continually until the sauce begins to thicken. Stir in the sour creme and mix well; season with salt and pepper to taste.

Add the seitan and onion/leek/mushroom mixture to the sauce. Stir well to combine and keep on low heat until the noodles are prepared. Arrange the cooked eggless noodles on a plate and top with the Stroganoff. Garnish with parsley and serve.

Stuffed Portabella Mushrooms

The largest of the cultivated mushrooms, portabellas (aka portobellos) have open veils and flat caps that can measure up to six inches in diameter. To maintain their high quality, refrigerate portabellas as soon as you get them home. Store the mushrooms in paper bags, never in plastic which retains too much moisture. Or, if the portabellas are covered with plastic, remove and wrap loosely with paper towels. When ready to use, wipe off the portabellas with a damp towel. This recipe serves two. Simply multiply the recipe for additional servings.

Ingredients:

- 2 large portabella mushrooms, stems removed
- 2 slices whole grain bread, lightly toasted and processed into crumbs
- 2 T extra-virgin olive oil
- 1/2 onion or 2 shallots, finely chopped
- 1/4 cup shredded or finely chopped carrot
- 1 stalk celery, finely diced
- 2 tsp minced garlic (2 cloves)
- 4 white or brown mushrooms, diced
- 1/2 tsp poultry seasoning
- 2 T minced fresh parsley or 2 tsp dried
- 2 T nutritional yeast
- 1/4 cup vegetable broth or chik'n broth (see pg. 121-122 for broth options)
- 1/2 tsp salt
- freshly ground black pepper
- 2 tsp extra-virgin olive oil
- 1 cup white wine (dry, not sweet) or additional broth

Technique:

Preheat oven to 375°F.

Remove the gills from portabella mushrooms with a sharp spoon. Set aside.

Heat the extra-virgin olive oil in a large skillet and sauté the onions, carrots and celery until tender. Add the mushrooms, garlic and poultry seasoning; continue to sauté for 2 minutes. Transfer to a large mixing bowl.

Add the parsley, bread crumbs, nutritional yeast and broth; season with salt and pepper to taste. Mix thoroughly until the ingredients begin to hold together. Let cool for about 15 minutes.

Mound a portion of stuffing into each mushroom cavity. Drizzle 2 tsp of extra-virgin olive oil into a shallow casserole dish; sprinkle the bottom of the dish with a pinch of salt and place the stuffed mushrooms into the dish. Pour the white wine (or broth) around the mushrooms. Bake uncovered about 30 minutes or until golden brown. Serve immediately.

Chesapeake Bay "Seafood" Cakes

These "seafood" cakes are reminiscent in taste and texture of New England crab cakes, and are sure to be an impressive first course or light entrée for your next vegan dinner party.

"Seafood" Cake Ingredients:

- 1 block (about 14 oz) firm or extra firm tofu, drained (do not use silken tofu)
- 2 T extra-virgin olive oil
- 1/4 cup finely diced green onion, including some of the green tops
- 1/4 cup finely diced onion
- 2 ribs celery, finely diced
- 1/2 sheet nori seaweed (optional)
- 2 tsp minced garlic (2 cloves)
- 2 T nutritional yeast flakes
- 1 T cornstarch (preferably non-GMO) or arrowroot powder
- 1 and 1/2 tsp Chesapeake Bay™ or Old Bay™ seasoning
- 1/2 tsp sea salt or kosher salt, or more to taste
- 1/4 tsp white pepper
- 2 T fresh lemon juice
- 1/2 cup plain dry breadcrumbs, regular or panko

For the breadcrumb coating, mix together in a bowl:

- 1 cup plain dry breadcrumbs, regular or panko
- 2 tsp Chesapeake Bay™ or Old Bay™ seasoning

In a separate bowl whisk together:

- 1/2 cup plain unsweetened non-dairy milk
- 2 T No Eggy Mayo (pg. 105) or commercial vegan mayonnaise

Technique:

Press the tofu to remove the excess moisture (see Preparing Tofu for Recipes, pg. 56).

Sauté the onion and celery with the extra-virgin olive oil in a skillet until the onion is translucent. Crumble or tear the optional seaweed into small pieces; add to the skillet with the garlic and sauté an additional minute. Set aside to cool.

Break up the tofu into a food processor and add the nutritional yeast, cornstarch or arrowroot powder, Chesapeake Bay™ or Old Bay™ seasoning, salt, white pepper and lemon juice.

Pulse the mixture several times until crumbly. The goal is to retain some texture, so avoid over-processing or you will end up with a paste. Transfer the mixture to a bowl and incorporate 1/2 cup of the bread crumbs. Mix thoroughly. Taste the mixture and add additional salt if needed.

Form patties from the mixture, about 3 to 4-inches in diameter and 1/2-inch thick.

Lay the patties on a plate or baking sheet lined with parchment or wax paper; cover with plastic wrap and refrigerate for at least one hour.

In a skillet, heat 1/4-inch of oil over medium heat. Dip the patties gently in the milk/mayo mixture and dredge in the breadcrumb/seasoning mixture. Handle them carefully to avoid breaking them. When the surface of the oil begins to shimmer, fry the patties until golden brown on both sides. Drain on a paper towel and keep warm in a low oven until you are finished cooking.

Top with Creamy Horseradish Sauce (pg. 205) or Rémoulade Sauce (pg. 211), if desired.

Scalloped Potatoes Gratin
An American favorite!

Ingredients:

- Better Butter (pg. 62) or vegan margarine
- 1 T flour (unbleached all-purpose wheat; rice or soy)
- 1 and 1/2 cups plain unsweetened non-dairy milk
- 1/4 cup nutritional yeast
- 1 sprig fresh thyme or 1/2 tsp dried thyme
- 2 garlic cloves, minced (about 2 tsp)
- 1/2 teaspoon ground nutmeg
- 2 pounds russet potatoes (about 4 potatoes)
- sea salt or kosher salt and ground black pepper
- 1 cup shredded vegan cheese that melts, your choice of flavor (i.e., Daiya™)

Technique:

Preheat the oven to 375° F.

In a saucepan over medium heat, melt 2 tablespoons of the butter or margarine and whisk in the flour to create a roux. Cook for a minute stirring constantly - do not let the roux turn brown. Slowly whisk in the milk. Add the nutritional yeast, thyme, minced garlic and nutmeg. Bring to a boil, stirring constantly. Remove from the heat, fold in the shredded cheese to melt, cover pot and set aside.

Now, peel and thinly slice your potatoes (about 1/8-inch thick). A mandoline works great for this, but watch your fingers!

Next, "butter" a casserole dish with the butter or margarine. Place a layer of potato slices in an overlapping pattern and season with salt and pepper. Spoon a little of the cheese mixture over the potatoes and spread evenly.

Continue to layer the potatoes with a sprinkle of salt and pepper and the cheese mixture.

Bake uncovered for 45 minutes. Set the oven on "broil" and cook an additional 5 minutes or until top begins to brown nicely.

Easy Skillet Chili

This recipe is easy to prepare; it's tasty and healthy, with just the right amount of spice. Chili Chedda' Cornbread (pg. 151) is a perfect accompaniment for this dish.

Ingredients:

- 2 T extra-virgin olive oil
- 1 large onion, diced
- 1/2 bell pepper, diced
- 1 stalk celery, diced
- 1 (4.5 oz) can diced green chilies
- 1 T minced garlic (3 cloves)
- 2 cups water
- 2 T tamari, soy sauce, Bragg Liquid Aminos™
  or 2 tsp Better Than Bouillon™ No Beef base
- 1 T chili powder
- 2 tsp oregano
- 1 bay leaf
- 1 tsp ground cumin
- 1/4 tsp ground red pepper, or to taste (optional)
- 1 cup TVP granules (textured vegetable protein)
- 1 large can (28 oz) organic diced tomatoes
- 1 can pinto beans (15 oz), rinsed very well and drained
- sea salt or kosher salt to taste

Technique:

In a skillet over medium heat, sauté the onion, green pepper and celery in oil until the onion is translucent. Add the green chilies and garlic; sauté for a minute or two more.

Add the water, tamari/soy sauce/liquid aminos or bouillon paste and additional spices/seasonings.

Increase the heat, bringing the mixture to a boil. Add the TVP, stir well and then reduce heat to a simmer.

Add the tomatoes with their liquid and the rinsed pinto beans and simmer for about 30 minutes to blend the flavors.

Taste and adjust seasonings if necessary. Remove the bay leaf before serving.

Garnish with a dollop of vegan sour cream if desired.

Chili Chedda' Cornbread

A moist, savory cornbread flavored with green chilies, jalapeno, onion and vegan cheddar cheese. This bread is the perfect accompaniment for my Easy Skillet Chili on pg. 150.

Ingredients:

- 1 and 1/4 cup plain unsweetened soymilk (sorry, no substitutions)
- 2 tsp raw apple cider vinegar
- 2 T Better Butter (pg. 62) or vegan margarine
- 1 small onion, finely chopped (about 1 cup)
- 1 small can (4 oz) diced mild green chilies, drained
- 1 fresh jalapeno, seeded and minced
- 1 and 1/4 cups unbleached all-purpose wheat flour
- 3/4 cup corn meal
- 1/4 cup nutritional yeast
- 2 tsp baking powder
- 1 tsp onion powder
- 1 and 1/2 tsp fine sea salt or kosher salt
- 1/4 cup (4 T) Better Butter (pg. 62) or vegan margarine
- 1/2 cup shredded vegan cheddar cheese that melts (i.e. Daiya™)

Technique:

In a small bowl, mix together the soymilk and raw apple cider vinegar and set aside to curdle and thicken for a minimum of 15 minutes.

Lightly oil an 8 or 9-inch square baking pan. Preheat oven to 375°F.

In a skillet over medium heat, melt 2 tablespoons of the butter or margarine and sauté the onions, green chilies and jalapeno until the onions are lightly browned, about 5 minutes. Add the 1/4 cup butter or margarine to the skillet to melt. Remove from heat and set aside.

Combine the flour, corn meal, yeast, baking powder, onion powder and salt in a large mixing bowl. Mix thoroughly.

Pour the curdled soymilk mixture into the dry ingredients and stir just enough until ingredients are moistened. Fold in the skillet mixture and the vegan cheddar cheese. Stir to combine but do not over mix or the cornbread will be dense.

Spoon the batter into an 8" baking pan. Smooth the top and place into oven. Bake about 25 to 30 minutes until the bread feels firm to the touch and the top just begins to crack. DO NOT over bake.

Cool for a minimum of 15 to 20 minutes before slicing and serving.

Grilled Portabella Mushrooms

Ingredients:

- 4 large portabella mushrooms
- sea salt or kosher salt and pepper, to taste

For the marinade, whisk together:

- 1/2 cup extra-virgin olive oil
- 1/4 cup red wine vinaigrette or balsamic vinaigrette
- 1/4 cup tamari or soy sauce
- 2 T homemade vegan Worcestershire Sauce (pg. 206) or commercial
- 1 tsp onion powder
- 2 tsp fresh garlic, minced
- 1/4 tsp ground black pepper
- 2 tsp prepared Dijon mustard

Technique:

Gently remove the stems from the mushrooms. Remove the gills from the mushrooms by scraping with the edge of sharp spoon. Place in a roomy plastic container (or zip-lock bag) and pour the marinade over the mushrooms. Seal with a lid, gently turn upside down and right-side up a few times to coat evenly and let stand for a minimum of 30 minutes before grilling.

Spray a non-stick skillet or grill pan with cooking oil spray (for an outdoor grill, "season" the rack with a paper towel dipped in vegetable oil) and place the skillet or grill pan over medium-high heat.

Grill the mushrooms hollow side down 5-8 minutes and turn. Baste the mushrooms with the marinade while grilling.

Continue to grill hollow side up another 5-8 minutes until juices are evident. Serve with potatoes, rice, risotto, couscous or quinoa and vegetables of your choice.

Note: The mushrooms can also be broiled in the oven.

Shepherd's Pie

Ingredients:

- 4 cups diced potatoes
- 2 T vegetable oil
- 1 large onion
- 2 tsp minced garlic
- 1 cup baby peas (from a can or thawed from frozen)
- 2 cups sliced mushrooms

- a pinch or two of thyme
- 2 tsp dried parsley
- salt and pepper to taste
- 2 cups Golden Gravy (pg. 205)
- 10 oz thinly sliced Beaf Seitan (pg. 9)
- 1 sheet puff pastry dough, thawed (such as Pepperidge Farms™)

Technique:

Add the onions and potatoes to a skillet with the vegetable oil; cover and cook over medium heat until the potatoes are tender, about 20 to 25 minutes, stirring every 5 minutes or so.

Add the garlic, thyme, parsley, peas and mushrooms and cook until the mushrooms have released most of their moisture; season with salt and pepper to taste.

Transfer the mixture to a lightly oiled shallow casserole dish. Top with the sliced seitan and golden gravy. Place the pastry sheet on top, cut off the excess and tuck in the edges. Brush with a small amount of extra-virgin olive oil or melted Better Butter (pg. 62) or vegan margarine.

Bake uncovered at 350°F for approximately 30-40 minutes or until the pastry is golden.

Herbed Scallion Rice

*Cooking the rice in a puree of fresh cilantro, parsley
and scallions adds flavor and a vibrant green color.*

Ingredients:

- 1 and 2/3 cups water
- 1/2 cup packed fresh parsley
- 1/4 cup packed fresh cilantro
- 3 scallions (including green) chopped

- 2 garlic cloves (or 2 tsp minced garlic)
- 1 T vegetable oil
- 1 cup white jasmine rice
- 1 tsp sea salt or kosher salt

Technique:

In a blender, purée the parsley, cilantro and garlic with the water until smooth.

Heat the oil in a small saucepan over high heat. Add the rice and stir to coat with the oil. Cook until slightly toasted, about 1 to 2 minutes. Add the herb purée and salt. Bring to a boil, cover and reduce heat to low. Cook for 20 minutes. Remove from the heat and let stand for 10 minutes. Fluff with a fork before serving.

Yankee Pot Roast

Hearty and satisfying; this is vegan comfort food at its best! Prepare the seitan a day before final preparation of your gravy and vegetables to allow sufficient refrigeration time. Refrigeration will firm the seitan and optimize its texture.

Ingredients:

- 1 recipe Beef Seitan (pg. 9)
  or Seitan Mignon (pg. 13),
  thinly sliced (about 20 oz)
- 4 T vegetable oil (1/4 cup)
- 3 T flour (unbleached all-purpose wheat;
  rice or soy)
- 5 cups beef broth
  (see pg. 123 for broth options)
- 1 cup tomato juice
- 1 large onion, chopped
- 2 large carrots, chopped

- 2 ribs celery, chopped
- 1 T minced garlic (3 cloves)
- 2 large russet potatoes, peeled and cut into
  chunks
- 1 tsp dried thyme or 3 sprigs fresh
- 1 bay leaf
- 8 oz white or brown mushrooms, quartered
- 1/2 cup baby peas
  (fresh, frozen or canned)
- 1 tsp Gravy Master™ - optional
- 1/2 tsp ground black pepper

Technique:

Brown the seitan slices in a cooking pot with a small amount of vegetable oil over medium heat. Remove and set aside.

In the same pot over medium heat, combine 3 T oil and flour together to make a paste (roux). Cook for about two minutes to eliminate any raw flour taste. SLOWLY but vigorously whisk in the beef broth until smooth. Stir in the tomato juice and bring to a boil.

Now add the remaining ingredients (except for the seitan). Bring back to a gentle simmer, cover the pot and cook until the vegetables are very tender and the potatoes are beginning to break down, about 1 hour. Add salt to taste as needed.

Add the seitan slices and simmer an additional 10 minutes. Remove the bay leaf.

Transfer the seitan, vegetables and gravy to a serving dish.

Battered or Breaded "Seafood" Fillets

Delicate tofu "fillets" are dredged in your choice of a pub-style beer batter or breaded with a crispy breadcrumb coating and then fried.

For the "fillets", drain and press 1 block (about 14 oz) firm or extra-firm tofu (do not use silken tofu), removing as much water as possible (see Preparing Tofu for Recipes, pg. 56). Slice the tofu into 6 - 8 pieces. You can also slice each "fillet" in half lengthwise to create "sticks".

1) Pub-Style Beer Batter

Whisk together the batter ingredients:

- 1/2 cup unbleached all-purpose wheat flour
- 2/3 cup beer (alcoholic or non-alcoholic)
- 1 T Old Bay™ or Chesapeake Bay™ seasoning
- 1/2 sheet nori seaweed*, finely ground (optional)

Technique:

Dip the tofu slices in the batter and fry in 1/2-inch hot vegetable oil until browned and crispy, about 1 to 2 minutes for each side. Watch them because they cook quickly. Drain on paper towels. Serve while still hot with vegan tartar sauce (vegan mayo and dill relish) or malt vinegar for dipping.

*To grind the nori seaweed, tear 1/2 sheet nori seaweed into pieces; place with the flour and seasoning into a mini-blender and pulse to a fine powder.

2) Breadcrumb Coating

Ingredients:

- flour (unbleached all-purpose wheat; rice or soy)
- 1 T Old Bay™ or Chesapeake Bay™ seasoning
- 1/2 sheet nori seaweed*, finely ground (optional)
- 2 T No-Eggy Mayo (pg. 105) or commercial vegan mayonnaise 1/2 cup plain unsweetened non-dairy milk
- unseasoned regular or Panko breadcrumbs

Technique:

In one bowl, combine 1/2 cup flour with the seasoning and the ground nori seaweed*.

In another bowl, slowly whisk the milk into the mayonnaise until smooth. And in a third bowl, place 1/2 cup breadcrumbs (replenish as needed). Dip your cutlets or nuggets first into the seasoned flour, coating well, then into the milk/mayonnaise mixture and then into the breadcrumbs, again coating well.

Fry in 1/2-inch hot vegetable oil until browned and crispy, about 1 to 2 minutes for each side. Watch them because they cook quickly. Drain on paper towels. Serve hot with vegan tartar sauce (vegan mayo and dill relish) or cocktail sauce (prepared horseradish and ketchup).

Garden Seitan Meatloaf

This is an original recipe created after many trials and disappointments with other vegan meatloaf recipes. It's firm, yet tender and moist with a nice balance of seasonings. This meatloaf takes longer to bake than most other meatloaf recipes, but is well worth the wait. Like most seitan recipes, it's even better reheated the next day.

Dry ingredients:

- 1 and 1/2 cup vital wheat gluten
- 2 T garbanzo bean (chickpea) flour
- 1 tsp onion powder
- 1 tsp cornstarch (preferably non-GMO), potato starch or arrowroot powder

Wet ingredients:

- 2 cups water
- 1/4 cup nutritional yeast
- 2 T soy sauce, tamari or Bragg Liquid Aminos™
- 1 T homemade vegan Worcestershire Sauce (pg. 206) or commercial
- 1 T prepared yellow or golden mustard
- 1/2 tsp Gravy Master™ or other browning liquid - optional

Sauté ingredients:

- 2 T vegetable oil
- 1/2 cup finely diced onion (about 1 small onion)
- 1/2 cup green or red bell pepper, very finely diced (about 1/2 of a pepper)
- 1 average sized carrot, shredded
- 1 rib celery, very finely diced
- 1 T minced garlic (3 cloves)
- 2 tsp dried parsley
- 1/2 tsp dried thyme
- 1/4 tsp ground black pepper, or more to taste

Technique:

Preheat the oven to 350°F. Oil a 9x5 metal loaf pan and set aside. Alternately, you can line the loaf pan with a strip of parchment paper; this way the meatloaf can be easily lifted out when done.

Sift together the dry ingredients in a large mixing bowl; set aside.

Combine the wet ingredients in a large bowl or measuring cup. Don't worry about dispersing the mustard completely. Set aside.

In a skillet over medium heat, sauté the onion, bell pepper, celery and carrot in the vegetable oil until the onion is translucent. Add the minced garlic, thyme and black pepper and sauté just until the vegetables are beginning to lightly brown. Mix the vegetables into the wet ingredients (this will also help disperse the mustard into the liquid).

Add the liquid ingredients with the mixed vegetables to the dry mixture. Mix until thoroughly combined. The dough will be very wet; this is normal.

Transfer the dough (including all of the liquid that may not have absorbed into the dough) to the loaf pan, spreading and packing evenly. Seal the loaf pan securely with foil. Place in the oven and bake for 90 minutes.

While the meatloaf is baking, mix together 1/4 cup ketchup, 2 tsp prepared yellow or golden mustard and a dash of homemade vegan Worcestershire Sauce (pg. 206) or commercial vegan Worcestershire in a small bowl. Set aside.

After 90 minutes, remove the pan from the oven, remove the foil and brush on the ketchup/mustard mixture (the meatloaf will still be very soft at this point - don't panic); return to the oven and bake uncovered for 30 minutes.

Remove the meatloaf from the oven and let cool for about 15 minutes before slicing and serving. The meatloaf will have an even better texture after refrigeration and reheating the following day (which is typical of many seitan recipes).

Sautéed Peppers and Onions

Use as a topping for your favorite sandwich or as a garnish for rice, quinoa or couscous.

Ingredients:

- 1 T Better Butter (pg. 62), vegan margarine or extra-virgin olive oil
- 1 large onion
- 1 large red bell pepper or Hungarian sweet wax pepper, seeded
- 1 large green bell pepper, seeded

- 3 large banana peppers, seeded (or 1 yellow bell pepper)
- 2 tsp brown sugar
- 2 tsp white wine vinegar
- 1/2 tsp crushed red pepper
- sea salt or kosher salt, to taste

Technique:

Julienne the onion and peppers (thinly slice). Place a skillet over medium-high heat. Add the butter, margarine or extra-virgin olive oil. Add the onion and sauté until softened. Reduce heat to medium, and add the peppers. Add salt to taste, and sauté until the peppers begin to soften. Add the brown sugar, vinegar, and crushed red pepper. Continue cooking over medium heat until the liquid has reduced significantly, and the peppers and onions are tender and lightly caramelized.

Fried Chik'n

Golden, crispy and delicious! Serve with your favorite dipping sauce, if desired. This breading recipe is also excellent for tofu or tempeh cutlets or nuggets. You can also use any commercial variety of vegan chicken. The secret for the breading is the mayonnaise, which helps the breadcrumbs adhere very well. My stepson, who is a very fussy eater, loved these chik'n nuggets. I like mine served cold too - there's nothing better than cold fried chik'n at a Summer picnic.

Ingredients:

- 1 recipe (about 20 oz) Chik'n Seitan cutlets or nuggets (pg. 11) or commercial vegan chicken
- flour (unbleached all-purpose wheat; rice or soy)
- 2 T No-Eggy Mayo (pg. 105) or commercial vegan mayonnaise
- 1/2 cup plain unsweetened non-dairy milk
- seasoned (or unseasoned) regular or Panko breadcrumbs
- vegetable oil for frying

Technique:

In one bowl, place about 1/2 cup flour. In another bowl, slowly whisk the soymilk into the mayonnaise until smooth. In a third bowl, place 1/2 cup breadcrumbs (replenish as needed).

In a large skillet over medium heat, heat about a 1/2-inch of vegetable oil until the oil begins to shimmer. Test with a few breadcrumbs; if they brown quickly, the oil is hot enough. The goal is to brown the coating quickly so the seitan does not dry out; so be sure the oil is sufficiently heated.

Dip your cutlets or nuggets first into the flour, coating well, then into the milk/mayonnaise mixture and then into the breadcrumbs, again coating well.

Fry in the hot oil, turning occasionally, until golden brown. Remove to a plate lined with paper towels.

Serve with a dipping sauce of your choice, if desired, such as Skye's Best BBQ Sauce (pg. 208) or "Buttermilk" Ranch Dressing (pg. 111).

Creole Jambalaya

Jambalaya originated in the Caribbean Islands. The Spanish culture mixed with the native foods and created what we know as Jambalaya. The Chik'n Seitan and Andouille Sausage in this recipe should be prepared a day ahead; the Jambalaya itself is quick and easy to prepare; serves 4.

Ingredients:

- 1 cup enriched white or brown rice
- 1/4 cup (4 T) Better Butter (pg. 62), vegan margarine or extra-virgin olive oil
- 10 oz Chik'n Seitan cutlets (pg. 11) or commercial vegan chicken, thinly sliced and cut into bite-sized pieces
- 4 Andouille Sausage (pg. 45), sliced
- 1 medium onion, diced
- 1 rib celery, diced
- 1/2 green bell pepper, diced
- 1 bay leaf
- several drops red hot sauce or 2 pinches cayenne pepper
- 2 T flour (unbleached all-purpose wheat; rice or soy)
- 1 (14-ounce) can diced tomatoes in juice
- 2 cups chik'n broth (see pg. 121-122 for broth options)
- 1 tsp cumin
- 1 tsp chili powder
- 1 tsp poultry seasoning
- 1 tsp homemade vegan Worcestershire Sauce (pg. 206) or commercial
- coarse salt and black pepper
- chopped scallions or snipped chives, for garnish (optional)
- fresh thyme, chopped for garnish (optional)

Technique:

Cook the rice according to package directions. Heat 2 tablespoons of the butter, margarine or oil in a large, deep skillet over medium-high heat. Add the chik'n and Andouille sausage and brown, about 5 minutes. Transfer to a bowl and set aside. Heat an additional 2 tablespoons of the butter, margarine or oil in the skillet. Add the onion, celery, green pepper and hot sauce or cayenne to the same skillet. Sauté until the vegetables are tender and the onions are beginning to caramelize.

Sprinkle the flour over the vegetables in the skillet and cook 1 or 2 minutes more. Stir in the tomatoes (with liquid) and the chik'n broth. Add the bay leaf, cumin, chili powder, poultry seasoning and vegan Worcestershire. Bring the mixture to a boil and then reduce heat to a simmer. Add the chik'n and sausage and simmer uncovered for 10 minutes.

Remove the skillet from the heat and place on a trivet. Ladle the jambalaya into shallow bowls. Using an ice cream scoop, place a scoop of rice in the center of the bowls of jambalaya. Sprinkle with salt, pepper, chopped scallions or chives, and thyme leaves.

Easy Stuffed Bell Peppers

Tender bell peppers are stuffed with a mixture of seasoned vegan "ground beef", rice and onions and topped with a tangy tomato sauce.

Ingredients:

- 3 large or 4 average-size green bell peppers
- extra-virgin olive oil
- 1 medium onion, finely diced
- 3 cloves finely minced garlic (3 T)
- 2 T tamari, soy sauce or Bragg Liquid Aminos™
- 1/2 tsp ground cumin
- 1/4 tsp ground black pepper, or more to taste
- pinch of red pepper flakes
- 1 tsp Gravy Master™ or other browning liquid
- 1 cup TVP granules (textured vegetable protein) - I use Bob's Red Mill™ brand
- 1 can (about 15 oz) tomato sauce
- 1/2 cup dry white basmati rice*
- 1/4 cup chopped fresh parsley
- additional sea salt or kosher salt and coarse ground black pepper to taste

*You can also use 2 cups cooked rice, couscous or quinoa of your choice and omit cooking the basmati rice according to the recipe.

Technique:

Remove the tops and seeds from the bell peppers. Parboil the peppers in rapidly boiling water in a large pot for about 4 to 5 minutes. Remove to drain and set aside.

In a small saucepan, bring 1 cup water to a boil and add the 1/2 cup basmati rice with 1 T extra-virgin olive oil. Reduce heat to a gentle simmer (low heat), cover and cook for 15 minutes or until all of the water is absorbed.

Preheat the oven to 350°F.

Meanwhile, while the rice is cooking, sauté the onions and garlic in a skillet with 2 tablespoons extra-virgin olive oil until tender. Add 1 and 1/3 cups water, the tamari/soy sauce or Liquid Aminos, cumin, black pepper, red pepper flakes and optional Gravy Master™. Bring to a boil and add the TVP. Reduce heat to low and cover for 10 minutes. After 10 minutes, remove the lid and continue to cook on low for an additional 5 to 10 minutes, stirring occasionally, until the mixture resembles moist ground beef.

When the rice is finished cooking, fluff the rice with a fork and add to the skillet with the TVP mixture. Stir in 1/2 can tomato sauce and the chopped parsley. Mix well. Taste and add additional salt if needed.

Lightly oil a baking dish that will accommodate the bell peppers. Pack the bell peppers with the TVP/rice mixture and place into the dish. Top with the remaining tomato sauce, season with salt and pepper and bake uncovered for 30 minutes.

Chik'n Fried "Steak" with Country Gravy

An American diner classic!

Ingredients:

- vegetable oil
- 1 recipe (about 20 oz) simmered Beaf Seitan cutlets (pg. 9)
- 2/3 cup flour (unbleached all-purpose wheat; rice or soy) or more as needed
- 2 T No-Eggy Mayo (pg. 105) or commercial vegan mayonnaise
- 2/3 cup non-dairy milk
- 2 cups chik'n broth (see pg. 121-122 for broth options)
- 2/3 cup plain dry fine breadcrumbs, or more as needed
- 3 sprigs fresh thyme or 1/2 tsp dried
- ground black pepper
- sea salt or kosher salt

Technique:

In one bowl, place the flour. In a second bowl, place the fine breadcrumbs. In a third bowl, add the mayonnaise and then slowly whisk in the non-dairy milk until smooth. Dredge one of the steaks in the flour, then in the milk/mayo mixture and finally in the breadcrumbs, coating well. Season with salt and pepper and set aside. Repeat with the remaining steaks.

Add enough of the vegetable oil to cover the bottom of a large skillet (about 1/2 cup) and place over medium heat.

Once the oil begins to shimmer, add the breaded "steaks". Cook each piece on both sides until golden brown, approximately 3 to 4 minutes per side. They will brown fairly quickly, so keep an eye on them.

Remove the "steaks" to a plate lined with a paper towel and cover with another towel to keep warm. Leave the residual oil in the skillet.

In the same skillet over medium heat, whisk 4 T of flour left over from the dredging (there should be sufficient, if not, use additional) into the residual oil. Stir until smooth and cook for about a minute. S-l-o-w-l-y whisk in the broth, stirring vigorously until the mixture is smooth (there will be fine flecks of fried breadcrumbs in the gravy but this just adds to its country-style character).

Add the thyme and stir frequently until the gravy comes to a boil and begins to thicken. Add the milk and stir until combined. Reduce heat and simmer approximately 5 to 10 minutes. Season the gravy to taste with ground black pepper and additional salt if needed.

Arrange the "steaks" on a plate and ladle the gravy on top (you can slice them into quarters for presentation, or leave them whole). There should be ample gravy to dress mashed potatoes as well.

Caraway Cabbage

The perfect accompaniment for Corned Beaf (pg. 20).

Ingredients:

- 1 head green cabbage
- 1 large onion, sliced
- 1 tsp caraway seeds
- 1 T raw apple cider vinegar
- Better Butter (pg. 62) or vegan margarine
- salt and pepper to taste

Technique:

Clean the cabbage by removing the outer layer of leaves. Cut the cabbage head into quarters and then rinse under cold running water.

Using a stainless steel knife cut the stem off of each cabbage quarter. To shred by hand, place the cabbage with flat side down on a cutting board. Cut the cabbage in slices to desired thickness. You can also shred the cabbage by using a kitchen mandoline or a food processor.

Add the cabbage to a large cooking pot and cover completely with cold water. Add vinegar and caraway seeds. Bring to boil then reduce heat, cover and simmer about 30 – 40 minutes or until the cabbage is tender but not mushy.

Drain in a colander. Caraway seeds that remain with the cabbage are desired for flavor, so do not rinse them out (unless you absolutely cannot tolerate a caraway seed getting stuck in your teeth).

Next, in a skillet over medium heat, sauté the onion in 4 tablespoons of the butter or margarine until the onion is translucent. Add the cabbage and continue to sauté, about 10 minutes, until the flavors are blended; season with salt and pepper to taste. Serve piping hot.

Slow-Cooker Stuffed Cabbage Rolls

Cabbage rolls bring back fond childhood memories of time spent on my aunt's farm. My aunt called them 'golumpkis', which is a rural Pennsylvania twist of the Polish 'golabkis'. My father and I always made these around the holidays too, and we would compete to see whose rolls were the tastiest. Here is my vegan version of this nostalgic and timeless recipe. I'm pleased to say these rolls are very similar to the original in both taste and texture. I hope you enjoy them too.

For the slow-cooker ingredients you will need:

- 1 head green cabbage
- 2 cans (28oz each) diced or crushed tomatoes with juice
- 2 T tamari, soy sauce or Bragg Liquid Aminos™
- 1 large onion sliced thin
- 1/4 cup fresh lemon juice
- 1/4 cup brown sugar
- sea salt or kosher salt and ground black pepper to taste

Thoroughly stir together the following dry ingredients in a large mixing bowl:

- 1 cup vital wheat gluten
- 1/2 cup dry "instant" or "quick cooking" brown or white rice
- 2 T nutritional yeast
- 2 T garbanzo bean (chickpea) flour
- 1 T dried minced or flaked onion
- 1 tsp onion powder
- 1 tsp garlic powder
- 1/4 tsp ground black pepper

For the wet ingredients, mix together the following in a separate bowl or measuring cup:

- 3/4 cup water
- 2 T tamari, soy sauce or Bragg Liquid Aminos™
- 1 T vegetable oil
- 2 tsp minced garlic (2 cloves)
- 1/2 tsp sea salt or kosher salt

Technique:

Core the cabbage and simmer whole in water in a large stockpot until the leaves begin to loosen. Remove the leaves as they loosen with tongs and drain on paper towels. Cut the tough rib from each leaf using a "V" shaped cut. Set aside.

In a large bowl combine the dry ingredients. Pour the wet ingredients (not the slow-cooker ingredients) into the dry ingredients. Mix thoroughly to combine (it may seem a bit dry) but DO NOT knead the dough, as kneading will make the filling less tender.

Tear off a small amount of the filling mixture and place onto a cabbage leaf and roll up, folding in the sides as you roll. Do not use too much filling, as the filling will expand to twice its size when slow-cooked. Roll the cabbage loosely to allow for expansion. Continue until all the filling is used. Set aside.

Place excess cabbage leaves into the bottom of the slow-cooker. Top with the cabbage rolls, sliced onion, diced tomatoes with juice, tamari/soy sauce or Liquid Aminos, brown sugar, lemon juice, a sprinkle of salt and a generous amount of ground pepper. Do not stir the slow-cooker contents as the ingredients will combine while slow-cooking.

Slow-cook on high for 2 hours and then reduce heat to low for an additional 2 hours or until the cabbage is very tender and the heavenly aroma fills the kitchen. About halfway through cooking time, taste the sauce and add salt if necessary. Adjust sweet and sour flavor by adding a little more lemon juice or brown sugar as necessary. Continue to slow cook until time is complete.

Roasted Cauliflower

Simple and wonderful! Roasting brings out the sweet flavor of the cauliflower.

Ingredients:

- 1 head of cauliflower, cut into florets
- 2 T extra-virgin olive oil
- 3 tsp minced garlic (3 cloves)
- sea salt or kosher salt and coarse ground black pepper

Technique:

Preheat the oven to 425°F. Toss the cauliflower, extra-virgin olive oil and garlic together in a large bowl. Season generously with salt (course ground is best) and pepper.

Spread the cauliflower in a single layer on a baking sheet and roast 20 to 25 minutes until browned on the edges. Serve hot. If desired, drizzle with a little balsamic vinaigrette before serving.

Perfect Asparagus

Asparagus is a wonderful vegetable that can be briefly simmered, roasted, grilled, sautéed or steamed. Overcooking asparagus makes it stringy and unappetizing, so here I've included two of my favorite methods for preparing crisp yet tender asparagus.

Preparation: First you will need to prepare your asparagus by trimming off any woody ends. For thicker stalks, peel the woody exterior a bit with a potato peeler.

Simmer Method

For the simmer method, the secret is a brief cooking time. I prefer thin asparagus, but for thicker varieties, increase the simmering time by about 30 seconds to 1 minute.

Fill a large skillet with about 2 inches of water, or enough to cover the asparagus when added. Do not add salt at this time; it will toughen the asparagus.

Bring the water to a boil in the skillet. Add the asparagus; reduce heat and simmer for 3-4 minutes. DO NOT exceed 4 minutes unless the asparagus is extremely thick.

Quickly remove the asparagus with a slotted spoon to a serving plate. Sprinkle with a little coarse sea salt, a squeeze of lemon and coarse ground pepper. Serve immediately.

Roast Method

Trim your asparagus as described above. Preheat the oven to 425°F. Place the asparagus in a single layer on a cookie sheet. Drizzle generously with a good quality extra-virgin olive oil and toss to coat; season with coarse ground salt and pepper. Roast for exactly 18 minutes. Sprinkle with a squeeze of lemon and serve immediately.

Crisp tender-cooked asparagus is also wonderful chilled and served as an appetizer (drizzle with a little fresh lemon juice or balsamic vinaigrette, if desired.) Lemon Mustard Sauce (pg. 218) or Hollandaise Sauce (pg. 216) pairs well with asparagus too.

Green Bean Casserole

A timeless holiday favorite!

Ingredients:

- 2 T Better Butter (pg. 62) or vegan margarine
- 1 and 1/2 cups minced white mushrooms
- 2 T flour (unbleached all-purpose wheat; rice or soy)
- 1 and 1/2 cups plain unsweetened non-dairy milk
- 1 T tamari, soy sauce or Bragg Liquid Aminos™
- 1 tsp garlic powder
- 1 tsp onion powder
- 2 cans (14oz each) organic cut green beans, well drained - or 1 and 1/2 lbs. cooked fresh green beans trimmed into bite-size pieces
- 1 and 1/3 cups French-fried onions (from canned - French's™ are vegan) - or make your own, the recipe and technique follows this recipe
- sea salt or kosher salt and ground black pepper to taste

Technique:

Preheat the oven to 350°F.

In a skillet over medium heat, melt the butter or margarine. Add the mushrooms and sauté until the excess liquid has evaporated from the mushrooms. Whisk in the flour and continue to cook for about a minute.

Slowly whisk in the milk. Add the tamari/soy sauce or Liquid Aminos, garlic powder, onion powder and a pinch of black pepper and bring to a boil, stirring constantly.

Reduce heat and simmer an additional 2 to 3 minutes. Taste and add salt to your liking and additional black pepper, if desired. Remove from the heat.

Lightly "butter" a casserole dish with the butter or margarine and combine the mushroom creme mixture with the green beans and 2/3 cup French-fried onions in the casserole dish.

Bake uncovered for 25 minutes or until the bean mixture is hot and bubbling. Stir and top with the remaining 2/3 cup onions. Bake for an additional 5 minutes or until the onions are golden brown.

French-Fried Onions

Golden, crispy and delicious!

Ingredients:

- 2 or 3 large or 5 medium sweet yellow onions
- plain unsweetened non-dairy milk for soaking the onions
- 1 and 1/2 to 2 tsp sea salt or kosher salt (try the first batch and adjust the salt to taste)
- ground black pepper
- pinch of cayenne pepper
- 1 and 1/2 cups unbleached all-purpose wheat flour
- vegetable oil for frying

Technique:

Mix the flour, salt, and ground peppers in a large bowl. Slice the onions and separate into rings. Soak the onions in the milk. Heat about 1/2-inch of oil in a large skillet over medium-high heat until it begins to shimmer.

Dredge the onions in the seasoned flour. Give them a good coating of flour. Place the onions into the hot oil in the skillet. Don't try to do all the onions at one; just one batch at a time.

When the onions begin to brown around the edges, turn them over and cook an additional minute or so (they cook very quickly!) Remove the rings and lay them on a paper bag or paper towels to cool/drain. Serve immediately or store in an air-tight container for topping your casseroles.

Flash Sautéed Kale

The seasonings add a wonderful flavor to the kale; serves 2 to 4.

Ingredients:

- fresh kale, washed and dried thoroughly, leaves removed from stems and chopped into pieces (about 10 cups)
- 3 T extra-virgin olive oil
- 1/4 cup finely chopped shallot or red onion
- 3 cloves garlic, finely minced (1 T)
- 2 T balsamic vinegar
- sea salt or kosher salt and coarse ground black pepper to taste

Technique:

In a skillet or wok over medium heat, sauté the shallot or onion in the extra-virgin olive oil until translucent. Add the garlic and cook for a minute more. Turn the heat up to high and add the kale. Toss to coat well and cook just until the kale begins to wilt, about 1 minute. Add the balsamic vinegar and a few pinches of salt and pepper. Toss well and continue to sauté another minute or two until tender but not mushy. The leaves should retain their vibrancy. Remove from the heat and serve immediately.

Mac' and Cheese

American comfort food at its finest!

You will need:

- 2 cups dry elbow macaroni
- salted water

Ingredients for the roux:

- 1/4 cup vegetable oil
- 1/4 cup flour (unbleached
  all-purpose wheat; rice or soy)

Sauce ingredients to be whisked together in a large measuring cup:

- 2 cups plain unsweetened non-dairy milk
- 1/2 cup nutritional yeast
- 1 tsp onion powder
- 1 tsp ground dry mustard
- 1/2 tsp sea salt or kosher salt or to taste
- 1/2 tsp garlic powder
- 1/2 tsp paprika
- 1/4 tsp freshly grated nutmeg
- pinch of white pepper

Technique:

Prepare your macaroni according to package directions and until desired tenderness.

While the macaroni is cooking, prepare the roux by heating the oil over medium heat in a medium saucepan. Add the flour and stir until smooth. Cook until the roux turns a light, golden color, about 3 to 4 minutes.

Reduce the heat to medium-low and incorporate the milk mixture SLOWLY to the roux, a little bit at a time, while whisking continuously and vigorously until very smooth. If you add the milk mixture too fast, the sauce will get lumpy; so I repeat: add S-L-O-W-L-Y. Bring to a boil, stirring constantly and then reduce to a simmer. Cook for about 5 minutes, stirring frequently.

Season with salt if needed and keep warm on low heat until ready to use, stirring occasionally.

Drain your macaroni into a colander and add back to the cooking pot. Stir in the cheese sauce.

At this point, you can serve immediately; or transfer the macaroni and cheese to a lightly oiled 8-inch baking dish and top with 2 T fine breadcrumbs. Broil for 5 minutes or so until lightly browned on top and serve immediately.

British Fare

"Bangers" and Mash

Bangers and mash, also known as sausages and mash, is a traditional English dish made with mashed potatoes and sausages smothered with rich onion gravy. This dish has particular iconic significance as traditional British working-class fare. Presented for you is my vegan version of this traditional dish.

Ingredients:

- 3 pounds Yukon Gold potatoes, peeled and quartered (or substitute with russet)
- sea salt or kosher salt and ground black pepper
- 1/4 cup (4 T) Better Butter (pg. 62) or vegan margarine
- 1 cup Heavy Creme (pg. 64) or commercial vegan cream substitute (or substitute with plain unsweetened non-dairy milk)
- 3 T Dijon mustard
- 1 T vegetable oil
- 1 recipe "Bangers" sausage (pg. 46)
- 1 recipe Savory Onion Gravy (pg. 207)

Technique:

Place the potatoes in a large pot; cover with water. Add 2 tsp salt. Bring to a boil and cook until tender, 20 to 25 minutes.

While the potatoes are cooking, prepare the onion gravy and set aside on low heat to stay warm.

Drain the potatoes and transfer to a large mixing bowl, and mash with the butter or margarine. Mix in the milk and mustard. Season with salt and pepper to taste and whip with an electric beater until smooth. Cover to keep warm.

Heat the oil in a skillet over medium-high heat; brown the sausages on both sides, about 5 minutes. Remove to a dinner plate.

To serve, spoon the mashed potatoes onto a plate, top with sausages and smother in onion gravy.

Beaf Wellington with Mushroom Pâté

This is an elegant entree for a holiday dinner or any special occasion. This dish may sound rather complex, but if you follow the directions exactly, you cannot go wrong. The roast needs to be prepared the night before and then refrigerated before assembling this dish, so plan accordingly. Beaf Wellington is excellent served with Golden Gravy.

Ingredients:

- 1 Seitan Mignon (pg. 13)
- 2 T Dijon mustard
- 2 T vegetable oil
- 1/2 lb fresh mushrooms of your choice
- 2 T red wine (dry, not sweet) - for pan searing the roast
- 2 cloves chopped garlic

- 1/2 tsp dried thyme
- 6 ultra-thin slices of peppered Smoked Turk'y Roast (pg. 32), or Tofurky™ peppered deli slices
- 1 vegan puff pastry sheet, such as Pepperidge Farm™ , thawed from frozen
- coarse sea salt or kosher salt

Technique:

Prepare the Seitan Mignon and refrigerate for a minimum of 8 hours. To prepare your Wellington, brown the Seitan Mignon in 1 tablespoon vegetable oil. Set aside to cool.

Once cooled, brush the seitan on all sides with the mustard. Set aside.

Preheat the oven to 400°F. Chop the mushrooms and garlic. Place them into a food processor with the thyme and process into a paste. Heat the skillet on medium-high heat with 1 T vegetable oil. Scrape the mushroom purée into the skillet and cook down, allowing the mushrooms to release their moisture. When the excess moisture from the mushrooms has sufficiently simmered away, set aside the purée to cool.

Lay out a large piece of plastic wrap. Lay the deli slices on the plastic wrap so that they overlap slightly. Spread the mushroom mixture over the deli slices.

Place the Seitan Mignon in the middle, roll the mushroom pâté and deli slices over the roast, using the plastic wrap so that you can do this tightly.

Wrap into a tight barrel shape, twisting the ends of the plastic wrap to secure. Refrigerate for 10 minutes.

On a lightly floured work surface, lay out the puff pastry sheet. Unwrap the roast from the plastic wrap and place in the middle of the pastry dough. Fold the pastry around the roast, tucking in the ends. Gently stretch the dough if necessary to completely cover the roast.

Place the pastry-wrapped roast on a baking sheet, seam side down. Score the top of the pastry lightly with a sharp knife. Sprinkle the top with coarse salt. Bake for 25-35 minutes. The pastry should be nicely golden when done.

Remove from the oven and let rest for 10 minutes before slicing. Slice in 1/2-inch thick slices and serve with gravy if desired. To reheat, wrap in foil and warm in the oven - do not microwave.

South of the Border Cuisine

Seitan Asada Tacos

These tacos are reminiscent of the authentic Baja Mexican cuisine I enjoyed while living in Southern California. Asada is traditionally served with diced onion and fresh chopped cilantro on a warm corn tortilla, but a flour tortilla makes a great soft taco too. Additional toppings can be added if desired. This recipe makes 4 to 6 seitan asada tacos.

Ingredients:

- 1 recipe prepared Beaf Seitan cutlets (pg. 9), sliced lengthwise into strips; or commercial vegan "steak" strips
- vegetable oil to coat bottom of skillet
- 1 T minced garlic (3 cloves)
- 2 T fresh lime juice (and additional wedges of lime as a garnish)
- handful of fresh cilantro, chopped
- 1 onion, chopped or thinly sliced
- corn or flour tortillas
- salsa, Pico de Gallo and/or sliced avocado as extra toppings (optional)

In small dish, mix together dry spice ingredients:

- 2 tsp ground cumin
- 1 tsp onion powder
- 1 tsp oregano
- 1/2 tsp chili powder
- 1/4 to 1/2 tsp cayenne pepper or red pepper flakes (depending on how spicy you prefer)
- 1/4 tsp black pepper

Technique:

Heat the oil in a skillet over medium-high heat. Add the garlic and sauté for about 30 seconds. Add the "steak" strips and sprinkle with some of the dry spice mixture. Turn with a spatula to coat with the spice, vegetable oil and garlic and continue to add remaining spice.

Sauté until the strips begin to brown and add the lime juice. Continue to sauté, turning occasionally, until lime juice evaporates and the strips become a little crispy on the edges. Transfer to a serving plate and add another squeeze of lime juice.

To assemble the tacos:

Heat the corn (or flour) tortillas on a dry griddle or skillet over medium-high heat. Tortillas can also be warmed in the microwave or directly on the stove burner. Place some of the Seitan Asada on the tortilla; add some onion, cilantro and optional toppings if desired. Serve with rice and pinto or black beans on the side. Garnish with extra wedges of lime.

South of the Border Casserole

This is my version of a tamale pie/casserole using TVP (textured vegetable protein) as a meat replacement. Even the most die-hard meat lover would have a hard time distinguishing this from ground beef. The TVP is combined with beans, corn and vegetables, fragrantly seasoned with Tex-Mex spices and then topped off with a polenta crust and optional vegan cheese. Don't be put off by the long list of ingredients - this casserole comes together rather quickly and makes a hearty and satisfying meal for the entire family.

Ingredients:

- 2 T vegetable oil
- 1 medium onion, diced
- 1/2 green bell pepper, diced
- 3 cloves garlic (3 tsp) finely minced
- 1 jalapeno pepper, seeded and minced (optional)
- 1 cup water
- 1 can (14 to 15 oz) diced tomatoes with liquid
- 2 tsp chili powder
- 2 tsp onion powder
- 1 tsp garlic powder
- 1 tsp dried oregano
- 1 tsp ground cumin
- 1/4 tsp red pepper flakes
- 3 T tamari, soy sauce or Bragg Liquid Aminos™
- 1 T homemade vegan Worcestershire Sauce (pg. 206) or commercial - optional
- 1 tsp Gravy Master™ or other browning liquid- optional
- 1 cup dry TVP granules (textured vegetable protein) – I use Bob's Red Mill™
- 1 can (about 15 oz) cooked beans such as pinto, red beans or black beans - rinsed very well and drained
- 1 can (about 15 oz) cooked corn
- 1 small can (about 2.25 oz) sliced black olives (optional)
- 1 packaged roll (about 1 lb) of polenta (in some regions this is called corn mush)
- 1 cup shredded vegan cheese that melts (optional; may I suggest Daiya™ shredded cheddar)
- garnish with chopped cilantro, vegan sour cream and/or sliced avocado (optional)

Technique:

In a large skillet over medium heat, sauté the onion, bell pepper, garlic and optional jalapeno pepper in 2 tablespoons of vegetable oil until the vegetables are tender and the onions are just beginning to caramelize.

Add the water and diced tomatoes with their liquid. Bring to a simmer.

Stir in the spices, tamari/soy sauce or Liquid Aminos™ and the optional vegan Worcestershire and Gravy Master™.

Now add the TVP granules and stir thoroughly to combine. Turn the heat to low, cover the skillet and let cook for about 10 minutes until the TVP is tender and a good deal of the liquid has been absorbed.

Stir in the corn, beans and optional black olives. Remove from heat, cover the skillet and set aside.

Cut the polenta (corn mush) into chunks, add to a food processor and pulse until you have coarse crumbs. If you don't have a food processor, cut the polenta into small chunks and mash with a potato masher or ricer. If you are going to use vegan cheese, transfer to a mixing bowl and combine with the shredded cheese.

Lightly oil a medium-sized baking dish (about 10 inches) and add the contents of the skillet, distributing evenly. Top with the polenta and optional cheese. Lightly pack down the polenta and sprinkle lightly with a little chili powder.

Bake uncovered at 375°F for about 45 minutes or lightly golden brown on top. Serve and garnish with sliced avocado, chopped cilantro and a dollop of vegan sour cream if you like.

Sizzlin' Fajitas

Marinated strips of vegan chicken or steak are grilled with onions and peppers and served sizzling hot on warm tortillas. Garnish with additional squeezes of fresh lime, cilantro and creamy guacamole.

Fajita Marinade Ingredients:

- 1/4 cup vegetable oil
- 2 T fresh orange juice
- 1 T fresh lime juice
- 1 T finely chopped cilantro (optional)
- 2 garlic cloves, finely minced
- 3/4 tsp sea salt or kosher salt
- 1 to 3 chipotle chilies (depending on heat desired) from a can in adobo sauce
- 1/2 tsp ground cumin
- 1/2 tsp coarse ground black pepper

Fajita Ingredients:

- 1 recipe (about 20 oz) prepared Beaf Seitan cutlets (pg. 9), cut into strips; or Chik'n Seitan cutlets (pg. 11), cut into strips
- sea salt or kosher salt and coarse ground black pepper to taste
- 1 red bell pepper, thinly sliced
- 1 green bell pepper, thinly sliced
- 1 large onion, thinly sliced
- vegetable oil
- lime wedges
- flour tortillas, warm
- Wholly Guacamole! (pg. 98)
- salsa of your choice

Technique:

In a blender (mini-blenders work great for this), process all the marinade ingredients until smooth.

Transfer to a re-sealable plastic bag and add the "steak" or chik'n, seal and shake to coat. Refrigerate for a minimum of 30 minutes.

Preheat a skillet or grill pan on medium-high heat. Season the pan liberally with salt and ground black pepper. Shake off excess marinade back into the bag and add the "steak" or chik'n. Grill over medium-high heat until nicely browned. Transfer to a bowl and set aside.

Season the same skillet with 2 T vegetable oil and a little more salt and pepper. Add the bell peppers and onions and grill for 7 to 8 minutes or until the vegetables are just barely limp.

While the peppers and onions are cooking, heat up the tortillas. Turn any free burners on a medium low flame. Place a tortilla on each flame and let it char about 30 seconds to 1 minute, flip the tortilla and repeat on the second side. Once heated and charred slightly, remove the tortilla to a clean kitchen towel and wrap to keep warm. Repeat until you have warmed all of your tortillas.

You can also heat your tortillas in a microwave: lightly dampen a kitchen towel with some water, wrap the tortillas in the damp towel and heat in the microwave for about 1 minute. Check to see if they are warm; if not, repeat the heating at 1 minute intervals until they are warm and pliable.

Now, add the "steak" or chik'n back to the pan with the vegetables to quickly reheat and add a squeeze of fresh lime juice to create the "sizzle".

To serve:

Spread some guacamole on a tortilla, top with a few slices of "steak" or chik'n, peppers, onions, and salsa. Roll up the tortilla to enclose the filling.

Fajitas can also be served with vegan sour cream and shredded vegan cheese if you desire.

Italian Cuisine

Pasta Primavera

Since "Primavera" means the season of Spring, the vegetable choices for this dish should be the crisp new vegetables of Springtime. This dish is wonderful served warm, but leftovers are equally nice served as a chilled pasta salad.

Ingredients:

- vegetables of your choice: asparagus, peas, broccoli, zucchini, yellow squash, carrots, onions, and green, red, yellow or orange bell peppers. The peppers, carrots, zucchini and squash should be julienned; onions sliced thin and broccoli cut into florets. If asparagus is used, trim the fibrous ends.
- 1/4 cup extra-virgin olive oil
- 1 cup vegetable broth (see pg. 121 for broth options)
- sea salt and freshly ground black pepper to taste
- 1 tsp dried oregano or 1 T fresh, chopped
- 1 tsp dried basil or 1 T fresh, chopped
- 1 tsp dried parsley or 1 T fresh, chopped
- 10 cherry tomatoes, halved
- 1 pound farfalle (bowtie pasta)
- 1/4 cup Golden Parmesan (pg. 65) or commercial vegan parmesan

Technique:

Preheat the oven to 450° F. On a large heavy baking sheet, toss all of the vegetables with the oil, salt, pepper, and herbs. Arrange evenly over the baking sheet. Bake until the carrots are tender and the vegetables begin to brown, stirring after the first 10 minutes, about 20 minutes total.

Meanwhile, cook the pasta in a large pot of boiling salted water according to package directions until done to desired tenderness. Drain and return to the cooking pot.

Add 1/2 cup of the vegetable broth to the pasta with the roasted vegetables and cherry tomatoes. Toss well. Add the remaining broth if necessary to moisten.

Season the pasta and vegetables with salt and pepper, to taste. Transfer to a large serving bowl. Sprinkle with the parmesan and serve immediately.

Broccoli Mushroom Alfredo

*Tender fettuccini noodles, broccoli and sautéed mushrooms
are topped with a rich and creamy vegan Alfredo sauce.*

Ingredients:

- Alfredo Sauce (pg. 216)
- 1/2 box (about 1/2 lb) dry fettuccini noodles
- 2 T extra-virgin olive oil
- 1 small onion, thinly sliced
- 2 cups broccoli florets
- 2 cups sliced mushrooms
- ground black pepper
- optional garnish: Golden Parmesan (pg. 65) or commercial vegan parmesan

Technique:

Prepare the Alfredo sauce according to directions and keep warm over low heat.

Meanwhile, in a skillet, sauté the onions in extra-virgin olive oil until translucent. Add the mushrooms and sauté until tender. Add to the Alfredo sauce in saucepan.

Bring 2 to 3 quarts water to a boil. Add a few generous pinches of salt. Cook the noodles according to package directions until desired tenderness. In the last 3 to 4 minutes of cooking time, add the broccoli to the pasta water.

Cook the broccoli for 1 to 2 minutes or until desired tenderness. Drain the noodles and the broccoli in a colander and return to the stock pot.

Top with the Alfredo sauce and mix well. Transfer to serving plates and garnish with fresh ground black pepper and additional Parmesan if desired; serve immediately.

Eggplant Rollatini

Tender slices of eggplant are rolled around vegan ricotta, topped with tomato sauce, vegan mozzarella and parmesan, and then baked.

Ingredients:

- 2 large eggplants, peeled and ends removed
- extra-virgin olive oil
- 2 cups Tofu Ricotta (pg. 68) or commercial vegan ricotta
- 3 T Golden Parmesan (pg. 65) or commercial vegan parmesan
- 1/4 cup fresh, finely chopped basil or 1 T dried basil
- sea salt or kosher salt and black pepper to taste
- 1 and 1/2 cups shredded vegan mozzarella that melts (i.e., Daiya™)
- 2 cups prepared tomato pasta sauce or marinara sauce, commercial or homemade

Technique:

Preheat oven to 450°F.

Peel and slice the eggplant lengthwise, about 1/4 to 1/2-inch thick. Oil a baking sheet (or two sheets if available to accommodate all the eggplant slices) and lay the slices in a single layer. Brush lightly with extra-virgin olive oil and sprinkle with salt.

Bake about 10 to 12 minutes or until the eggplant is softened. This ensures easy rolling. Remove to a plate.

Reduce oven heat to 400°F.

In a bowl, combine the ricotta, 3 tablespoons parmesan, 1/2 cup shredded mozzarella, basil and salt and pepper to taste.

In a shallow casserole dish, spread about 1/2 cup tomato sauce evenly on the bottom. Set aside.

On a work surface, spread about 2 tablespoons of the ricotta mixture on an eggplant slice. Roll up and place into the casserole dish, seam side down. Repeat with each slice.

Top the rollatini with the remaining mozzarella and then with the remaining sauce. Bake uncovered for about 30 minutes.

Chik'n Piccata

"Piccata" in Italian, is used in reference to a way of preparing food. It means "sautéed and served in a sauce containing lemon, butter and herbs, usually parsley." This dish is wonderful served with your favorite pasta.

Ingredients:

- 4 to 6 Chik'n Seitan cutlets (pg. 11) or commercial vegan chicken
- sea salt or kosher salt and freshly ground black pepper
- flour (unbleached all-purpose wheat; rice or soy), for dredging
- 1/4 cup (4 T) Better Butter (pg. 62) or vegan margarine
- 1/4 cup (4 T) extra-virgin olive oil
- 1/4 cup fresh lemon juice
- 1/2 cup chik'n broth (see pg. 121-122 for broth options)
- 2 or 3 T capers, drained
- 1/4 cup fresh parsley, chopped

Technique:

Season the chik'n with salt and pepper. Dredge in the flour and shake off excess.

In a large skillet over medium-high heat, melt 2 tablespoons of the butter or margarine with 4 tablespoons extra-virgin olive oil. When the butter/margarine and oil start to sizzle, add the chik'n cutlets and sauté, turning every few minutes until the chik'n is browned nicely. Remove and transfer to a plate. Remove the pan from the heat.

Into the pan add the lemon juice, chik'n broth and capers. Return the pan to the heat and bring to a boil.

Adjust salt and pepper to taste. Return the chik'n to the pan and simmer for 5 minutes.

Remove the chik'n to a platter.

Add the remaining 2 tablespoons butter or margarine to the sauce and whisk vigorously. Pour the sauce over the chik'n and garnish with parsley. *Buono Appetito!*

Eggplant Parmigiana

The classic Italian dish; vegan-style.

Ingredients:

- extra-virgin olive oil
- 2 large or 3 medium-sized eggplant, about 2 pounds
- salt and pepper
- 1 large onion, chopped
- 2 tsp minced garlic (2 cloves)
- 2 cups marinara or tomato sauce
- 1 tsp dried oregano
- 1 bunch fresh basil leaves, chiffonade*
- 1 and 1/2 cups shredded vegan mozzarella that melts (i.e., Daiya™)
- 1/2 cup Golden Parmesan (pg. 65) or commercial vegan parmesan
- 1 cup dry bread crumbs

*Chiffonade is a French cooking term and technique in which herbs or leafy green vegetables (such as spinach and basil) are cut into long, thin strips. This is generally accomplished by stacking leaves, rolling them tightly, and cutting across the rolled leaves with a sharp knife, producing fine ribbons.

Technique:

Set the oven on "Broil".

Lightly toast the breadcrumbs on a baking sheet about 1 minute under the broiler. Do not burn! Remove and set aside. Lightly oil the baking sheet(s) with extra-virgin olive oil.

Peel and slice each eggplant into 1/2 inch thick slices. Place slices in a single layer on the oiled sheet(s), lightly mist or brush with extra-virgin olive oil and lightly season with salt and pepper. Broil the eggplant until the slices begin turning lightly brown on top, about 10 min. Remove and turn the slices and continue to broil until lightly browned and the eggplant is tender. Remove the slices from the baking sheet and place them on to a plate to cool.

Lower the oven temperature to 350°F.

In a skillet, sauté the onions in a tablespoon of extra-virgin olive oil until translucent. Add the garlic and oregano and sauté another minute or two. Add the sauce and combine well. Turn off heat.

In a medium-sized, lightly oiled baking dish (about 8×12), spread a thin layer (1/2 cup) of sauce on the bottom. Arrange a single layer of eggplant slices, slightly overlapping. Over the slices, sprinkle 1/2 cup breadcrumbs. Evenly spread about 3/4 cup of tomato sauce and sprinkle the chopped fresh basil. Sprinkle with 1/2 of the vegan parmesan and 1/2 of the vegan mozzarella, spreading evenly.

Repeat with another layer of eggplant, remaining breadcrumbs and then mozzarella. Top with the remaining sauce and parmesan. Cover with foil and bake 30 minutes. Remove foil and continue baking another 15 minutes. Remove from the oven and let set about 5 to 10 minutes before slicing and serving.

Garden Lasagna

Tender lasagna noodles are layered with fresh garden vegetables, rich tomato sauce and vegan cheeses and then baked to perfection.

Ingredients:

- 8 to 10 eggless lasagna noodles
- 2 T extra-virgin olive oil
- 1 large onion, chopped
- 2 tsp minced garlic (2 cloves)
- 1 tsp each dried oregano, basil and parsley
- 1/4 tsp ground black pepper, or to taste
- 1/2 cup dry TVP (textured vegetable protein)
- 1/2 cup vegetable broth (see pg. 121 for broth options)

- 1 jar or can (about 10 oz) favorite chunky-style tomato pasta sauce
- 2 packed cups fresh baby spinach
- 1 large zucchini, sliced very thin lengthwise
- 1 and 1/2 cups Tofu Ricotta (pg. 68) or commercial vegan ricotta cheese
- 1 and 1/2 cups shredded vegan mozzarella that melts (i.e., Daiya™)
- 1/2 cup Golden Parmesan (pg. 65) or commercial vegan parmesan

Technique:

Prepare the lasagna noodles according to package directions. Add a tablespoon of vegetable oil to the water when boiling to prevent sticking after draining. Drain and set aside.

Place a layer of paper towels in a colander. Place a layer of zucchini slices on the paper towels and sprinkle lightly with sea salt. Place another layer of paper towels on top and then something heavy on top of the towels (heavy ceramic bowl, etc.) This helps remove excess moisture from the zucchini.

Steam the spinach and press in a sieve or tofu press to remove excess moisture. Set aside. Bring the vegetable broth to a boil and add to the TVP in a bowl, stir well to reconstitute. Set aside.

Sauté the onion in extra-virgin olive oil until translucent; add the garlic, herbs and pepper. Sauté for another minute or two and add the pasta sauce. Remove from heat and stir in the rehydrated TVP. Set aside. Preheat the oven to 350°F.

Lightly oil a lasagna pan with extra-virgin olive oil or vegetable oil cooking spray. Add a thin layer of pasta sauce to the bottom of the lasagna pan. Lay half the noodles over the sauce. Spread the ricotta over the noodles; use the back of a spoon to evenly distribute. Use a little more ricotta if necessary. Evenly spread the steamed spinach on top.

Add another layer of sauce (1/2 of the remaining sauce) and layer with the remaining noodles. Pat the zucchini dry and brush off excess salt with paper towels over the sink; layer the slices over the noodles. Sprinkle evenly with mozzarella. Top with another layer of remaining sauce. Sprinkle generously with vegan parmesan.

Cover with foil and bake for 1 hour. Let cool for 10-15 minutes before serving.

German Fare

Sauerbraten (German Pot Roast)

This is a traditional German favorite, vegan-style. In German, "sauerbraten" means "sour roast". Actually, the roast and gravy offer a wonderful combination of sweet and sour flavors. Begin a day ahead, as the simmered "roast" needs to refrigerate for a minimum of 8 hours to marinate and firm its texture. Serve with mashed potatoes and German Red Cabbage. Wunderbar!

First, prepare Seitan Mignon (pg. 13) according to the directions. When finished simmering, remove the pot from the heat and let the seitan rest in the broth until it cools to room temperature. Remove the cheesecloth and place the seitan in an airtight container or zip-lock bag. Add 1/4 cup of the cooled simmering broth and 1 tablespoon of red wine vinegar. Refrigerate for a minimum of 8 hours to marinate the seitan. Reserve the broth for the Sauerbraten gravy but be sure to add back a little water, if necessary, because the broth may have become very salty from evaporation during simmering.

Next, prepare your Sauerbraten gravy; the ingredients are:

- Better Butter (pg. 62) or vegan margarine
- 1/4 cup flour (unbleached all-purpose wheat; rice or soy)
- 4 cups reserved beaf broth
- 1/4 cup red wine vinegar
- 2 T brown sugar
- 1 medium onion, chopped
- 1 large carrot, chopped

- 1 bay leaf
- 12 juniper berries (optional)
- 1 tsp Dijon mustard
- 1 tsp ground ginger
- 1/2 tsp ground cloves
- 1/2 tsp ground black pepper
- 1/4 cup dark seedless raisins
- sea salt or Kosher salt, to taste

Technique:

In a large pot, heat 1 tablespoon of the butter or margarine over medium heat. Add the seitan and roll it around to coat with the butter or margarine. Sauté, turning frequently, until the seitan begins to lightly brown. Add a dash of tamari or soy sauce and continue to roll the seitan until nicely browned and lightly crisp. Transfer to a cutting board and with a serrated knife, slice into thin medallions. Cover with plastic wrap to avoid drying out and set aside.

Add 1/4 cup butter or margarine to the same pot and melt over medium heat. Whisk in the flour to create a smooth paste (roux), incorporating any browned bits left in the pot. Cook until the roux turns golden brown. Slowly whisk in the reserved broth (to avoid lumps) and stir vigorously. Add all other ingredients, increase heat and bring mixture to a boil, stirring frequently. Now reduce the heat to a simmer and cook partially covered for 45 minutes.

Taste the gravy and add salt or additional brown sugar if desired. Add the roast slices to the gravy and simmer an additional 10 minutes. Transfer the roast slices to a serving platter. Strain the gravy through a sieve and discard the solids. Ladle some gravy over the sliced sauerbraten and place additional into a gravy boat to serve with the potatoes.

You can store the sauerbraten for up to 10 days in the refrigerator, or freeze for up to 3 months.

German Red Cabbage

Ingredients:

- 2 T vegetable oil
- 1 onion, thinly sliced
- 1 small red cabbage, shredded
- 1/3 cup raw apple cider vinegar
- 2 T brown sugar
- 1 tsp mustard seed (optional)
- sea salt or kosher salt and black pepper to taste

Technique:

Place a skillet over medium high heat. Add the oil and onion and sauté for 2 minutes. Add the cabbage, sautéing until it wilts, about 5 minutes. Add the vinegar and stir to combine. Sprinkle the sugar over the cabbage and mix well to combine. Season with mustard seed, salt and pepper and reduce heat a bit. Let cabbage continue to cook 10 minutes or until tender, stirring occasionally.

Brats and Sauerkraut

Ingredients:

- 6 German Bratwurst (pg. 43) or commercial vegan bratwurst
- 3 T vegetable oil
- 1 large onion, thinly sliced
- 1 (15 oz) can or jar sauerkraut, drained
- 2 tsp brown sugar
- 1 cup of beer (alcoholic, or non-alcoholic)

Technique:

In a large skillet, brown the brats in 2 tablespoons of vegetable oil over medium heat. Remove the brats and set aside. Add the onion and 1 T of vegetable oil to the skillet and sauté until translucent. Add the sauerkraut and brown sugar. Continue to sauté over medium heat until the sauerkraut begins to caramelize.

Add the beer, cover the skillet and simmer about 20 to 30 minutes. Uncover and add back the brats. Continue to simmer until the liquid reduces but do not let the sauerkraut dry out.

Serve over mashed potatoes. *Wunderbar!*

Indian Cuisine

Delhi Delight

Creamy coconut milk tempers the heat of Indian spices in this fragrant and savory dish.

Ingredients:

- 2 T Better Butter (pg. 62) or vegan margarine
- 1 large onion sliced thin
- 10 oz thinly sliced Chik'n Seitan (pg. 11); or commercial vegan chicken or extra-firm tofu
- 2 tsp minced garlic (2 cloves)
- 2 tsp fresh grated ginger root
- 1 (8 oz) can tomato sauce
- 1 can (14 oz) coconut milk (regular or lite)*
- 2 tsp ground cumin
- 2 tsp paprika
- 1 tsp sea salt or kosher salt, or to taste
- 1/2 tsp ground coriander (optional)
- 1/2 tsp turmeric (optional)
- 1/2 tsp cayenne pepper (or more for additional heat)
- 2 cups steamed cauliflower florets
- 1/4 cup chopped fresh cilantro or pinch of dried parsley for garnish (optional)

*Do not use Coconut Milk Beverage; it lacks the distinct coconut flavor essential for this recipe.

Technique:

In a skillet over medium heat, sauté the onion in the butter or margarine until the onion is translucent. Add the sliced chik'n and sauté until firm and lightly browned.

Add garlic and ginger, stir to coat and cook 1 or 2 more minutes. Add the remaining ingredients and simmer on low to blend flavors, about as long as it takes to prepare your rice.

Adjust seasonings if necessary. Serve over basmati rice. Garnish with cilantro or parsley if desired.

Saag Tofu Paneer (Creamed Spinach with Tofu Cheese)

This is one of my favorite ways to prepare spinach. Tofu replaces the paneer, which is an Indian dairy cheese. The recipe calls for garam masala, which is an Indian spice blend containing cardamom, cinnamon, cloves, cumin, black pepper and coriander. It can be found in specialty food stores or in the ethnic section of some supermarkets; or you can blend your own using Skye's Garam Masala (recipe following). You really have to try this dish; the flavors are amazing!

Ingredients:

- 1 block (about 14 oz) firm or extra-firm tofu (do not use silken tofu)
- approx. 1 lb fresh spinach (or 2 packages frozen and thawed)
- 1 large onion, diced
- 1 T fresh grated ginger root (about a 2-inch piece)
- 2 T tomato paste
- 2 tsp minced garlic
- 1/4 cup (4 T) Better Butter (pg. 62) or vegan margarine
- 1/2 tsp salt, or more to taste
- 1 tsp Skye's Garam Masala (pg. 187) or commercial garam masala
- 1 tsp ground cumin
- 1/4 tsp cayenne pepper
- 1/2 cup Heavy Creme (pg. 64) or commercial vegan cream substitute

Technique:

Drain and press the tofu to remove as much water as possible and then cut into bite-size cubes (see Preparing Tofu for Recipes, pg. 56).

Spray a non-stick skillet with a little cooking oil spray and sauté the tofu cubes over medium-high heat until firm and lightly golden brown. Sprinkle with a little salt and set aside in a bowl.

Steam the fresh spinach (this can be done in the microwave if desired) and then place in a strainer. With a wide spoon, press out extra moisture. It doesn't need to be completely dry; the excess moisture just needs to be removed. If using thawed frozen spinach, press in a strainer to remove excess moisture in the same manner. A tofu press also works great for quickly and easily removing the excess moisture from the spinach. Add the spinach to a food processor and pulse to puree the spinach. Set aside.

Add the butter or margarine to the skillet and sauté the onions over medium heat until translucent. Add the ginger, tomato paste, garlic, salt and spices and sauté for a few more minutes. Do not let the garlic and spices burn. Add the spinach to the skillet and blend well. Reduce heat to low and let cook until the flavors combine and the spinach begins to change from a bright green to a darker green color. Fold in the creme and blend well. Add a little water to thin consistency if necessary and adjust salt as needed. Add the tofu cubes and carefully incorporate so as not to break up the cubes too much. Heat through. Serve over basmati rice.

Tandoori Chik'n Skewers

Chik'n Seitan "tenders" are marinated in tandoori spices, skewered and then grilled until crispy. Eggplant chunks, onion, mushrooms, cherry tomatoes or bell peppers can also be added to the skewers, if desired. Natural tandoori spice blend (which lacks the artificial red dye) can be found in specialty food markets, or online. Traditionally, the base for the marinade is plain yogurt; but since seitan is plant-based and contains virtually no fat, I've substituted with vegan mayonnaise to provide the oil (fat) which will keep the seitan flavorful and moist when grilled. For a more authentic red "tint" to the tandoori chik'n, add 2 tsp of beet powder to the marinade, but this is completely optional (and beet powder isn't always easy to find).

Ingredients:

- 1 recipe Chik'n Seitan "tenders" (pg. 11)
- 1/2 cup No-Eggy Mayo (pg. 105) or commercial vegan mayonnaise
- 2 T raw apple cider vinegar
- 2 T fresh lemon juice
- 1 T natural tandoori spice blend
- 1 T fresh grated ginger root
- 1 tsp garlic powder
- 1 tsp onion powder
- 1/2 teaspoon sea salt
- 1/4 tsp cayenne pepper (optional, for extra heat)
- 2 tsp beet powder (optional, for color)
- steel skewers for grilling, or bamboo skewers pre-soaked in water

Technique:

Prepare the chik'n seitan "tenders" according to the recipe on pg. 11, and then let them cool in the broth until they reach room temperature (or cool enough to handle).

Whisk together all other ingredients until well combined. Add the seitan, covering well with the marinade. Refrigerate for at least 1 hour. A zip-lock bag works great for this purpose.

Remove the "tenders", shaking off any excess marinade and thread on to the skewers. Brush generously with vegetable oil and add additional vegetables as desired.

Place on a pre-heated oiled grill, or under the broiler, turning once or twice until the seitan is lightly crisp on the outside. Brush again generously with vegetable oil while grilling or broiling – this is very important. Do not overcook or the seitan will dry out. Squeeze a little lemon juice over the chik'n before serving.

Serve with basmati rice or Biryani (recipe follows) and fresh Indian Raita (pg. 219).

Skye's Garam Masala (Indian Spice Blend)

Ingredients:

- 1 T ground coriander
- 1 T turmeric
- 2 tsp ground cardamom (if you cannot find cardamom, substitute with ground ginger)
- 1 tsp ground cinnamon
- 1 tsp ground cloves
- 1 tsp ground nutmeg
- 1/2 tsp ground black pepper

Mix the spices together in a bowl. Place in an airtight container, and store in a cool, dry place.

Mango Lassi (Yogurt Drink)

Lassi is an Indian beverage made from yogurt and the pulp from fresh or frozen mangoes. It's wonderful for cooling the heat of spicy Indian cuisine.

Ingredients:

- 2 ripe, sweet mangos
- 1 and 1/2 cups plain or vanilla vegan yogurt
- 2 T brown rice syrup or 1 T organic sugar, or to taste (optional)
- 2 cups crushed ice

Technique: Peel and dice the mango and add to the blender. Add the rest of the ingredients and purée until smooth and frothy. Serve immediately.

Aloo Gobi (Indian-Spiced Potatoes and Cauliflower)

Tender potatoes and cauliflower seasoned with curry - a very popular Indian dish.

Ingredients:

- 2 T vegetable oil
- 1 tsp Indian curry powder
- 1/2 tsp Skye's Garam Masala (pg. 187) or commercial garam masala
- 2 tsp fresh grated ginger root
- 1/4 tsp ground red pepper, or more to taste
- 1 T minced garlic (3 cloves)
- 1 large sweet yellow onion
- 2 large russet potatoes (about 1.5 lbs.), peeled and cut into small chunks
- 2 cups cauliflower florets (1 small head of cauliflower)
- 1/2 tsp sea salt or kosher salt, or more to taste
- chopped cilantro as a garnish (optional)

Technique:

In a large skillet over medium heat, stir the curry powder, garam masala, ginger and red pepper together with the vegetable oil. Add the onion and cook for about 2 minutes and then add the garlic and cook for an additional minute.

Add the potatoes and cauliflower and season with the salt. Toss thoroughly to coat the potatoes and cauliflower with the vegetable oil and spices.

Cover and reduce heat to medium-low and cook, stirring occasionally until the cauliflower is tender and the potatoes are just beginning to break apart (about 25 to 30 minutes).

Taste and add additional salt if needed. Garnish with chopped cilantro if desired and serve.

Biryani (Indian Rice)

This is a classic dish of seasoned basmati rice and vegetables cooked in broth.

Ingredients:

- 2 T Better Butter (pg. 62)
  or vegan margarine
- 1 medium onion, finely diced
- 1 carrot, shredded
- 1/3 cup unsalted cashews (raw or roasted; whole or pieces)
- 1/2 tsp ground coriander
- 1/2 tsp ground turmeric
- 1/2 tsp ground cumin
- 1/4 tsp ground black pepper
- 2 tsp minced garlic (2 cloves)
- 1/2 cup baby peas (fresh, canned or frozen)
- 1/4 cup seedless raisins
- 2 cups vegetable broth or chik'n broth
  (see pg. 121-122 for broth options)
- 1 cup basmati rice
- optional garnish: chopped cilantro

Technique:

Melt the butter or margarine in a medium-sized saucepan over medium heat. Add the onion, carrot, cashews and spices and sauté until the onion is translucent.

Add the garlic, peas and raisins and sauté an additional minute.

Add the broth and bring to a boil. Stir in the rice, lower heat to a simmer, cover and cook for 20 minutes.

Fluff the rice with a fork before serving.

Channa Masala (Indian-Spiced Chickpeas)

This dish is a classic in Indian cuisine. Garbanzo beans (chickpeas) are packed with protein essential to the vegan diet. The balance of spice in this recipe adds a wonderful fragrance and flavor. If you'd like to add more heat, include some ground red pepper to spice things up.

Ingredients:

- 2 T Better Butter (pg. 62) or vegan margarine
- 1 medium onion, finely chopped
- 1 T minced garlic (3 cloves)
- 2 tsp Skye's Garam Masala (pg. 187) or commercial garam masala
- 1 tsp paprika
- 2 tsp fresh grated ginger root
- 1 green chili, seeded and minced
- 1/2 tsp sea salt or kosher salt, or to taste
- 1 can (15 oz) garbanzo beans (chickpeas), rinsed very well
- 1 cup diced tomatoes (fresh or canned)
- 1/4 cup water
- 1 T lemon juice (about 1/2 lemon)

Technique:

Measure out all your ingredients and set aside. In a skillet with a lid, melt the butter or margarine over medium heat. Add the onion and cook, stirring frequently until the onion is beginning to caramelize. Add the garlic and cook an additional minute or so, but do not let garlic burn.

Turn the heat to medium-low and add the spices, ginger, minced green chili and salt. The spices will become very fragrant when they come in contact with the heat. Stir for 1 minute and add the garbanzo beans, diced tomatoes, water and lemon juice.

Cover the skillet with a lid. Simmer, stirring occasionally, for an additional 40 minutes or until the sauce thickens and the garbanzo beans are very tender.

Serve with basmati rice or Biryani (pg. 189).

Dal (Indian-Spiced Lentils)

Every good cook has their own version of Indian Dal - this is my version. Your kitchen will be filled with the most heavenly aroma as the lentils gently simmer in the fragrantly-spiced sauce.

Ingredients:

- 2 T Better Butter (pg. 62) or vegan margarine
- 1 medium onion, diced
- 1 T minced garlic (3 cloves)
- 1 green chili, seeded and minced
- 1 and 1/2 tsp ground cumin
- 1 cup dry lentils (sort through the lentils to remove any foreign debris and then rinse in a strainer and drain)
- 1 T fresh grated ginger root
- 1 tsp Skye's Garam Masala (pg. 187) or commercial garam masala
- 1/4 tsp ground red pepper
- 2 tsp organic sugar
- 2 bay leaves
- 1 T tomato paste
- 1 T fresh lemon juice (about 1/2 lemon)
- 4 cups vegetable broth or chik'n broth (see pg. 121-122 for broth options)*

*If you prepare your broth yourself, don't make it too salty. This dish requires evaporating the broth down into a sauce, therefore it will become very concentrated during cooking. You can always add salt later but you cannot subtract it.

Technique:

In a large skillet, melt the butter or margarine over medium heat and sauté the onions until tender, but do not brown.

Add the garlic, green chili, cumin, lentils, ginger, garam masala, red pepper, sugar and bay leaves. Sauté for 1 to 2 minutes and add the tomato paste, lemon juice and broth. Bring to a boil and then lower to a gentle simmer.

Partially cover the skillet and cook for 90 minutes, stirring occasionally, or until the liquid is reduced into a sauce and the lentils are very tender.

Add salt if needed and additional red pepper for more heat if desired.

Serve with basmati rice or Biryani (pg. 189) and garnish with chopped cilantro.

Garlic Naan (Indian Flatbread)

Naan is a leavened bread which is traditionally cooked in a Tandoor, or earthen oven, but can also be made on your stovetop at home. This bread is wonderful for soaking up the flavorful sauces of Indian cuisine. The dough for naan needs to be made in advance, so allow a few hours of preparation time.

This recipe took numerous attempts to achieve the correct formula and technique. All of the naan recipes I came across while researching called for lengthy kneading in order to produce a very elastic dough. I found that odd because I always remembered naan to be very delicate and light. And after several failed attempts using the lengthy kneading method, I came to the conclusion that less kneading is the key to producing the best texture. Most of the recipes also included dairy and sometimes eggs, so I had to find the right balance of vegan ingredients to ensure success. Please be as precise as possible with measurements - this is essential! I hope you enjoy.

For the Naan Dough:

- 1 pkg active dry yeast (2 and 1/4 tsp)
- 1/2 cup warm water (not hot)
- 2 tsp organic sugar
- 1/4 cup plain unsweetened non-dairy milk
- 1 tsp vegetable oil
- 2 cups unbleached all-purpose wheat flour
- 1 tsp ground cumin
- 3/4 tsp fine sea salt
- 1/2 tsp garlic powder

For Garnishing the Naan:

- 1/4 cup (4 T) Better Butter (pg. 62) or vegan margarine
- 1 T minced garlic (3 cloves)
- 2 T finely chopped cilantro or parsley (optional)

Technique:

In a small bowl, add the dry yeast and sugar to the warm water and stir until the yeast is dissolved. Cover and set aside for 10 minutes or until the mixture begins to thicken. This indicates the yeast is active (proofing).

Sift the flour, salt and cumin (optional) into a large mixing bowl. Also, add a tablespoon of all-purpose flour to a small dish - you can keep this nearby and use it for flouring your work surface.

Stir the almond milk and 1 tsp vegetable oil into the yeast mixture and then add to the dry ingredients. Mix into a rough dough with a large spoon or rubber spatula.

Now, use your fingertips to mix all this into a soft dough. The dough will be somewhat dry but mix together as best as you can. Once mixed, lightly flour a clean, flat work surface and knead the dough using the heel of your hand about 25 strokes until it is smooth and just beginning to show signs of elasticity. DO NOT overwork the dough, as excessive kneading will make the naan tough. The goal is to produce a naan that is light and airy, not tough and chewy.

Grease the bottom of the mixing bowl with a few drops of vegetable oil and place the dough into it. Cover with a clean dish towel, set it in a warm place and allow to rise for 1 hour.

When the dough has finished rising, punch down the dough, turn out onto the lightly floured work surface and knead a few more times. Cut the dough in half and cut each half into thirds for a total of six pieces. Roll each piece into a round ball with your palms. Place onto a lightly oiled cookie sheet, cover with a towel and let rise for an additional 30 minutes.

Meanwhile, in a small saucepan, warm the vegan butter, margarine or oil over medium heat and add the garlic. Sauté until softened but do not brown or the garlic will become bitter. Remove from the heat and stir in the optional cilantro or parsley. Set aside.

Next, heat a dry skillet with a lid over medium heat until very hot (about 5 minutes). The skillet is hot enough if a drop of water instantly vaporizes upon contact.

Now, lightly flour the same surface on which you kneaded the dough. Flatten a ball of dough into a disc and with a lightly floured rolling pin roll out the disc until you have an oval shape - roll the dough as thin as you can without it tearing. Rolling may take some effort, as the dough is elastic, but persevere. Don't worry about the shape being somewhat irregular, that's actually ideal.

Lay the piece of rolled dough into the dry skillet and cover with its lid. When the dough begins to bubble on top, use a wide spatula to check and see if the bottom is browning. If so, flip the naan, cover with the lid and cook another minute or so to lightly brown the other side.

Remove and brush the bubbled side of the naan generously with the melted butter/garlic/herb mixture and place into a napkin-lined basket. Cover with a paper towel to keep warm while repeating the process with the remaining dough.

To reheat, wrap in foil and warm in a 350°F oven for a few minutes.

Thai Cuisine

Seitan Pad Thai

Delicate rice noodles are stir-fried with seitan, tofu scramble, vegetables, crushed peanuts and a spicy sweet vegan Thai sauce.

Ingredients:

- 2 T vegetable oil, plus extra as needed
- 1 T chopped garlic (3 cloves)
- 2 tsp fresh grated ginger root
- 1 and 1/2 cup Basic or Beaf Seitan (pg. 9), thinly sliced
- 8 oz medium-size dried rice noodles
- Pad Thai sauce, recipe follows
- 1/2 block (about 7 oz) soft to firm tofu, (do not use silken tofu)
- 1 T nutritional yeast
- pinch of turmeric
- 1/4 cup finely chopped roasted peanuts or cashews
- 3/4 cup chopped green onion including the greens
- 2 cups bean sprouts, rinsed, plus more for garnish
- wedges of lime and chopped cilantro as a garnish

Pad Thai Sauce:

- 1 T tamarind paste* (available at Asian/East Indian food stores)
- 1/3 cup vegetable broth (see pg. 121 for broth options) or water
- 3 T tamari, soy sauce or Bragg Liquid Aminos™
- 1 tsp Thai chili sauce, or to taste - or - 1/2 tsp red pepper flakes
- 3 T organic sugar, or more to taste

*If you absolutely cannot locate tamarind paste, try substituting with 1 T dark molasses and the juice of 1 lime.

Technique:

Drain and lightly press the tofu to remove excess moisture. Crumble the tofu into a small bowl and stir in the nutritional yeast and a pinch or two of turmeric. Set aside.

Bring a pot of water to a boil and turn off the heat. Soak the noodles in the hot water for 5 minutes, or until limp but still firm. Drain and rinse with cold water. The noodles must be slightly under-cooked at this stage as they will finish cooking later when they are stir-fried.

Combine the Pad Thai sauce ingredients in a cup, stirring well to dissolve the paste and sugar. Heat the sauce gently in the microwave until warm (or a small saucepan on the stove). Set aside.

Heat the oil in a wok over medium-high heat. Add the garlic, ginger and seitan and stir fry until the seitan is just beginning to brown. Remove and set aside.

Add the noodles to the hot wok. They will stick together, so stir fast and try to separate them. Add a little water, stirring a few times. Then add the Pad Thai sauce, and keep stirring until everything is thoroughly mixed. The noodles should appear soft and moist. Return the seitan to the wok.

Push the contents of the wok up around the sides to make room to "scramble" the tofu. If the pan is very dry, add 1 more tablespoon of oil. Add the tofu mixture and "scramble" until heated through. When the tofu has cooked a bit, stir the noodles over until everything is well mixed.

Add the chopped peanuts, green onions and bean sprouts. Mix well and cook for an additional minute or two or just until bean sprouts are lightly cooked. Transfer to a platter. Garnish with raw bean sprouts, cilantro and a squeeze of lime juice.

Japanese and Pacific Cuisine

Tempura Vegetables

For the best results, prepare the tempura batter just before frying the vegetables. Serve with Tempura Sauce (pg. 218) for dipping.

Ingredients:

- vegetables of your choice, sliced or cut into chunks*
- canola or peanut oil for deep-frying
- 1 cup rice flour or unbleached all-purpose wheat flour
- 1 T cornstarch (preferably non-GMO) or arrowroot powder
- 1 and 1/2 cups chilled club soda or sparkling water (Perrier™, for example)
- 1/2 tsp sea salt or kosher salt
- pinch or two of ground red pepper (optional)

*Some tempura favorites include: mushrooms, onions, bell pepper, potato, zucchini, squash, sweet potato, okra, green beans, asparagus, broccoli, cauliflower, carrot, and eggplant; Chinese-style tofu is also wonderful when prepared as tempura.

Technique:

Whisk together the flour, cornstarch, soda water and salt until a smooth batter is formed. Heat a sufficient amount of oil for deep-frying in a skillet or deep-fryer. Test the temperature with a drop of water - if it crackles and dances on the oil, the oil is sufficiently hot (360°F to 375°F is ideal).

Dip the vegetables in the batter to coat and shake off the excess. Add to the hot oil, trying to ensure that the vegetables do not touch when adding so they don't stick together. Cook root vegetables for about 4 minutes and all others for about 3 minutes. The time might differ if your oil is at a different temperature.

Remove the tempura from the oil with a slotted spoon or other deep-fryer utensil made for this purpose. Place on a few layers of paper towels to allow the remaining oil to drain. Sprinkle with salt and serve immediately with tempura dipping sauce.

Sesame Miso Tofu with Vegetables

Main Ingredients:

- 1 block (about 14 oz) firm or extra-firm tofu (do not use silken tofu)
- 1 onion, sliced thin
- 2 T peanut or canola oil
- 1 T tamari, soy sauce or Bragg Liquid Aminos™
- 1 T mirin (sweet rice wine)
- drizzle of toasted sesame oil
- assorted vegetables and greens as desired; such as julienned carrots and zucchini; sliced red or green bell peppers; sliced mushrooms; baby corn; bamboo shoots; sliced water chestnuts; green beans; tender asparagus; snow peas; bok choy; napa cabbage; spinach; kale; beet greens; bean sprouts; broccoli, etc.

Marinade:

- 1 T mellow white miso paste
- 1 T sesame tahini
- 1 T fresh grated ginger root
- 2 T rice vinegar
- 2 T organic sugar or brown rice syrup
- 1/4 cup water

Technique:

Drain and press the tofu to remove as much water as possible (see Preparing Tofu for Recipes, pg. 56). Cut into 1-inch cubes and pat dry with a paper towel. In a large bowl, whisk together the marinade ingredients and add the tofu cubes. Marinate for at least 30 minutes in the refrigerator.

Preheat the oven to 400°F. Transfer the tofu to a baking dish (but do not discard the marinade) and bake for 15 minutes. Turn the pieces, coat with more marinade and bake an additional 15 minutes. Remove from the oven and set aside. Discard the remaining marinade.

Heat the peanut or vegetable oil in a large skillet or wok until very hot but not smoking. Add the firmer vegetables first (onions, carrots, bok choy, broccoli, etc). Stir fry just until tender. Add the tofu cubes, tender vegetables, sprouts and greens last.

Add the tamari/soy sauce or Liquid Aminos and the mirin. Toss and stir fry about 1 minute until the greens wilt. Do not overcook. Remove from the heat and drizzle with a small amount of toasted sesame oil. Serve over rice or soba noodles (Japanese buckwheat noodles).

Sushi

Ingredients:

- sushi nori sheets (seaweed)
- 1 and 1/2 cups dry short-grain Japanese sushi rice (white sticky rice), rinsed well in a strainer and drained; do not use long grain rice - it will not work.
- 2 cups water
- 3 T rice vinegar (no substitutions)
- 3 T organic sugar or brown rice syrup
- 1 tsp sea salt or kosher salt
- assorted fillings, such as: blanched asparagus spears; julienned carrot, zucchini and/or daikon radish (matchstick-size pieces); shredded napa cabbage; assorted sprouts; green onions (scallions); avocado; cucumber; marinated or glazed tofu strips; thin slices of seitan; thin strips of roasted red pepper; thin strips of sautéed or roasted portabella mushrooms; tempura-battered and fried eggplant, etc.

Optional Garnish:

- toasted sesame seeds

Condiments:

- wasabi paste (Japanese horseradish) - check ingredients; some wasabi products contain milk derivatives
- tamari, soy sauce or Bragg Liquid Aminos™
- pickled ginger

You will also need:

- plastic wrap and a bamboo mat or cloth napkin for rolling

Technique:

Warm the vinegar; add the salt and the sugar and mix well to completely dissolve. Set aside.

Cook your rice in the water according to the directions on the package. Cook until tender but firm.

Place the cooked rice in a glass, ceramic or wooden bowl (no metal, as this will react with the vinegar). Sprinkle the vinegar/sugar/salt mixture over the rice. Mix thoroughly but gently with a large wooden or plastic spoon. Cover the rice bowl with plastic wrap and wait until the rice cools to slightly above room temperature. Do not refrigerate the rice or it will be impossible to roll.

Lay a sheet of plastic wrap over the bamboo mat (or cloth napkin). Place one sheet of nori, shiny side down, on the plastic wrap, making sure the wide edge of the nori is nearest you.

With fingertips dipped lightly in water, spread about 1/2 cup of the prepared sticky rice evenly over the bottom 2/3 of the nori, leaving about 2 inches exposed on the side furthest from you. The layer of rice should be thin enough so that you can see the nori underneath.

Add desired fillings horizontally in the middle of the rice, making sure that ingredients are spread evenly and touch both side edges of the nori.

Lightly dampen the exposed edge of the nori with wet fingers. This will help seal the roll when finished.

Hold the edge of the plastic and mat nearest you and lift up and over the filling, encasing the filling inside the sushi rice. Make sure the edge of the nori gets tucked under the rice.

Lift the edge of the rolling mat/plastic wrap and roll the nori encased filling with the palms of your hands until it reaches the top edge of the nori. Tighten the roll, by pressing with your fingers on the bamboo mat, the same way you would a rug to minimize excess space. Be careful not to make it too tight, however, or the fillings may fall out. This whole process takes a little practice, so be patient.

Let the roll rest seam side down on a cutting board at least 2 minutes. Slice it first down the middle with a sharp serrated knife. From there you can cut it into sixths or eighths, whichever you prefer.

For the dipping sauce, mix a little wasabi with the tamari or soy sauce. Sprinkle some toasted sesame seeds over the sushi if you like and serve with pickled ginger to cleanse the palate. I like to put the ginger on my sushi before dipping in the sauce -the flavors are amazing!

Douzo omeshiagari kudasai! (Enjoy your meal!)

Pineapple Teriyaki Chik'n

Pineapple adds a hint of tropical sweetness to this easy-to-make island-inspired dish. For those who don't care for meat analogues, sliced portabella mushrooms, firm tofu or tempeh make an excellent substitute.

Ingredients:

- 10 oz thinly sliced Chik'n Seitan (pg. 11) or commercial vegan chicken
- 2 T vegetable oil
- 1 onion chopped into 1 inch pieces
- 1 bell pepper, chopped into 1 inch pieces
- 2 cups broccoli florets
- 2 cups sliced mushrooms
- 1 and 1/2 cups pineapple chunks in natural juice, drained
- 2 tsp minced garlic (2 cloves)
- 1 T fresh grated ginger root
- 1/4 cup homemade Teriyaki Sauce (pg. 206) or commercial
- 1 tsp sesame oil (optional)
- black pepper to taste

Technique:

Heat the oil in a skillet over medium-high heat. Add the peppers and sauté until slightly softened.

Add the onion and broccoli. Sauté until the onion becomes translucent and the broccoli is tender crisp.

Add the chik'n, mushrooms, ginger, garlic, pineapple, optional sesame oil and black pepper. Continue to stir fry, stirring occasionally until onions begin to caramelize and chik'n begins to brown a bit.

Add the teriyaki sauce and stir to combine. Serve over jasmine or brown rice.

Island Grilled Pineapple

Sweet pineapple spears are marinated in a tangy sauce and then grilled. Wonderful when served as an accompaniment to Asian and Island inspired entrees.

Ingredients:

- 1 pineapple
- 2 T homemade Teriyaki Sauce (pg. 206) or commercial
- juice of 2 limes
- 2 T finely minced cilantro
- 1/2 tsp Thai red chili paste

Technique:

Peel and core the pineapple. A pineapple slicer makes an easy job of this, if you have one. Cut the pineapple lengthwise into 8 to 10 spears.

Mix the remaining ingredients and then pour over the pineapple spears in a zip-lock bag. Marinate for several hours in the refrigerator, turning occasionally.

Grill on the BBQ or a lightly oiled grill pan, turning occasionally, until the pineapple is lightly caramelized or until grill marks appear. Serve hot.

Chinese Cuisine

Mongolian Beaf

Ingredients:

- 1 T vegetable oil
- 2 tsp fresh grated ginger root
- 1 T minced garlic (3 cloves)
- 2 tsp cornstarch (preferably non-GMO) dissolved in 1 T water
- 1/3 cup tamari, soy sauce or Bragg Liquid Aminos™
- 2/3 cup water
- 1/3 cup light brown sugar
- vegetable oil, for frying (about 1/4 cup)
- 10 oz thinly sliced Beaf Seitan (pg. 9)
- whole green onions, sliced lengthwise (or try thinly sliced yellow onion; lightly steamed broccoli; or steamed green beans)

Technique:

Make the sauce by heating 1 tablespoon of vegetable oil in a medium saucepan over medium-low heat. Don't get the oil too hot.

Add the ginger and garlic to the pan, cook for 30 seconds to 1 minute. Quickly add the tamari/soy sauce or Liquid Aminos, water and cornstarch mixture before the garlic scorches. Whisk well to combine.

Dissolve the brown sugar in the sauce. Raise the heat to medium and rapid simmer the sauce for 2-3 minutes or until the sauce thickens. Remove from the heat and set aside.

In a skillet or wok, heat 1/4 cup oil over medium heat until it's nice and hot, but not smoking. Add the sliced seitan to the oil and sauté for a few minutes until nicely browned. Be careful turning, as to not break the seitan up too much.

After a couple minutes, use a large slotted spoon to transfer the seitan onto paper towels to drain any excess oil. Discard the oil out of the wok or skillet.

Place the pan back over the heat, add the seitan back in the pan with the sauce and cook for one minute while stirring.

Add the green onions and cook for a few more minutes until the onions are just tender, then remove the seitan and onions with tongs or a slotted spoon to a serving plate.

Leave the excess sauce behind in the pan. Serve over jasmine rice.

Ginger Garlic Chik'n

This is a very quick and easy stir-fry dish.

Ingredients:

- juice of 1 lemon (about 2 T)
- 1 T tamari, soy sauce or Bragg Liquid Aminos™
- 1/4 tsp red pepper flakes, or more to taste
- 2 T vegetable oil
- 1 onion, thinly sliced
- 10 oz thinly sliced Chik'n Seitan (pg. 11) or commercial vegan chicken
- 2 tsp minced garlic (2 cloves)
- 1 T fresh grated ginger

Technique:

In a small bowl, mix the lemon juice with the tamari/soy sauce or Liquid Aminos and the red pepper flakes. Set aside.

Heat the vegetable oil in a skillet over medium heat. Add the onion and sauté until the onion becomes translucent. Add the chik'n and cook until golden.

Add the ginger and garlic and cook for an additional minute.

Turn the heat up to medium-high and add the lemon juice/tamari mixture. Stir fry until the onions and chik'n begin to brown nicely.

Serve with stir-fry Asian vegetables over jasmine or sticky rice.

Sweet and Sour Orange Chik'n

This dish is a classic restaurant-style favorite. Try substituting the chik'n seitan with sliced tofu or tempeh.

Ingredients:

- 10 oz Chik'n Seitan nuggets (pg.11) or commercial vegan chicken cut into bite sized pieces
- 2 T cornstarch (preferably non-GMO), plus more for dusting the chik'n
- 1/3 cup vegetable broth (see pg. 121 for broth options) or water
- 1 T vegetable oil
- 2 tsp minced garlic (2 cloves)
- 1 tsp fresh grated ginger root
- 1 cup orange juice (or try pineapple, passion fruit or mango)
- 1/4 cup rice vinegar
- 2 T organic ketchup
- 2 T brown sugar, or more to taste
- 1 tsp sesame oil
- 2 T tamari or soy sauce
- 1/2 to 1 tsp red chili sauce (or to taste)

Technique:

Dissolve the cornstarch in the vegetable broth or water. Set aside.

In a saucepan, heat the oil over medium heat and sauté the garlic until golden. Add the remaining ingredients (except for the chik'n) and whisk to combine. Now whisk in the cornstarch mixture. Bring to a boil, stirring frequently, and then reduce heat to a slow simmer.

Continue to cook until the mixture thickens nicely. Add more sugar or chili sauce to taste if desired.

Meanwhile, lightly dust your chik'n pieces with cornstarch or all-purpose flour and fry in very hot vegetable oil until golden brown (the goal is to brown the exterior of the nuggets quickly, so the seitan does not dry out). Remove to a plate lined with paper towels to drain.

In a bowl, toss your fried chik'n pieces with the sweet and sour glaze. Serve over jasmine rice with an Asian vegetable medley.

Chapter 9

Sauces and Gravies

Golden Gravy

You may want to include Gravy Master™ in your gravy, depending on the depth of color you are trying to achieve. Gravy Master™ is an animal-free product used to enhance the brown color of gravies, producing a more appetizing appearance.

Ingredients:

- 2 cups beef broth (see pg. 123 for broth options); vegetable broth or chik'n broth (see pg. 121-122 for broth options)
- 1/4 cup (4 T) Better Butter (pg. 62), vegan margarine or vegetable oil
- 1/4 cup flour (unbleached all-purpose wheat; rice or soy)
- 1 tsp Gravy Master™ - optional

Technique:

In a saucepan, melt the vegan butter or margarine (or heat the oil) over medium-low heat. Add the flour and whisk vigorously to create a roux (a smooth paste used for thickening). Continue to heat for a few minutes to remove any raw flour taste. Slowly add the broth, a little at a time, whisking vigorously as you incorporate to eliminate lumps. Add Gravy Master™ if desired. Continue to cook and whisk until mixture thickens and just begins to come to a boil; reduce heat to low until ready to serve.

Creamy Horseradish Sauce

This creamy sauce tempers the strong bite of horseradish and is wonderful served with Corned Beef (pg. 20), Seitan Mignon (pg. 13) or Chesapeake Bay "Seafood" Cakes (pg. 148).

Whisk together in a small bowl until smooth and creamy.

- 1 cup No-Eggy Mayo (pg. 105) or commercial vegan mayonnaise
- juice of 1 lemon
- 1 or 2 T prepared horseradish (not creamed), or to taste
- salt and pepper, to taste

Tip: Homemade No-Eggy Mayo is much more economical than commercial vegan mayonnaise and tastes better too!

Worcestershire Sauce

This is my version of the classic sauce which is indispensable as a flavoring for beaf broth, beaf seitan, seitan meatloaf, and several vegan cheeses and salad dressings. Non-vegan commercial Worcestershire contains anchovy paste and thus is not suitable for vegans. There are a few brands of vegan Worcestershire sauce on the market, and they are very good, but they're not readily available to everyone. I hope you enjoy this recipe.

Ingredients:

- 1 and 1/2 cups apple cider vinegar
- 1/2 cup dark balsamic vinegar
- 1/2 cup tamari or soy sauce
- 3 T dark brown sugar
- 1 medium onion, chopped
- 1 piece ginger root (about 1 and 1/2 inch), peeled and sliced

- 1 tsp ground dry mustard
- 1 tsp lemon zest, loosely packed
- 1 tsp orange zest, loosely packed
- 1 tsp liquid smoke
- 3 cloves garlic, crushed
- 5 whole cloves
- 5 whole peppercorns

Technique:

Place all of the ingredients in a medium saucepan and bring to a boil over medium-high heat. Reduce the heat to a rapid simmer and cook until the sauce is reduced by half volume, about 45 minutes. Strain through a fine mesh sieve or a double layer of cheesecloth and cool completely before using. Store the sauce in the refrigerator in an airtight container for up to 3 months.

Teriyaki Sauce/Glaze

Ingredients:

- 1 T vegetable oil
- 2 tsp fresh grated ginger root
- 2 tsp cornstarch (preferably non-GMO) or arrowroot powder

- 1/3 cup tamari soy sauce or Bragg™ Liquid Aminos
- 2/3 cup water
- 1/3 cup light brown sugar

Technique:

Heat the vegetable oil in a small saucepan over medium-low heat. Don't get the oil too hot. Add the ginger and garlic to the pan, cook for 30 seconds to 1 minute. Quickly add the tamari/soy sauce or Liquid Aminos, water and the cornstarch mixture before the garlic scorches. Whisk well to combine. Dissolve the brown sugar in the sauce. Raise the heat to medium and rapid simmer the sauce, stirring constantly, for 2-3 minutes.

You can strain the sauce if you like, but the bits of ginger and garlic add a nice touch. Remove from the heat and set aside. The sauce will thicken a bit upon cooling.

Savory Onion Gravy

Ingredients:

- 3 T Better Butter (pg. 62), vegan margarine or vegetable oil
- 2 medium onions, peeled and thinly sliced
- 3 T flour (unbleached all-purpose wheat; rice or soy)
- 3 cups vegetable broth (see pg. 121 for broth options) or beaf broth (see pg. 123 for broth options)
- 1 tsp organic sugar
- 1 tsp balsamic vinegar
- sea salt or kosher salt and ground black pepper, to taste

Technique:

In a saucepan, melt the vegan butter or margarine (or heat the oil) over medium heat. Add the onions and sauté until very tender and beginning to caramelize.

Whisk in the flour and stir until a smooth paste (roux) is achieved. Slowly whisk in the broth until smooth. Add the sugar and balsamic vinegar and bring the mixture to a boil, stirring frequently.

Reduce heat and simmer until the mixture is thickened nicely. Add salt and pepper to taste.

Ladle half of the mixture into a blender and process until smooth - be careful however, as hot liquids may expand explosively when a blender is suddenly turned on high. For safety, cover the lid with a dish towel, hold down firmly and start the blender on low-speed, gradually increasing speed. Return the blended gravy to the saucepan to keep piping hot until ready to serve.

For a velvety smooth gravy, process the entire contents in the blender.

You can also thicken gravies by using 2 tsp of potato starch for every tablespoon of flour called for in a recipe. Mix it with enough water to achieve a smooth liquid (slurry). Follow the recipe as usual but omit using the flour to create a roux.

As you are bringing the gravy to a boil, whisk in the starch mixture. Once you have reached a boil, reduce heat to a simmer and continue to cook until the mixture thickens. Bob's Red Mill™ produces an excellent unmodified potato starch.

Soy Ginger Dipping Sauce

This flavorful blend of ingredients makes a wonderful dipping sauce for Asian spring rolls.

Ingredients:

- 2 T organic sugar
- 1/4 cup soy sauce, tamari or Bragg Liquid Aminos™
- 3/4 cup water
- 2 tsp cornstarch mixed with 2 tsp water
- 1 T fresh lime juice
- 2 tsp fresh grated ginger root
- 1 clove garlic, minced (1 tsp)
- 2 T chopped green onions

Technique:

Combine the sugar, soy sauce, and water in a small saucepan. Bring to a boil. Stir in the cornstarch/water paste. Reduce heat to a simmer and add the garlic, ginger, lime juice and green onions. Continue to simmer, stirring frequently, for about 2 minutes to blend the flavors. Serve warm or cold.

Skye's Best BBQ Sauce

Rich, thick and tangy; this sauce is wonderful for brushing on seitan or tempeh when grilling or broiling; makes about 1 and 1/2 cup sauce.

Ingredients:

- 1/4 cup Better Butter (pg. 62) or vegan margarine
- 2 T minced garlic (6 cloves)
- 1 can (6 oz) organic tomato paste
- 1/2 cup water
- 1/2 cup dark brown sugar
- 1/4 cup raw apple cider vinegar
- 1 T dried minced or flaked onion
- 1 T homemade vegan Worcestershire Sauce (pg. 206) or commercial
- 1 T liquid smoke
- 1 tsp sea salt or kosher salt
- 1 tsp prepared spicy mustard
- 1/2 tsp hot red pepper sauce - optional

Technique:

Melt the butter or margarine in a small saucepan over medium-low heat. Sauté the garlic for about 1 minute; whisk in the remaining ingredients and bring the mixture to a simmer. Reduce heat to low and cook uncovered, stirring occasionally, for about 1 hour until the sauce is thickened. Let cool and refrigerate to further thicken before using.

Tzatziki Sauce (Greek Cucumber Sauce)

Tzatziki sauce is used as a condiment for Greek and other Mediterranean cuisine and is traditionally made with a thick plain dairy yogurt. Vegan plain yogurt would seem to be the obvious choice as a dairy replacement, however, it often contains a very noticeable amount of sugar (this sugar is necessary to culture the yogurt since the lactose, or milk sugar, of dairy milk is absent). This noticeable sweetness does not work well with this sauce; therefore it does not make a suitable dairy replacement. So the best option is to use vegan sour cream. This recipe makes about 2 cups.

Ingredients:

- 1 cup Sour Creme (pg. 65) or commercial vegan sour cream
- 1 cucumber, peeled or unpeeled, seeded and diced
- 1/4 cup finely minced onion
- 2 cloves garlic, finely minced
- 2 T extra-virgin olive oil
- 1 T fresh lemon juice
- 2 tsp red wine vinegar or raw apple cider vinegar
- 1/2 tsp sea salt or kosher salt, or to taste
- 1/4 tsp black pepper, or more to taste
- 1 tsp chopped fresh dill (optional)
- non-dairy milk, to thin consistency but only if necessary

Technique:

Thoroughly stir together all the ingredients in a bowl (except for the non-dairy milk). Taste the mixture and add a little more lemon juice or salt and pepper, if needed.

Chill for at least two hours to blend the flavors. The moisture from the onion and cucumber should dilute the sauce to a nice consistency. However, if it is still too thick for your liking, stir in a little non-dairy milk, a tablespoon at a time, until the desired consistency is achieved.

Garnish with a sprig of fresh dill just before serving, if desired.

Classic "Cheese" Sauce

This is the ultimate non-dairy cheese sauce for pouring over noodles, vegetables or baked potatoes. It's perfect for macaroni and cheese and cheesy rice. I think you'll love it! This recipe makes about 2 and 1/2 cups of sauce.

Ingredients for the roux:

- 1/4 cup (4 T) Better Butter (pg. 62), vegan margarine or vegetable oil
- 1/4 cup flour (unbleached all-purpose wheat; rice or soy)

Ingredients to be whisked together in a large measuring cup:

- 2 cups plain unsweetened non-dairy milk
- 1/2 cup nutritional yeast
- 1 tsp onion powder
- 1 tsp ground dry mustard
- 1/2 tsp sea salt or kosher salt or to taste
- 1/2 tsp garlic powder
- 1/2 tsp paprika
- 1/4 tsp freshly grated nutmeg
- pinch of white pepper

Technique:

Prepare the roux by melting the vegan butter or margarine (or heat the oil) over medium-low heat in a medium-size saucepan. Add the flour and stir until smooth. Cook for 3 to 4 minutes to eliminate any raw flour taste.

Begin to incorporate the milk mixture SLOWLY to the roux, a little bit at a time, while whisking continuously and vigorously until very smooth. If you add the milk mixture too fast, the sauce will get lumpy, so I repeat: add S-L-O-W-L-Y.

Bring to a boil, stirring constantly and then reduce to a simmer. For extra cheesiness, stir in a 1/2-cup of shredded vegan cheese that melts (i.e., Daiya™).

Cook for about 5 minutes, stirring frequently. Season with salt if needed and keep warm on low heat until ready to use, stirring occasionally.

Rémoulade Sauce

A piquant sauce with complex flavors that pairs well with pan-seared Beaf Seitan (pg. 9) or Seitan Mignon (pg. 13). It's also a wonderful accompaniment for Chesapeake Bay "Seafood" Cakes (pg. 148); or try it on Frankfurters (pg. 53) as a gourmet touch.

Ingredients:

- 1 cup No-Eggy Mayo (pg. 105) or commercial vegan mayonnaise
- 2 T minced fresh onion
- 2 T minced capers
- 2 T minced celery
- 1 T fresh lemon juice

- 1 T Louisiana-style hot sauce, or to taste
- 1 T homemade vegan Worcestershire Sauce (pg. 206) or commercial
- 1 tsp grainy mustard
- 1 tsp minced garlic (1 clove)
- 1/4 tsp ground black pepper

Technique:

Whisk together and refrigerate at least 1 hour for the flavors to combine.

Tip: Homemade No-Eggy Mayo is much more economical than commercial vegan mayonnaise and tastes better too!

Spicy Thai Peanut Sauce

Serve with fried tofu, chik'n seitan, vegetable stir fry, Asian noodles or Asian greens.

Ingredients:

- 2 T vegetable oil
- 3 scallions, chopped
- 1 T minced garlic (3 cloves)
- 1 T fresh grated ginger root
- 1 cup water (or 1/2 cup water and 1/2 cup coconut milk)
- 1 cup creamy or chunky peanut butter

- 2 T fresh lime juice
- 2 T tamari, soy sauce or Bragg Liquid Aminos™
- 2 T rice vinegar or raw apple cider vinegar
- 1 T brown sugar or agave syrup (optional)
- 1/2 tsp dried red pepper flakes or 1/2 tsp Thai red chili paste (or more if you like it hot!)

Technique:

In a saucepan, heat the oil over medium heat and sauté the scallions, garlic and ginger, stirring until fragrant, about 1 minute. Do not let the garlic brown or it will turn bitter. Stir in the remaining ingredients and bring to a simmer, stirring often until the mixture is smooth. Thin with a little water if necessary. The sauce can be made ahead, covered and chilled. If the sauce is too thick after chilling, stir in 1 to 2 tablespoons hot water until the sauce reaches the desired consistency; or simply warm in the microwave or reheat on low in a saucepan.

Indian Curry Simmering Sauce

This fragrant and flavorful sauce is excellent for simmering tofu, tempeh, vegetables or pan-seared seitan.

Ingredients:

- 2 T Better Butter (pg. 62) or vegan margarine
- 2 tsp minced garlic (2 cloves)
- 1 Serrano chili, seeds removed and finely chopped
- 1 T fresh grated ginger root
- 1 (8 oz) can tomato sauce
- 1 can (13.5 oz) full fat or lite coconut milk*
- 2 tsp Indian curry powder
- 2 tsp tamarind paste (optional)
- 1/2 tsp salt, or to taste
- 1/2 tsp ground dry mustard

Technique:

In a skillet, sauté the Serrano chili in the butter or margarine over medium heat until softened; add the garlic and ginger and continue to sauté another minute or two. Do not let the garlic burn.

Whisk in the remaining ingredients and simmer for 10 minutes to blend flavors before using as a simmering sauce.

*Do not use Coconut Milk Beverage; it lacks the distinct coconut flavor essential for this recipe.

Balsamic Gastrique

This sauce, or more accurately "reduction", can be used in small amounts to liven up everything from fresh fruit (especially nice drizzled over cubed watermelon) to fresh, steamed or sautéed vegetables and seitan.

Ingredients:

- 1 cup balsamic vinegar
- 2 T organic sugar

Technique:

In small saucepan, stir together vinegar and sugar over medium-high heat. Cook until syrupy and reduced by 2/3, about 15 minutes.

Red Pepper Aioli

This sauce pairs beautifully with many recipes, such as Fried Green Tomatoes (pg. 97), grilled vegetables, bruschetta, Chesapeake Bay "Seafood" Cakes (pg. 148) and as a dipping sauce for artichoke leaves. Fill an applicator bottle with the aioli to decoratively garnish your favorite dish.

Ingredients:

- 2 tsp minced garlic or 2 cloves
- 1 large red bell pepper or sweet Hungarian red wax pepper
- 1/2 cup No-Eggy Mayo (pg. 105) or commercial vegan mayonnaise
- salt and freshly ground black pepper, to taste

Technique:

Split the red pepper in half and remove the membrane and seeds. Lay the pepper cut-side down on a lightly oiled baking sheet. Mist with a little vegetable oil spray and broil until the skin begins to blacken.

Remove from the broiler and wrap the pepper in foil to hold in the steam (be careful, it's hot!) Let set for 15 minutes, unwrap and remove the skin; pat dry with a paper towel.

Add the cooked red pepper, garlic and mayonnaise to a food processor or mini-blender and process until smooth. Season the aioli, to taste, with salt and pepper.

Transfer the aioli to a small bowl or applicator bottle. Cover and refrigerate. The aioli can be made up to 2 days ahead.

Béarnaise Sauce

Tarragon adds a flavorful note to this sauce. It's delicious served over cooked vegetables or pan-seared seitan; or as an alternate sauce for Eggless Benedict (pg. 85). I highly recommend only using the mayonnaise suggested in the recipe - other vegan mayonnaise may not be thick enough to hold up in the sauce.

Ingredients:

- 1 cup No-Eggy Mayo (pg. 105) or Vegenaise™
- 1 T nutritional yeast
- pinch of black pepper
- pinch of turmeric for color (optional)
- 1 shallot, finely minced or 2 T minced red onion
- 1/4 cup white wine (dry, not sweet such as Chardonnay)
- 2 tsp minced fresh tarragon or 1/2 tsp dried
- sea salt or kosher salt to taste (only if necessary)

Technique:

In a small bowl, combine the mayonnaise, nutritional yeast, pepper and optional turmeric.

In a very small saucepan over medium-low heat, simmer the shallot (or red onion) and the tarragon in the wine until the wine is reduced by half. Do not let the wine evaporate completely. Reduce heat to the lowest setting.

Whisk the mayonnaise mixture into the saucepan and heat gently on low until warm. Taste and add salt, but only if necessary. Do not simmer or boil.

Tip: Homemade No-Eggy Mayo is much more economical than commercial vegan mayonnaise and tastes better too!

Easy Cheesy Sauce

A quick sauce that is perfect for hot sandwiches. This recipe makes about 1 cup of cheese sauce.

Ingredients for the roux (thickener):

- 2 T vegetable oil
- 2 T flour (unbleached all-purpose wheat; rice or soy)

Ingredients to be whisked together in a measuring cup:

- 1 cup plain unsweetened non-dairy milk
- 1/4 cup nutritional yeast
- 1 tsp raw apple cider vinegar
- 1/2 tsp onion powder
- 1/2 tsp ground dry mustard
- 1/2 tsp paprika
- 1/4 tsp sea salt or kosher salt, or more to taste
- 1/4 tsp garlic powder
- pinch of white pepper

Technique:

Prepare the roux by heating the oil over medium-low heat in a small saucepan. Add the flour and stir until smooth. Cook for 2 minutes, stirring frequently.

Remove the saucepan from the heat and incorporate the milk mixture SLOWLY to the roux, a little bit at a time, while whisking continuously and vigorously until very smooth. If you add the milk mixture too fast, the sauce will get lumpy, so I repeat: add S-L-O-W-L-Y.

Place the saucepan over medium-high heat and stir constantly until the mixture begins to bubble and thicken, then reduce to low to keep warm. For extra cheesiness, stir in a 1/4-cup of shredded vegan cheese that melts (i.e., Daiya™).

Season the sauce with additional salt if needed and stir occasionally until ready to use.

Alfredo Sauce

A rich and creamy sauce traditionally served over fettuccini.

Ingredients:

- 2 cups Béchamel Sauce (pg. 217)
- 2 T white wine (optional)
- 2 tsp onion powder
- 1 tsp garlic powder or 2 tsp finely minced garlic (2 cloves)
- 1/2 tsp sea salt or kosher salt, or to taste
- 1/2 tsp black pepper, or to taste
- 1/4 cup Golden Parmesan (pg. 65) or commercial vegan parmesan
- 1/4 cup chopped fresh flat-leaf parsley (optional)

Technique:

Warm the Béchamel sauce in a saucepan. Whisk in all the other ingredients except for the parsley. Cook over medium-low heat just until it begins to bubble. Adjust seasonings to taste, if necessary. Reduce heat to low to keep warm and stir in the optional parsley just before serving.

Hollandaise Sauce

Excellent served over grilled vegetables or Eggless Benedict (pg. 85). I highly recommend only using the mayonnaise suggested in the recipe - other vegan mayonnaise may not be thick enough to hold up in the sauce.

Ingredients:

- 1 cup No-Eggy Mayo (pg. 105) or Vegenaise™
- 1 T fresh lemon juice (or more to taste)
- 1 T nutritional yeast
- pinch of cayenne pepper
- pinch of turmeric for color (optional)
- sea salt or kosher salt to taste (only if necessary)

Whisk the ingredients together in small microwave-safe bowl. Add salt to taste. Cover and microwave for 30 seconds to 1 minute (or a bit longer if necessary) to gently warm. Do not boil. Whisk again and serve.

Tip: Homemade No-Eggy Mayo is much more economical than commercial vegan mayonnaise and tastes better too!

Béchamel Sauce

Béchamel Sauce, also known as "white sauce", is one of the classic French "mother" sauces and may be used "as is" or as the base for many other sauce variations, such as Alfredo sauce. Incorporate sautéed mushrooms for a creamy mushroom sauce or blend in roasted red peppers for an elegant and smooth red pepper sauce - the possibilities are limited only by your imagination.

Ingredients:

- 1/4 cup (4 T) Better Butter (pg. 62) or vegan margarine
- 3 T flour (unbleached all-purpose wheat; rice or soy)
- 2 cups plain unsweetened non-dairy milk
- 1/2 tsp sea salt or kosher salt, or more to taste
- 1/4 tsp freshly grated nutmeg (optional)
- ground black pepper (optional)

Technique:

In a medium saucepan, melt the vegan butter or margarine over medium-low heat. Add the flour and stir until smooth. Turn up the heat to medium and cook until the mixture turns a light, golden color, about 3 minutes - but DO NOT let it brown.

Incorporate the soy or nut milk SLOWLY to the mixture, whisking continuously and vigorously until very smooth. Bring to a boil and then reduce to a simmer. Cook for about 5 minutes, stirring constantly and then remove from heat. Season with salt and nutmeg, and set aside until ready to use.

Tempura Sauce

In Japanese cooking, tempura sauce usually includes "dashi", a Japanese broth which is sometimes made with fish. I offer here a vegan sauce perfect for dipping your tempura vegetables.

Ingredients:

- 1 cup vegetable broth (see pg. 121 for broth options)
- 1/4 cup sweet mirin (Japanese rice wine)
- 1/4 cup tamari, soy sauce or Bragg Liquid Aminos™
- 1 and 1/2 tsp organic sugar

Technique:

Combine ingredients in a sauce pan and bring to a boil on medium heat. Remove from heat and let cool to room temperature. Serve into individual small bowls. Add some grated daikon radish if desired as a garnish. Refrigerate any unused portion.

Lemon Mustard Sauce

Excellent served over grilled asparagus or steamed broccoli.

Ingredients:

- 1/4 cup (4 T) Better Butter (pg. 62) or vegan margarine
- 1 tsp cornstarch (preferably non-GMO), arrowroot powder or potato starch
- 1 cup dry white wine
- juice of 1 lemon (about 2 T)
- 2 tsp Dijon mustard
- chives, snipped (for garnish, optional)
- salt and pepper to taste

Technique:

Melt the vegan butter or margarine in a saucepan over medium-low heat and whisk in the starch until smooth. Add the remaining ingredients and continue to cook until the sauce thickens a bit. Serve and garnish with snipped chives if desired.

Indian Raita

Raita is an Indian, Pakistani and Bangladeshi condiment consisting of yogurt (dahi), cucumber and seasonings and used as a sauce or dip to temper the heat of Indian spices. Raita is traditionally made with a thick plain dairy yogurt. Vegan plain yogurt would seem to be the obvious choice as a dairy replacement, however, it often contains a very noticeable amount of sugar (this sugar is necessary to culture the yogurt since the lactose, or milk sugar, of dairy milk is absent). This noticeable sweetness does not work well with this sauce; therefore it does not make a suitable dairy replacement. So the best option is to use vegan sour cream. This recipe makes about 2 cups.

Ingredients:

- 1 cup Sour Creme (pg. 65) or commercial vegan sour cream
- 1 cucumber, peeled or unpeeled, seeded and diced
- 1/4 cup finely chopped scallions (green onions) including green tops
- 2 T extra-virgin olive oil
- 1 T fresh lemon juice
- 1/2 tsp sea salt or kosher salt, or more to taste
- 1/4 tsp ground cumin
- 2 T chopped fresh mint (optional)
- non-dairy milk, to thin consistency but only if necessary

Technique:

Thoroughly stir together all the ingredients in a bowl (except for the non-dairy milk). Taste the mixture and add a little more lemon juice or salt and pepper, if needed.

Chill for at least two hours to blend the flavors.

The moisture from the green onion and cucumber should dilute the sauce to a nice consistency. However, if it is still too thick for your liking, stir in a little non-dairy milk, a tablespoon at a time, until the desired consistency is achieved.

Garnish with a sprig of fresh mint if you like.

Chapter 10

Sweets and Treats

Mike's Best Brownies

Mike is my partner and a professional chef, so he loves to cook too. These brownies are chocolaty, chewy and decadent. Serve with a cold glass of non-dairy milk.

Ingredients:

- 1 cup unbleached all-purpose wheat flour
- 1 cup organic sugar
- 1/3 cup unsweetened cocoa powder
- 1/2 tsp baking powder
- 1/2 tsp fine sea salt
- 1/2 cup water
- 1/2 cup vegetable oil
- 1/2 cup vegan chocolate chips
- 1 tsp real vanilla extract

Technique:

Preheat the oven to 350°F.

Combine the flour, sugar, cocoa powder, baking powder, and salt in a mixing bowl.

In a separate bowl combine the water, vegetable oil, and vanilla extract. Add this to the dry ingredients and mix well. Incorporate the chocolate chips. Allow to rest for 15 minutes (this is very important!)

Pour into an 8-inch square pan lined with parchment paper. Bake for 25 to 30 minutes. Allow to cool for at least 10 minutes before cutting.

Peach Upside-Down Cake

My partner Mike and I worked diligently to create the perfect vegan upside-down cake. We think you'll enjoy it! You can substitute pineapple for the peaches if you prefer.

Ingredients:

- 1/2 cup organic brown sugar
- 1/4 cup (4 T) Better Butter (pg. 62) or vegan margarine
- fresh peach or pineapple slices; or canned peach or pineapple slices in own juice, drained well
- 2 cups plain unsweetened soymilk (sorry, no substitutions)
- 2 tsp raw apple cider vinegar
- 2 and 1/2 cup unbleached all-purpose white wheat flour
- 1 and 1/2 tsp baking powder
- 1 tsp baking soda
- 1/2 tsp salt
- 2/3 cup canola oil
- 1 and 1/2 cups organic granulated sugar
- 2 T real vanilla extract

Technique:

Re-slice the canned peaches if necessary so that slices are no more than 1/4 inch thick. To ease peeling of fresh peaches, blanch in boiling water for one minute, and immerse in an ice water bath to cool. The skins should slip off easily. If using fresh pineapple, slice no more than 1/4-inch thick. For canned sliced pineapple, drain very well.

Whisk together the soymilk and vinegar in a non-metallic bowl and set aside to curdle for at least 1 hour. Preheat the oven to 350°F. Line the bottom of a 10-inch round cake pan with parchment paper, lightly grease with butter or margarine and flour the sides.

Melt the butter or margarine and pour into the bottom of the cake pan. Sprinkle the brown sugar evenly over the bottom of pan and arrange the peach slices (or pineapple slices) on top of the brown sugar. Set aside.

Beat together the soymilk/vinegar mixture, oil, granulated sugar and vanilla extract in a large mixing bowl.

In a separate bowl, sift together the dry ingredients. Incorporate the dry ingredients a bit at a time into the wet ingredients and mix with a rubber spatula until no large lumps remain (small lumps are okay). Pour the batter gently into the pan covering the peach (or pineapple) slices. Bake for 40 to 45 minutes or until a toothpick inserted in the center comes out clean.

Remove from the oven and let cool for 10 minutes. Run a butter knife around the sides of the pan to loosen the cake. Invert onto a serving tray and carefully lift the pan (tap if necessary). If the parchment comes out with the cake, slowly peel away. Serve at room temperature but refrigerate any leftovers.

Lemon Cupcakes

Refreshingly light and lemony cupcakes are topped with lemon icing and optional shredded coconut flakes; makes 24 cupcakes.

Ingredients:

- 2 cups plain unsweetened soymilk
- 2 tsp raw apple cider vinegar
- 2 and 1/2 cups unbleached all-purpose white wheat flour
- 1 and 1/2 tsp baking powder
- 1 tsp baking soda
- 1/2 tsp salt
- 2/3 cup canola oil
- 1 and 1/2 cups granulated sugar
- 1 T vanilla extract
- 1 T lemon extract
- 2 T finely grated lemon zest
- optional garnish: shredded coconut

Technique:

Whisk together the soymilk and vinegar in a large bowl and set aside to curdle for at least 1 hour.

Preheat the oven to 350°F. Line the pans with paper cupcake liners. Beat together the soymilk mixture, oil, sugar, vanilla and lemon extracts.

In a separate bowl, sift together the dry ingredients. Incorporate the dry ingredients a bit at a time into the wet ingredients and mix with a rubber spatula until no large lumps remain. Try not to over-mix or the cupcakes will be dense. A few small flour lumps are okay. Fold in the lemon zest.

Fill the cupcake liners 2/3 full and bake for 20-22 minutes. Remove and let cool completely before frosting (see following page for frosting recipe). Top with shredded coconut if desired.

Lemon Frosting

This recipe makes about 3 cups which is enough to frost 1 cake or 24 cupcakes.

Ingredients:

- 1/2 cup Better Butter (pg. 62) or vegan margarine, softened
- 2 cups organic sugar
- 2 T fresh lemon juice
- 2 T cold non-dairy milk

Technique:

In a dry blender, pulse process the sugar until it becomes a fine powder. Set aside.

In a large mixing bowl, beat the butter or margarine with an electric hand mixer until smooth. Add the powdered sugar with the remaining ingredients, beating for about 2 minutes on a medium-speed setting until the mixture resembles a thick frosting. Chill briefly before using. Make sure the cake or cupcakes are completely cool before frosting.

Mike's Gingerbread Cookies

Ingredients:

- 1/2 cup brown sugar
- 3/4 cup dark molasses
- 1/4 cup Better Butter (pg. 62) or vegan margarine (softened)
- 1/3 cup cold water
- 1 tsp vanilla
- 3 and 1/2 cups unbleached all-purpose white wheat flour
- 2 tsp baking soda
- 2 tsp baking powder
- 1 tsp ground ginger
- 1/2 tsp salt
- 3/4 tsp ground cinnamon
- 1/2 tsp ground allspice
- 1/2 tsp ground cloves

Technique:

Mix all ingredients thoroughly. Cover dough and refrigerate for 1 1/2 to 2 hours. Preheat oven to 350°F. Remove dough from refrigerator. Roll dough out to 1/4 inch in thickness on a lightly floured surface. Cut into desired shapes, and place on a lightly greased cookie sheet (or a cookie sheet lined with parchment paper). Bake for 10 to 12 minutes and cool on a wire rack.

Chocolate Cake

Moist and tender every time!

Ingredients:

- 1 and 1/2 cups unbleached all-purpose white wheat flour
- 1 cup organic sugar
- 1/3 cup cocoa powder
- 1 tsp baking soda
- 1/4 tsp fine sea salt
- 1 cup water
- 1/4 cup light-tasting vegetable oil
- 1 T raw apple cider vinegar (you will not taste the vinegar, so don't worry)
- 2 tsp real vanilla extract

Technique:

Preheat oven to 375°F.

Grease an 8″x 8″ square pan with Better Butter (pg. 62) or vegan margarine and then flour the bottom and sides. Shake out the excess flour. If you have parchment paper, cut to fit the bottom of the pan (this will assist removal of the cake).

Sift the dry ingredients together. Whisk the wet ingredients together. Add the wet ingredients to the dry ingredients and mix well (don't worry about any tiny lumps in the batter). Pour into the pan and bake 30 to 35 minutes, or until a toothpick inserted in the center comes out clean.

Let cool at least 20 minutes before removing. To remove, run the blade of a butter knife around the edges to loosen (if you have not used parchment paper, strike the pan sharply against the countertop to loosen the bottom). Place your hand over the cake and invert to remove. Place gently onto serving plate.

Do not frost/ice the cake until completely cooled.

Frost or ice the cake with Chocolate Ganache Frosting (pg. 225) or your favorite vegan frosting or icing.

For a double layer cake, grease and flour two round 8"cake pans. Double the recipe and divide the batter between the two pans. Follow the directions as described above.

Chocolate Ganache Frosting

This semi-sweet chocolate frosting is creamy and rich yet very easy to make. Most ganache recipes call for semi-sweet chocolate. This is a potential problem for strict ethical vegans because commercial semi-sweet chocolate contains refined white sugar, and refined white sugar is usually filtered through bone char to make it white. I solved that problem by using pure unsweetened baker's chocolate. By adding your own organic sugar (evaporated cane juice), the ganache remains 100% vegan. This recipe yields about 2 and 2/3 cups of frosting, which is enough to frost a double layer cake or 24 cupcakes.

Ingredients:

- 8 oz (1 pkg) unsweetened baker's chocolate (8 squares, 1 oz each)
- 1 and 1/3 cup non-dairy milk
- 1 cup organic sugar
- 1/4 cup (4 T) Better Butter (pg. 62) or vegan margarine
- 2 tsp real vanilla extract

Technique:

Break the chocolate squares in half and place in a mixing bowl.

Add the milk, sugar and butter or margarine to a small saucepan and cook over medium heat, stirring frequently to dissolve the sugar and just until the mixture begins to bubble. Do not leave unattended or the milk may boil over.

Pour the milk mixture over the chocolate, add the vanilla, and stir until the chocolate is completely melted and smooth. At this point, you can use the ganache as a glaze; just let it sit at room temperature until it cools and thickens slightly but is still pourable.

For frosting, transfer the mixture to a container with a lid and refrigerate until cooled and semi-firm.

If the frosting has been chilling for more than a few hours, let it sit at room temperature until slightly softened, then stir thoroughly or whip with an electric mixer. Make sure your cake is completely cooled before frosting.

Mike's Best Ever Pumpkin Pie

A favorite Autumn and Winter treat, perfect for celebrating the Equinox, Halloween, Thanksgiving, Yule and Christmas.

Ingredients:

- 16 oz canned pumpkin purée
- 1 carton (about 12 oz) extra-firm Mori-Nu™ silken tofu
- 3/4 cup organic sugar
- 1/2 tsp salt
- 1 tsp ground cinnamon
- 1/2 tsp ground ginger
- 1/4 tsp ground cloves
- 9-inch vegan pie shell

Technique:

Preheat the oven to 425°F. Combine the pumpkin purée, sugar, salt, spices, and silken tofu in a blender. Blend until smooth. Pour into the pie shell and bake for 15 minutes. Reduce oven temperature to 350°F, and continue baking for an additional 40-45 minutes. Cool on a wire rack for up to 2 hours. Refrigerate until completely chilled, and serve.

Cranberry Creme Cheese Tartlets

These tartlets make a simple yet elegant holiday dessert.

Ingredients:

- 1 cup (8oz) Creme Cheese (pg. 69) or commercial vegan cream cheese
- 1/4 cup whole cranberry sauce (canned or freshly made) plus more to top tartlets
- 1 pkg (15 count) mini fillo cups, frozen

Technique:

Thoroughly stir the cranberry sauce into the cream cheese. Cover and refrigerate until ready to serve. Fill the frozen fillo cups just before serving with the mixture (try using a pastry bag to pipe the mixture, if you have one). The fillo cups will defrost very quickly, so there's no need to thaw them before filling and serving.

Top with an additional small dollop of cranberry sauce. Serve immediately.

Coconut Creme Pie

A graham cracker pie shell is filled with a velvety coconut creme, and then crowned with vegan whipped topping and toasted coconut. Everyone deserves to indulge now and then, especially when this pie is so easy to make. This is one of my best desserts.

Ingredients:

- 1 cup coconut flakes, sweetened or unsweetened - your choice
- 1 can (about 13 to 14 oz) full fat coconut milk - DO NOT substitute with lite coconut milk or coconut milk beverage
- 1 carton (about 12 oz) firm/extra-firm Mori-Nu™ silken tofu
- 1/2 cup plain unsweetened non-dairy milk
- 2/3 cup organic sugar
- 1/4 cup (4 T) cornstarch (preferably non-GMO) or arrowroot powder
- 1/4 tsp sea salt
- 1 tsp real vanilla extract
- 1 graham cracker pie crust 9″ (make sure it's vegan)
- Heavenly Whipped Creme (pg. 66) or commercial vegan whipped dessert topping of choice

Technique:

Spread the coconut flakes on a cookie sheet and bake in the oven at 350°F for about 7 minutes.. The coconut should be turning a light golden brown just around the edges. Set aside to cool.

Pre-bake your pie crust at the same time, but bake for 15 minutes.

In a blender, process the coconut milk, silken tofu, non-dairy milk, sugar, cornstarch or arrowroot powder, salt and vanilla until smooth.

Transfer to a large saucepan and cook over medium heat, stirring frequently, until the mixture begins to bubble. The mixture will begin to lump as it heats up - this is normal, as the mixture is beginning to thicken. Just keep stirring and eventually it will smooth out. Continue to cook, stirring constantly, until the mixture becomes a very thick pudding.

Remove from the heat and add 3/4 cup of the toasted coconut (reserving 1/4 cup for the topping on the pie). Stir well. Pour into the pie crust, smooth the top gently with a rubber spatula or the back of a spoon and place in the refrigerator uncovered for 1 hour until the top of the pie is set. Cover with plastic wrap and chill the pie for an additional 2 hours minimum, or until completely firm.

Remove from the refrigerator and spread a layer of the whipped creme or topping evenly over the pie. Sprinkle with the remaining 1/4 cup toasted coconut.

Banana Date Bread

There's no need to discard over-ripe bananas when you can make this incredibly moist bread. Flavored with tropical cinnamon and cardamom, the kitchen will be filled with a wonderful aroma as it bakes. You can also add a 1/2 cup chopped unsalted walnuts or pistachios if you desire.

Ingredients:

- 1 and 1/2 cups unbleached all-purpose white wheat flour
- 1/2 cup whole wheat flour
- 1 tsp baking powder
- 1/2 tsp baking soda
- 1 tsp ground cinnamon
- 1 tsp ground cardamom
- 1/4 tsp fine sea salt
- 3 over-ripe bananas
- 1/2 cup REAL maple syrup, dark amber variety
- 1/2 cup chopped dates
- 1/2 cup vegetable oil, such as sunflower or safflower

Technique:

Preheat the oven to 350°F and lightly oil a small metal loaf pan (about 4x8").

Measure out your dry ingredients into a large bowl.

Mash the bananas in a separate large mixing bowl. Stir in the maple syrup, vegetable oil and chopped dates until well blended.

Sift the dry ingredients into the banana mixture. Gently fold the ingredients together with a rubber spatula or wooden spoon just until all the ingredients are moistened and combined. Do not over-mix or the bread will be dense.

Bake uncovered for 1 hour. Cool on a wire rack then invert the pan to remove the loaf. Slice and serve.

Banana Creme Pie

Fresh sliced bananas are layered in a graham cracker pie shell, then bathed in a creamy vanilla pudding and crowned with vegan whipped topping and additional sliced bananas. Everyone deserves to indulge now and then, especially when this pie is so easy to make.

Ingredients:

- 3 ripe bananas plus an additional banana for garnishing the pie
- 1 carton (about 12 oz) firm/extra-firm Mori-Nu™ silken tofu
- 1/2 cup plain unsweetened non-dairy milk
- 1/2 cup organic sugar
- 1 T plus 2 tsp cornstarch (preferably non-GMO) or arrowroot powder
- 1/4 tsp sea salt
- 1 and 1/2 tsp real vanilla extract
- 1 graham cracker pie crust 9″ (make sure it's vegan)
- Heavenly Whipped Creme (pg. 66) or commercial vegan whipped dessert topping of choice

Technique:

Preheat your oven to 350°F. Bake the pie crust for 15 minutes. Remove and set aside but leave the oven on.

In a blender, process the silken tofu, non-dairy milk, sugar, cornstarch or arrowroot powder, salt and vanilla until smooth.

Transfer to a large saucepan and cook over medium heat, stirring frequently, until mixture begins to bubble. The mixture will begin to lump as it heats up - this is normal, as the mixture is beginning to thicken. Just keep stirring and eventually it will smooth out. Continue to cook, stirring constantly, until the mixture becomes a very thick pudding. Remove from the heat and set aside.

Place a layer of sliced bananas on the bottom of the pie shell and spoon in about 1/3 of the pudding mixture, spreading evenly. Add another layer of bananas and half of the remaining mixture, again spreading evenly.

Repeat with the last layer of bananas and finish with the remaining pudding mixture. Smooth the top gently with a rubber spatula or the back of a spoon and place in the oven for 10 minutes. Remove and let cool for about 10 minutes.

Place in the refrigerator uncovered for 1 hour until the top of the pie is set. Cover with plastic wrap and chill the pie for an additional 2 hours minimum, or until completely firm.

Remove from the refrigerator and spread a layer of the whipped creme or topping evenly over the pie. Garnish with sliced bananas just before serving. This pie should be consumed within a couple of days before the bananas turn brown.

Truffles

Many thanks to my friend Andy Eastman, for sharing his recipe for this decadent treat.

Ingredients:

- 1 (12 oz) package vegan chocolate chips
- 1 cup Creme Cheese (pg. 69) or commercial vegan cream cheese
- 2 cups Organic Powdered Sugar (pg. 232)
- 2 T flavored syrup, such as hazelnut or vanilla (optional)

- chopped nuts (optional topping)
- coconut flakes (optional topping)
- 1 cup vegan chocolate chips (optional topping)

Technique:

Melt the chocolate chips in a double boiler, saucepan, or microwave. Place the cream cheese in a food processor and slowly add the sugar. Blend until well mixed. Then add the melted chocolate chips to the cream cheese mixture and process until well mixed. If using flavored syrup, add the syrup to the mixture and blend for 30 seconds. Pour the blended mixture into a bowl and refrigerate for 2 hours. Once chilled, roll the mixture with your hands into bite-sized balls and place on a serving tray.

If using optional toppings, pour the nuts and/or coconut flakes into a shallow bowl and roll the chilled balls into them. Place the truffles on a tray and refrigerate for 30 minutes. For truffles with a hard chocolate coating: After the chilled mixture has been rolled into bite-sized balls, melt 1 cup of the vegan chocolate chips. Dip the balls into the melted chocolate, place on a tray, and refrigerate for 2 additional hours.

Pineapple Cooler (Beverage)

Fresh pineapple is always a treat, and with this recipe the rind doesn't have to go to waste. Be sure to wash the exterior of your pineapple thoroughly before peeling and using the rind for this recipe; makes 4 eight-ounce servings.

Ingredients:

- 4 cups water
- peel of 1 pineapple, washed
- 1/2 cup organic sugar or other natural sweetener of your choice

- 2 whole cloves
- 1 tsp fresh grated ginger root
- ice, for serving

Technique: Bring 4 cups of water to a boil in a medium saucepan over high heat. Place the pineapple peel, sugar, cloves, and ginger in a large heatproof pitcher. Pour the boiling water into the pitcher and stir to combine. Let stand at room temperature for 24 hours; strain. Transfer to the refrigerator to chill; serve over ice.

Organic Whole-Wheat Chocolate Chippers

These cookies couldn't be easier to prepare and they're simply awesome! Be sure to immediately wrap in plastic once they cool to retain freshness. Consume within a day or two for optimum freshness (they're always eaten quickly in our home anyways).

Ingredients:

- 1/2 cup Better Butter (pg. 62) or vegan margarine - room temperature
- 1 cup light organic brown sugar
- 1/2 tsp baking soda
- 2 tsp organic vanilla extract
- 1 and 1/4 cup organic WHOLE wheat flour
- 1/4 cup organic non-dairy milk
- 1 pkg (about 10 oz) semi-sweet organic chocolate chips (make sure they're vegan)

Technique:

Set the oven for 375°F.

Cream together the butter or margarine and the brown sugar.

Add the baking soda and vanilla and mix well.

Add the flour and milk and mix well.

Incorporate the chocolate chips into the batter.

Drop by the large tablespoonful onto a parchment-lined cookie sheet and bake for approximately 13 minutes.

Chocolate Pudding
Rich, creamy and delicious!

Ingredients:

- 4 tsp cornstarch (preferably non-GMO) or arrowroot powder
- 1 can (14oz) full fat organic coconut milk (do not use coconut milk beverage)
- 1/3 cup of unsweetened cocoa powder
- 1/2 cup organic sugar
  (or 1/3 cup for semi-sweet)
- 1 tsp real vanilla extract

Technique:

In a small bowl, dissolve the cornstarch or arrowroot powder in just enough water to make a smooth liquid. Set aside.

Add the remaining ingredients to a blender and process until smooth.

Pour the blender contents into a saucepan and cook over medium heat, stirring frequently, until the mixture begins to bubble. Vigorously whisk in the dissolved starch liquid. Continue to cook, stirring constantly, until the mixture thickens.

Pour into a heat-proof container and place a layer of plastic film directly in contact with the surface of the pudding. This will discourage a "skin" from forming on the surface. Refrigerate for several hours until chilled.

When ready to serve, vigorously stir the pudding and spoon into individual dessert cups.

Organic Powdered Sugar

Why make your own powdered sugar? Non-vegan commercial powdered sugar is made from refined white sugar which has typically been filtered through bone char during the refining process. Making your own is very simple. This recipe will make 1 lb of powdered sugar.

Ingredients:

- 2 cups organic sugar (evaporated cane juice)

Technique:

In a dry blender, add the sugar and pulse process at high speed into a fine powder. Store the sugar in a dry container until ready to use.

Flan

Smooth and creamy vanilla cashew custard is topped with a maple syrup glaze. This is my own signature recipe created after many disappointing results with other vegan flan recipes.

Ingredients:

- 1/4 cup real maple syrup
- 1 and 1/3 cup water
- 1 cup whole raw cashews
- 2/3 cup organic sugar
- 2 T agar flakes*
- 2 tsp real vanilla extract

Special items needed:

- any shallow round or square bowl that will hold a little over 2 cups liquid - or - 4 dessert ramekins (1/2 cup size each) which will act as the mold(s) for the custard.
- a high-powered blender (such as a Vitamix™)

*Agar is a tasteless seaweed derivative and a vegetarian replacement for gelatin; it can be purchased in most health food and natural food stores, or online.

Technique:

Soak the cashews for a minimum of 8 hours in the refrigerator with just enough water to cover; or, if you're in a hurry, place the cashews in a bowl, cover with near boiling water and let soak for about an hour.

Pour the maple syrup into the bottom of the container or distribute equally into the dessert ramekins. Set aside.

Process the cashews and 1 and 1/3 cup fresh water in the blender until completely smooth. Strain the creme through a fine mesh sieve to eliminate any residual particles.

In a saucepan, combine the strained cashew creme with the sugar, agar flakes and vanilla. Cook over medium heat, stirring frequently, until the sugar and agar are completely dissolved and the mixture is just nearing the boiling point. Return the hot mixture to the blender and process for about 30 seconds. This will ensure that the agar is completely emulsified into the mixture.

Warning! Hot liquids can sometimes expand explosively when a blender is suddenly turned on high speed. Hold the lid down with a dish towel and start the blender at low speed, then increase the speed slowly.

Gently pour the mixture into the bowl or ramekins over the syrup, cover with plastic wrap, and refrigerate for at least 2 hours. To remove from the bowl or ramekins, place a serving plate on top and quickly invert the custard onto the plate. The custard should remove easily.

Mousse au Chocolat

Fluffy whipped coconut cream is folded into semi-sweet chocolate ganache. The mousse is light and airy in texture yet very rich and decadent in taste - an elegant dessert that will surely impress. This recipe makes eight 1/2 cup servings.

Ingredients:

- 2/3 cup non-dairy milk
- 2/3 cup organic sugar
- 2 T Better Butter (pg. 62) or vegan margarine
- 6 oz unsweetened baker's chocolate (6 squares, 1 oz each)
- 2 tsp real vanilla extract or 1 T liqueur of your choice (Grand Marnier, for example)
- 2 cups Heavenly Whipped Creme (pg. 66)
- 8 dessert cups or ramekins

Technique:

Break the chocolate squares in half and place in a mixing bowl.

Add the milk, sugar and butter or margarine to a small saucepan and cook over medium heat, stirring frequently to dissolve the sugar and just until the mixture begins to bubble. Do not leave unattended or the milk may boil over.

Pour the scalding hot milk/sugar mixture over the chocolate. Add the vanilla or liqueur and whisk until the chocolate is completely melted and smooth.

Refrigerate until cooled and thickened but not firm, about 20 to 30 minutes. If it has not sufficiently cooled, chill a bit longer. Do not proceed to the next step if the ganache is still warm.

Now, whip the ganache until smooth. With a rubber spatula, fold (don't stir) the whipped creme into the ganache until completely incorporated.

Spoon the mousse into the dessert cups, dividing evenly. Cover the cups with plastic wrap and chill in the refrigerator for several hours until set. Before serving, garnish with optional ingredients as you desire, such as whipped creme (if you have any left), vegan chocolate shavings or fresh raspberry sauce.

Kheer (Indian Rice Pudding)

Kheer is prepared at festivals, in temples, and on all special occasions in India. The term 'kheer', as it is used in northern India, is derived from the Sanskrit word 'ksheeram', which means milk.

Ingredients:

- 1 cup water
- 1 cup non-dairy milk
- 1/2 cup basmati rice (for authentic flavor, do not substitute with other varieties)
- 1 can (14 oz) full fat organic coconut milk
- 1/4 cup organic sugar, or more to taste
- 1/2 tsp ground cardamom
- 1/3 cup seedless raisins
- 1/3 cup chopped or crushed pistachios, cashews or almonds

Technique:

In a large non-stick sauce pan, bring the water and milk just to a boil. Do not boil the mixture or the non-dairy milk may cause the pot to boil over. Immediately stir in the rice and cardamom.

Reduce heat to a simmer, partially cover and cook for 20 minutes, stirring occasionally. The cardamom will clump initially but will disperse upon cooking and stirring.

Increase the heat to medium and add the coconut milk, sugar and raisins. Cook uncovered, stirring frequently, until the mixture begins to thicken, approximately 10 minutes. Taste and add additional sugar, if desired.

Remove from the heat and stir in the pistachios, cashews or almonds. Transfer the mixture to a glass or ceramic bowl and place plastic wrap directly on the surface of the pudding. Cool at room temperature and then refrigerate until well chilled. Spoon the pudding into individual cups to serve.

Note: Indian rice pudding is meant to be somewhat milky and not as thick as American puddings, but once you refrigerate, the pudding will thicken substantially.

'Coconut Milk' Ice Cremes

Originally, my coconut milk ice creme recipes called for starch (cornstarch or arrowroot powder) to thicken the ice creme base, but this involved cooking the base to activate the thickening properties of the starch. Now, I use a small amount of guar gum as a thickener and the ice creme base can be prepared in one step without cooking.

Guar gum, also called *guaran*, is a natural substance derived from the ground seeds of the guar plant which grows primarily in Pakistan and the northern regions of India. It is used as a thickener and stabilizer in food applications. It also prevents ice crystallization in ice creme.

Guar gum can be found in most health food stores and natural markets, or online. Bob's Red Mill™ produces an excellent guar gum and this is what I use in my ice creme recipes, as well as for making Better Butter (pg. 62).

Placing the ice creme in the freezer after processing will further firm its texture. Extended freezing will make the ice creme very hard – simply thaw slightly to serve.

Chocolate (or Carob) 'Coconut Milk' Ice Creme

Ingredients:

- 2 cans (about 13 oz each) full fat organic coconut milk
  (do not use lite coconut milk or coconut milk beverage)
- 1/2 cup unsweetened cocoa or carob powder
- 3/4 cup organic sugar
- 2 tsp real vanilla extract
- 3/4 tsp guar gum

Technique:

Place all of the ingredients in a blender and process for about 30 seconds. This will ensure that the guar gum is completely incorporated and the sugar is completely dissolved. Pour into a container and stir in the remaining fruit; cover and refrigerate until very cold (or place in the freezer for about an hour).

When well chilled, process the mixture according to your ice cream maker's instructions. You can also stir in about a 1/4 cup of chopped chocolate or nuts (macadamias are great) just before placing in the ice creme maker.

For vanilla ice creme, omit the cocoa or carob powder and add the pulp from 2 vanilla beans. Simply split the vanilla beans lengthwise and scrape out the pulp (aka 'caviar') with the edge of a butter knife.

Pina Colada 'Coconut Milk' Ice Creme

*A sweet tropical taste of the islands! Mango purée or
mashed banana also makes a fantastic tropical ice creme treat.*

Ingredients:

- 1 can (about 13 oz) full fat organic coconut milk
  (do not use lite coconut milk or coconut milk beverage)
- 2/3 cup organic sugar
- 1 tsp real vanilla extract
- 3/4 tsp guar gum
- 2 cups crushed pineapple (fresh or 15 oz can, lightly drained); or mango purée or mashed banana*

*If using banana, mash and stir into the ice creme base just before processing in the ice cream maker. This will prevent it from turning brown.

Technique:

Place all of the ingredients and 1 cup of the fruit in a blender (reserving 1 cup of fruit) and process for about 30 seconds. This will ensure that the guar gum is completely dispersed and the sugar is completely dissolved.

Pour into a container and stir in the remaining fruit; cover and refrigerate until very cold (or place in the freezer for about an hour).

When well chilled, process the mixture according to your ice cream maker's instructions.

Cashew Maple Pecan Ice Creme

Ingredients:

- 1 and 1/2 cup (7.5 oz by weight) whole raw cashews
- 2 cups water
- 1/2 cup real maple syrup
- 1/2 cup organic sugar
- 2 tsp real vanilla extract
- 1/4 tsp guar gum - optional (a natural thickener; see information on pg. 236)
- 1/2 cup finely chopped pecans

Technique:

Soak the cashews for a minimum of 8 hours in the refrigerator with just enough water to cover; or, if you're in a hurry, place the cashews in a bowl, cover with near boiling water and let soak for about an hour.

Drain the cashews, discarding the soaking water. Add the cashews to a high-powered blender with 2 cups fresh water and process until completely smooth.

Strain the cashew creme through a fine sieve and return the creme to the blender.

Add the remaining ingredients EXCEPT for the chopped pecans. Process the mixture until blended.

Transfer to a container and stir in the chopped pecans; refrigerate until very cold. When well-chilled, process the mixture according to your ice cream maker's instructions.

Notes:

1. Cashew ice creme will freeze hard when placed in the freezer for extended periods; therefore, it's best served immediately from the ice cream machine. To serve after hard freezing, simply thaw at room temperature until softened.
2. Cashew creme is essentially a suspension of micro-fine particles of cashew nuts and water. These micro-fine particles are what give the cashew creme its richness and body and make it suitable as an ice creme base. Sensitive palates, however, may detect these micro-fine particles as a subtle "grittiness" in the texture of the ice creme. If this is going to be an issue for you, you may want to experiment with full-fat coconut milk as an ice creme base. Try my 'Coconut Milk' Ice Cremes (pg. 236) for a very smooth and rich ice creme treat.